T0222267

# Swift Game Programming for Absolute Beginners

Arjan Egges

Apress®

**Swift Game Programming for Absolute Beginners**

ISBN-13 (pbk): 978-1-4842-0651-5

ISBN-13 (electronic): 978-1-4842-0650-8

Managing Director: Welmoed Spahr
Lead Editor: Jonathan Gennick
Development Editor: Douglas Pundick
Technical Reviewer: Stefan Kaczmarek
Editorial Board: Steve Anglin, Mark Beckner, Gary Cornell, Louise Corrigan, Jim DeWolf, Jonathan Gennick, Robert Hutchinson, Michelle Lowman, James Markham, Susan McDermott, Matthew Moodie, Jeffrey Pepper, Douglas Pundick, Ben Renow-Clarke, Gwenan Spearing, Matt Wade, Steve Weiss
Coordinating Editor: Jill Balzano
Copy Editor: Mary Behr
Compositor: SPi Global
Indexer: SPi Global
Artist: SPi Global
Cover Designer: Anna Ishchenko

*To Yfa*

# Contents at a Glance

# Contents

# About the Author

**Arjan Egges**, PhD, is an associate professor in Computer Science at Utrecht University in the Netherlands. He is responsible for research in the area of computer animation, and he heads the university's motion capture lab. Arjan has written many research papers on animation. He is the founder of the highly successful, annual ACM SIGGRAPH conference on Motion in Games, the proceedings of which have been published by Springer-Verlag. Arjan designed Utrecht University's computer animation course offerings in the Game and Media Technology master's program, and he is currently the leader of that master's program. In 2011 he designed the introductory programming course for the university's bachelor's degree offering in Game Technology. He is the main author of *Learning C# by Programming Games*, published in 2013 by Springer, and *Building JavaScript Games: for Phones, Tablets and Desktop*, published in 2014 by Apress.

# About the Technical Reviewer

 **Stefan Kaczmarek** has more than 15 years of software development experience, specializing in mobile applications, large-scale software systems, project management, network protocols, encryption algorithms, and audio/video codecs. As chief software architect and cofounder of SKJM, LLC, Stefan developed a number of successful mobile applications including iCam (which has been featured on CNN, Good Morning America, and The Today Show, and which was chosen by Apple to be featured in the "Dog Lover" iPhone 3GS television commercial) and iSpy Cameras (which held the #1 Paid iPhone App ranking in a number of countries around the world including the United Kingdom, Ireland, Italy, Sweden, and South Korea). Stefan resides in Phoenix, Arizona, with his wife, Veronica, and their two children.

# Acknowledgments

Many people have contributed to this book. First, I would like to thank Stefan Kaczmarek, the technical reviewer, for reading the chapters and providing lots of useful feedback during the writing process. I also want to thank the Apress team for helping this book become a reality. In particular, I want to thank Jonathan Gennick, Douglas Pundick, and Jill Balzano for their involvement in this book. My thanks go to Heiny Reimes, who designed the original sprites that formed the basis of the Painter, Penguin Pairs, and Tick Tick games. I'd like to thank Renske van Alebeek, who was responsible for editing and redesigning the sprites to be suitable for Apple devices, and who also designed a completely new set of sprites for the Tut's Tomb game.

# Introduction

Swift, the new programming language that replaces Objective C, was announced by Apple on June 2, 2014. Since then, there have been many updates to the language. At the time of writing of this book, we are at version 2. Swift is a very well-structured programming language that takes many features from existing modern languages such as C#, Haskell, and Python, and it introduces a few new features itself.

If you want to develop for the iOS, watchOS, or OS X platforms, you must learn Swift. This book teaches you the Swift language in depth; at the same time, you'll learn how to develop games for the iOS platform. Because this book was written with game development as its context, you will learn that many of the new features are very useful for designing game software. The book builds on the SpriteKit framework and shows you how to develop apps that are ready to be put in the App Store and to be played by everyone (and hopefully will make you a lot of money in the process)!

While reading this book, you will develop four games. Each of the four games uses professionally-developed artwork. Each game builds on the knowledge obtained while developing the previous one, going from a simple point-and-shoot game and a physics-based reaction game, to a puzzle game, and in the end, a full-fledged platform game with animation, intelligent enemies, and much more. As you'll see, building games can be as much fun as playing them.

Even though this book teaches you Swift in the context of game development, after reading the book you will be able to use the skills you acquired to develop any kind of application for Apple devices.

## Who This Book Is For

This book is for anyone who has an interest in learning how to create games. If you have no prior (Swift) programming experience, don't worry. This book teaches you all you need to know. If you already know how to program, then this book will still be interesting for you. I show you how to develop games using the latest features of the Swift 2.0 language and the SpriteKit framework. The book develops four different games for the iOS platform. The code for these games is carefully developed, taking into account the proper way of organizing code and making it clean, robust, and easily extensible.

## Structure of This Book

Each chapter in this book has its own collection of example programs. You can find the examples on the web site belonging to this book. I explain all the Swift programming concepts based on these examples. Throughout the book you will find many game design and development tips, such as how and when to use menus or tutorials, working in a team with artists, and publishing and marketing tips.

The book is globally divided into five parts. The following is an overview of what each part is about.

## Part I

This part provides an overview of the Swift programming language, along with an introduction to its main features. I introduce the most important game programming structure—the game loop. You will see how to use SpriteKit, which is the framework provided by Apply for developing Swift games. You will learn about variables and data structures that are useful for representing a game world, and you will see how to include game assets such as sprites and sounds in your programs.

## Part II

This part focuses on the first game: the *Painter* game. The goal of the game is to collect paint of three different colors: red, green, and blue. The paint is falling from the sky in cans that are kept floating by balloons, and you must make sure that each can has the right color before it falls through the bottom of the screen. I will show you how to react to what the player is doing by reading mouse, keyboard, or touch input. I will introduce the *class* as a blueprint for an object (also called an *instance* of that class). You will learn about constructor methods as the methods responsible for creating an instance of the class they belong to.

You will learn how to write your own methods, properties, and classes, and how to use these programming concepts to design different game-object classes. You will see how game objects should interact with each other. As an example of this interaction, you will see how to handle basic collisions between game objects. You will learn how inheritance is implemented in Swift so that game-object classes can be hierarchically built up. You will be introduced to the concept of polymorphism, which lets you call the right version of a method automatically. You will finish the Painter game by adding a few extra features, such as motion effects, sounds, music, and maintaining and displaying a score.

# Part III

The second game you develop in this book is *Tut's Tomb*: a game in which you have to collect treasures that fall down. This game illustrates how to use the physics engine that's a part of the SpriteKit framework. You will learn to program more advanced input handling such as dragging objects around on the screen and dealing with multiple touches at the same time. You will also learn about making your game look nicer by using a custom font.

# Part IV

This part introduces the game *Penguin Pairs*, a puzzle game in which the goal is to make pairs of penguins of the same color. Throughout the different levels of the game, you will introduce new gameplay elements to keep the game exciting. For example, there is a special penguin that can pair with any other penguin, penguins can get stuck in a hole, and you can place penguin-eating sharks on the board.

I will show you how to deal with structures and layouts in games such as a playing grid or a row of buttons. You will create a variety of useful GUI elements for menus, such as an on/off button and a slider button. You will learn about a class design for dealing with different game states such as menus, a title screen, and so on. And you will see how different states can be part of the game loop and how you can switch between them. Finally, you will learn about loading levels from a file, and how to store the player's progress through the game and recall that information when the game is started again.

# Part V

The final game you will develop in this book is a platform game called *Tick Tick*. I will show you how to create a tile-based game world, similar to what you learned while developing the previous game. You will see how to add animations like a running character. You will develop your own physics engine specifically tailored to platform games, which includes mechanisms for jumping, falling, and handling collisions between the character and other objects in the game. You will also add some basic intelligence to enemies in the game. As a result, the player will have different gameplay options and must develop different strategies to complete each level.

# Tools

In order to develop iOS games in Swift, you are going to need a Mac with Xcode installed on it. Xcode is the development environment provided by Apple that you use to create OS X, iOS, or watchOS applications. In order to be able to run the examples, you will need a version of Xcode that supports Swift 2.0 or higher (which is version 7 at the time of writing of this book). You need to enroll as an Apple developer to obtain Xcode, although you only need to take part in the paid program if you want to run apps on your iPad or iPhone and publish apps in the App Store. Xcode and the iOS simulator are free to use for any Apple developer.

# Example Games

I supply a large number of examples that show the various aspects of programming Swift games. Next to the code, you also get professionally developed game assets at two different resolutions. The collection of examples is contained in a single ZIP file, which you can find on the book's information page (www.apress.com/9781484206515), under the Source Code/Downloads tab. This tab is located beneath the Related Titles section of the page.

After you've downloaded the ZIP file, unpack it somewhere. When you look in the folder where you've unpacked the file, you'll see a number of different folders. Each chapter in the book has its own folder. For example, if you want to run the final version of the Penguin Pairs game, go to the folder belonging to Chapter 21 and open the PenguinPairsFinal Xcode project (this is the file ending with .xcodeproj). After Xcode has opened the project, run the game by pressing Command+R or the Play button on the top left of the window.

As you can see, there are quite a few different files pertaining to this particular example. A simpler example can be seen if you go the folder belonging to Chapter 1, where you will find two very basic examples of Swift applications: an OS X console application and an iOS game app.

# Contacting the Author

If you have any questions regarding the book, please feel free to contact me directly at the following e-mail address: j.egges@uu.nl.

# Getting Started

The first part of this book covers the basics of developing game applications in Swift. You will see a number of simple examples that show how to create apps using Swift. I will give you an introduction to the Swift language, as well as the SpriteKit engine, which is used to create 2D games. This part covers core Swift programming constructs such as instructions, expressions, objects, and methods. In addition, I will introduce the game loop and how to load and draw sprites (images).

# Chapter 1

# The Swift Language

This chapter provides an introduction to the Swift programming language. Swift is one of the more recent developments in the evolution of programming languages. In order to understand Swift, you need to first understand how computers (including iOS devices such as iPads or iPhones) work, and how the languages used to program them have evolved. After talking about computers and programs (including apps) in general, I'll give an introduction to Swift and how you can use some of its basic features to create your first program.

## Computers and Programs

This section briefly covers computers and programming in general. After that, you'll move on to programming your first application using Swift.

### Processors and Memory

Generally speaking, a computer consists of one or more *processors* and forms of *memory*. This is true for all modern computers, including game consoles, smartphones, and tablets. I define memory as something that you can *read information from and/or write things to*. Memory comes in different varieties, mainly differing in the speed of data transfer and data access. For example, a computer may have memory in the shape of (relatively slow) hard disk memory, much faster RAM (Random Access Memory), a USB flash drive that's connected to the machine, or an open network connection to a server that has memory itself. The main processor in the computer is called the *central processing unit (CPU)*. The most common other processor on a computer is a *graphics processing unit (GPU)*.

The main task of the processor is to execute *instructions*. The effect of executing these instructions is that the memory is changed. Especially with my very broad definition of memory, every instruction a processor executes changes the memory in some way. You probably don't want the computer to execute only one instruction. Generally, you have a very long list of instructions to be executed—"Move this part of the memory over there, clear this part of the memory, draw this image on the screen, check if the player is pressing a key on the gamepad, and make some coffee while you're at it"—and (as you probably expect) this list of instructions that is executed by the computer is called a *program*.

# Programs

In summary, a *program* is a long list of instructions to manipulate the computer's memory. However, the program itself is also stored in memory. Before the instructions in the program are executed, they're stored on a hard disk, a DVD, or a USB thumb drive; or on any other storage medium. When they need to be executed, the program is moved to the RAM memory of the machine.

The instructions that, combined together, form the program need to be expressed in some way. You could use gestures, or make weird noises. Unfortunately, the computer doesn't understand this very well (although with the motion tracking devices of today, perhaps it will understand in a couple of years). The computer also can't grasp instructions typed in plain English (yet), which is why you need programming languages such as Swift. In practice, the instructions are coded as text, but you need to follow a very strict way of writing them down, according to a set of rules that defines a programming language. Many programming languages exist, because when somebody thinks of a slightly better way of expressing a certain type of instruction, their approach often becomes a new programming language. It's difficult to say how many programming languages exist because that depends on whether you count all the versions and dialects of a language; but suffice to say that there are thousands.

Fortunately, it's not necessary to learn all these different languages because they have many similarities. In the early days, the main goal of programming languages was to use the new possibilities of computers. However, more recent languages focus on bringing some order to the chaos that writing programs can cause.

# Programming Languages

In the early days, programming computer games was a very difficult task that required great skill. A game console like the popular Atari 2600 had only 128 bytes of RAM, which is really small compared to today's computers (4GB of RAM is nearly 33,000 times as much as 128 bytes). It also used cartridges with at most 4,096 bytes of ROM (Read-Only Memory) that had to contain both the program and the game data. This limited the possibilities considerably, and the machines were also extremely slow.

Programming such games was done in Assembly, a very basic programming language that defined a set of instructions that a processor could execute. Each processor could have a different set of instructions, leading to different Assembly languages. As a result, every time a new processor came around, all existing programs had to be completely rewritten for that processor. Therefore, a need arose for processor-independent programming languages. This resulted in languages such as Fortran (FORmula TRANslating System) and BASIC (Beginners' All-purpose Symbolic Instruction Code). BASIC was very popular in the 1970s because it came with early personal computers such as the Apple II in 1978, the IBM-PC in 1979, and their descendants. Unfortunately this language was never standardized, so every computer brand used its own dialect of BASIC.

As programs became more complex, it became clear that a better way of organizing all these instructions was necessary. So, *procedural* languages were created; they grouped instructions into *procedures* (also called *functions*, or *methods*). A well-known example of a procedural language is C, which was defined by Bell Labs in the late 1970s. C is still used quite a lot, although it's slowly but surely making way for more modern languages, especially in the game industry.

Over the years, games became much larger programs, and teams rather than individuals created them. It was important that the game code be readable, reusable, and easy to debug. Object-oriented programming languages address this need, by letting programmers group methods into something called a *class*. The memory that groups of methods are related to is called an *object*. A class can describe something like the ghosts in a game of Pac-Man. Then each individual ghost corresponds to an object of the class. This way of thinking about programming is powerful when applied to games. Another powerful aspect of object-oriented programming is inheritance, which allows developers to extend existing code and add functionality to it. You'll read more about inheritance and how you use it in games in Chapter 10.

In the early eighties, two programmers named Brad Cox and Tom Love created a language called Objective-C, which was an extension of C in which object-oriented programming was possible. In 1988, the Objective-C language was licensed to NeXT, the company founded in 1985 by Steve Jobs after he was forced out of Apple. NeXT developed a lot of tools around the Objective-C language, such as a tool for building interfaces, as well as a development environment called Project Builder, the predecessor of what we now call Xcode. When Jobs returned to Apple in the nineties, the tools developed at NeXT became the foundation for Mac OS X.

Over the last two decades, new languages such as Java and C# have further introduced useful features. Apple realized that a new language was needed for their platform, one that profited from programming language advances made in the last decades. So, on June 2, 2014, Apple announced the Swift programming language as the new programming language for both OS X and iOS. Swift is a much more modern alternative to Objective-C. It takes many features from languages such as C# or JavaScript, which makes writing programs for OS X or iOS much more efficient. Since the market for iOS apps is huge, Swift is going to have a big impact on the industry. This book teaches you the Swift language in depth, with a special focus on developing games. Upon finishing this chapter, you will have created your first program in Swift.

# Programming Games

The goal of this book is to teach you how to program games. Games are very interesting (and sometimes challenging!) programs. They deal with a lot of different input and output devices, and the imaginary worlds that games create can be extremely complex.

Until the beginning of the 1990s, games were developed for specific platforms. For example, a game written for a particular console couldn't be used on any other device without major effort from the programmers to adapt the game program to the differing hardware. In the 1980s, arcade games were extremely popular, but almost none of the code written for them could be reused for newer games because of the constant changes and improvements in computer hardware.

As games grew more complex, and as operating systems became more hardware independent, it made sense for the game companies to start reusing code from earlier games. Why write an entirely new rendering program or collision-checking program for each game, if you can simply use the one from your previously released game? The term *game engine* was coined in the 1990s when first-person shooters such as Doom and Quake became a very popular genre. These games were so popular that their manufacturer, id Software, decided to license part of the game code to other game companies as a separate piece of software.

Many different game engines are available today. Modern game engines provide a lot of functionality to game developers, such as a 2D and 3D rendering engine, special effects such as particles and lighting, sound, animation, artificial intelligence, scripting, and much more. The main engine used for the games in this book is SpriteKit. SpriteKit is an engine developed by Apple targeted at game development. After reading this book, you will have seen all the major aspects of this engine and you will know how to use it to create your own games.

# Developing Games

Two approaches are commonly used in developing games. Figure 1-1 illustrates these approaches: the outer one encompasses the inner one. When people are first learning to program, they typically begin writing code immediately, and that leads to a tight loop of writing, then testing, and then making modifications. Professional programmers, by contrast, spend significant upfront time doing design work before ever writing their first line of code.

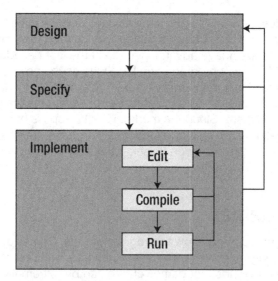

*Figure 1-1.  Programming on a small scale and on a large scale*

# Small Scale: Edit-Compile-Run

When you want to build a game in Swift, you need to write a program that contains many lines of instructions. Using the Xcode framework, you can edit the program you're working on. A program generally consists of different text files, each containing instructions. Once you're done writing down these instructions, you tell the Xcode program to *compile* the code you have written and execute the program. When all is well, the program is compiled and executed.

However, most of the time, things aren't that easy. For one thing, the text files you give to the compiler should contain valid Swift code because you can't expect the computer to compile files containing random blabbering. The Xcode program checks whether the source code adheres to the language specifications of the Swift language. If not, it produces an error, and the compilation process stops. Of course, programmers make an effort to write correct Swift programs, but it's easy to make a typo, and the rules for writing correct programs are very strict. So, you'll most certainly encounter errors during the compilation phase.

After a few iterations during which you resolve minor errors, the source code is compiled without encountering any problems. As the next step, the computer *executes* or *runs* the program it just created. In many cases, you then discover that the program doesn't exactly do what you want it to do. Of course, you made an effort to correctly express what you wanted the program to do, but conceptual mistakes are easy to make.

So you go back to the text editor, and you change the code. Then you try to compile and run the program again and hope you didn't make new typing mistakes. You may find that the earlier problem is solved, only to realize that although the program is doing something different, it still doesn't do exactly what you want. And it's back to the editor again. Welcome to life as a programmer!

# Large Scale: Design-Specify-Implement

As soon as your game becomes more complicated, it's no longer a good idea to just start typing away until you're done. Before you start *implementing* (writing and testing the game), there are two other phases.

First, you have to *design* the game. What type of game are you building? Who is the intended audience of your game? Is it a 2D game or a 3D game? What kind of gameplay would you like to model? What kinds of characters are in the game, and what are their capabilities? Especially when you're developing a game together with other people, you have to write some kind of design document that contains all this information, so that everybody agrees on what game they're developing! Even when you're developing a game on your own, it's a good idea to write down the design of the game. The *design* phase is actually one of the most difficult tasks of game development.

Once it's clear what the game should do, the next step is to provide a global structure for the program. This is called the *specification* phase. Do you remember that the object-oriented programming paradigm organizes instructions in methods and methods in classes? In the specification phase, you make an overview of the classes needed for the game and the methods in those classes. At this stage, you only need to describe what a method will do, not how it's done. However, keep in mind that you can't expect impossible things from methods: they have to be implemented later.

When the game specification is finished, you can start the *implementation* phase, which generally means going through the edit-compile-run cycle many times. After that, you can let other people play your game. In many cases, you'll realize that some ideas in the game design don't work that well. So, you begin again by changing the design, followed by changing the specification and finally doing a new implementation. You let other people play your game again, and then… Well, you get the idea. The edit-compile-run cycle is contained in a larger-scale cycle: the design-specify-implement cycle (see Figure 1-1). Although this book focuses mainly on the implementation phase, you will find game design tips and tricks in the various chapters of this book.

# Building Your First Swift Program

In this section, you will learn how to create a simple program in the Swift language (see also the HelloWorld example belonging to this chapter). Since you are going to use the Xcode development environment, start by launching the Xcode program. Click *Create a new Xcode Project*, displayed on the welcome screen. A dialog will appear that will allow you to choose between several template projects. By default, Xcode has templates for iOS projects (applications that run on iPhones or iPads), watchOS projects (applications that run on the Watch) and OS X projects (applications that run on Macs). Let's start by creating a simple OS X console application. In order to do this, click the Application item under OS X, and select the *Command Line Tool* project template (see Figure 1-2).

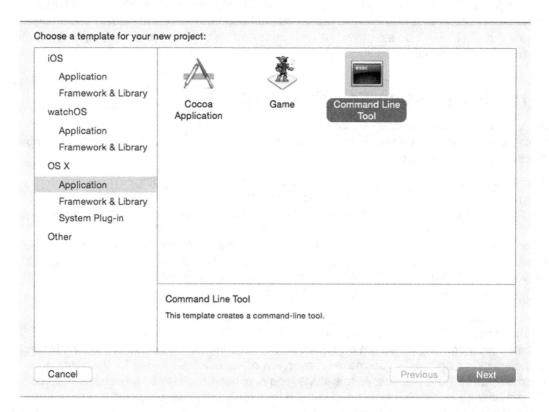

*Figure 1-2. The project template selection dialog*

A command line tool (also called a console application) is one of the most basic types of programs that exist. A command line tool is a simple program that reads and/or outputs text.

After you select the Command Line Tool option, click the Next button. Then, choose a product name (for example, HelloWorld). In that same window, make sure that the language selected for the project is Swift. After clicking Next, you must select a folder in which the project and the code will be stored; for example, you could save it to the Desktop. After you've selected a location for your project, click Create. You just created a basic project in which you can write code.

On the left side, you see the items associated with the project. There are two folders. One folder contains an item called `main.swift`, which is a text file containing the instructions that make up the program. The second folder (called `Products`) contains a single item carrying the name that you chose for the product. This item has a command line tool icon, meaning that the product that is created with the project is a command line tool.

If you click the item `main.swift`, you see that the file is opened in an editor. The template project has already added a few lines of code for you as a starting point. The most important line is the following one:

```
print("Hello, World!")
```

This instruction tells the computer to write a line of text to the console. The text that should be written can be found between the parentheses. In Swift, any text expression is always written between double quotes. To see what this program does, click the Play button in the top left of the Xcode window (see Figure 1-3). This compiles the program and runs it. When the program runs, you will see its output in the debug area at the bottom of the Xcode window (also shown in Figure 1-3). If you don't see a debug area, activate it by clicking the corresponding view button in the top right of the Xcode window. In Figure 1-3, you can see three view buttons in the top right of the window. The left one shows or hides the part of the window that lists the files and folders in the project. The right one toggles the panel showing the project properties. Finally, the middle one shows or hides the debug area. After the program has run, you'll see that the text *Hello, World!* has appeared there, as well as a message that the program has finished execution.

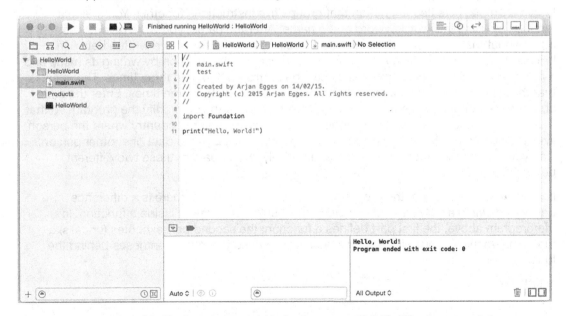

*Figure 1-3. A screenshot of the Xcode environment right after the program HelloWorld has been executed*

You can now start changing the code to change what the program is doing. For example, add the following line to your code:

```swift
print("Goodbye, World!")
```

When you run this program, two lines are printed in the debug area. Now change the code to the following two lines:

```swift
print("Hello, World!", appendNewline: false)
print("Goodbye, World!")
```

When you run this program, you'll see that the two texts are written behind each other. This is because print adds a *line break* after writing the text to the console, unless you say otherwise (which is what I did in the first print instruction above). The last program you executed consists of two instructions. Each instruction tells the compiler to execute a function (or method) that consists of other instructions. print is an example of a function. Here you can clearly see that Swift is indeed a procedural language. Instructions are grouped in functions/methods.

You can group your own instructions into your own functions/methods very easily. Have a look at the following program:

```swift
func printData() {
    print("Name: Shirley")
    print("Age: 26")
    print("Profession: Teacher")
    print("Married: yes")
    print("Children: 2")
}

printData()
printData()
printData()
```

In this example, I created a function that groups five instructions together. You create a function by using the func keyword and a name. After the name, you write parentheses (more about that later). The instructions that belong to the function are written between braces: { and }. After defining this function, you can call the function by writing its name and a pair of parentheses. In this example, I call the printData function three times. The result is that the instructions that make up the function are all executed three times. Enter the code above in the editor and see for yourself what it is doing. Can you modify the program so that the data is printed six times? Now modify the program so that the country where the person lives is also printed. Try to add a second function that displays the data of another person. Can you change the program so that it alternatively shows data of these two different persons?

If you take another look at the program, perhaps you realize that there is a difference between *defining* a function and *executing* the instructions written inside a function. In the program above, the first part defines a function; the second part executes (or calls) a function. Whenever you call a function, you always need to write parentheses behind the function call, like so:

```swift
printData()
```

The reason that these parentheses are there is because sometimes functions need extra information in order to be able to do their work. A good example of this is the print function, which requires text as extra information. After all, what good is a printing function if you can't tell it what it is supposed to print? Just like the printData function, the print function also has parentheses behind it when it is called. The difference is that in the case of print, there is actually information between the parentheses, namely the text that should be printed:

```
print("Hello, World!")
```

Later on, you will see many more examples of functions and how they are called. Since this book is about programming games, let's now make an actual iOS game application.

# Building Your First Swift Game

In order to get started with programming an iOS game, you need to create a suitable project. Since iOS games do much more than only print text, you need to create a Game project. This is very easy. In Xcode, go to the main menu and choose File ➤ New ➤ Project. Then, choose the Game template that you find in the iOS category. After pressing Next, enter a suitable name for your game, such as BasicGame. Again, make sure that Swift is selected as the main language. Also, make sure that SpriteKit is selected as the game technology that will be used. SpriteKit is a collection of functions and classes created by Apple that are useful for developing games. Finally, select a folder where your game project and its source code should be stored, and click Create. Alternatively, you can have a look at the BasicGame example belonging to this chapter, which already is in the right format.

If you take a look at the files in the game project you just created, you see that the basic iOS game is quite a bit more complicated than a command line tool application. The main file where you are going to make changes to the code is the file called GameScene.swift. The other files are there to set up the right environment for iOS games. Inside the GameScene.swift file, you write the code that is specific to your particular game. The most important part of the code is the following instructions:

```
import SpriteKit

class GameScene: SKScene {
    override func didMoveToView(view: SKView) {
        /* Setup your scene here */
        let myLabel = SKLabelNode(fontNamed:"Chalkduster")
        myLabel.text = "Hello, World!"
        myLabel.fontSize = 65
        myLabel.position = CGPoint(x:CGRectGetMidX(self.frame),
            y:CGRectGetMidY(self.frame))

        self.addChild(myLabel)
    }
    ...
}
```

Without going too much into detail, let's have a look at the structure of this code. The first instruction, import SpriteKit, is there to tell the compiler that the program needs functions and classes from SpriteKit. This is different from using a function such as print. The print function is built into the language itself. Functions and classes related to dealing with sprites (images) are rather specific and therefore they have been put in a separate collection, also called a *framework*. At the beginning of a program, you may see one or more of these import instructions, depending on what the program is going to need.

After the framework import instruction, you see a *class*. This is where you see that Swift is an object-oriented language. Instructions are grouped in methods, and methods in turn are grouped in classes. You see this same structure appearing in this example. There are three instructions grouped in a method called didMoveToView. This method belongs to a class called GameScene. When we define a function or a method, we use the func keyword. When we define a class, we use the class keyword. Programmers use methods and classes to better structure their code so that it is easier to understand what each part of the code does and how it is related to other parts of the program. In this case, the GameScene class groups methods that do something with the game scene (in other words, the game world). The method didMoveToView contains instructions that need to be executed when the game appears on the screen of the device.

## FUNCTIONS OR METHODS?

As discussed in this chapter, procedural programming languages group instructions into functions/methods. Functions and methods are grouped into classes in object-oriented languages. So what's the difference between functions and methods? Well, there really isn't one. In this book, only when a function is a part of class do I call it a method. So, didMoveToView from the iOS example is a method, and printData (from the command line tool example) is a function. They both group together instructions, but didMoveToView belongs to a class (GameScene) and printData doesn't.

The first line of code in the didMoveToView method (/* Setup your scene here */) is a written comment that the Xcode program ignores. The second line is an instruction that creates something called a label node. A label node represents a text label that you can place anywhere on the screen. The two instructions after that assign text and a font size to the label. Then, you see an instruction that assigns a position to this label node. This instruction looks rather complicated since it calculates what the middle of the screen is while defining the position. You could have also written a more simple instruction:

```
myLabel.position = CGPoint(x:500, y:300)
```

Try out a few different values for the x and y position of the text on the screen. Note that when you use the SpriteKit framework, the origin of the screen is on the bottom left, and follows the orientation of the device, as you can see in Figure 1-4.

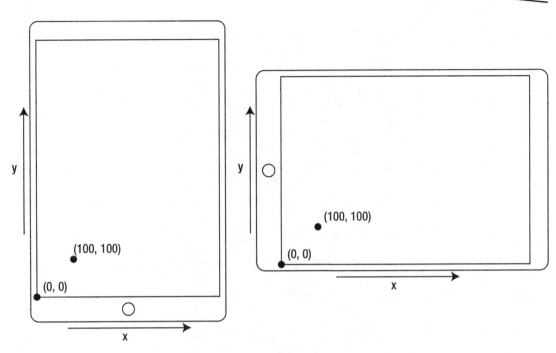

*Figure 1-4.* *The coordinate system of iDevices places the origin at the bottom left of the screen, regardless of the device orientation*

Also note that when you set the position of something like a text label, the position (500, 300) will be at the *bottom center* of the text that is placed on the screen.

The last instruction in the method tells the game engine that the label should be a part of the scene. If you omit that instruction, the text label will not be drawn. You can launch the application by pressing the Play button in the top left of the screen. To the right of that button, you can select for which device you would like to build the app. When you run the app, Xcode will start a simulator program that shows you what the app will look like on the device you selected. For example, Figure 1-5 shows the app running in the iPhone 4s simulator. Try to simulate the app on a few different platforms. If the simulator screen is too big, you can choose another scale by pressing Command+1, Command+2, or Command+3. You can also change the scale by selecting Window ➤ Scale in the iOS Simulator menu.

*Figure 1-5. A basic iOS game application (running in iPhone 4s mode)*

Again, try to play around with the program. Can you draw a different text on the screen? Change the position of the text and see how different *x* and *y* values result in different positions of the text on the screen.

# A Few Observations

In the iOS game example, the code contains a lot of things that you may not yet recognize. For example, behind the name of the class (GameScene), there is a colon and the word SKScene. What this means is that the GameScene class is based on an already existing class called SKScene. One could also say that GameScene *is a special version of* SKScene. Note that SKScene groups a number of methods. GameScene copies these methods but also replaces one of them, namely the didMoveToView method. That's why the word override is in front of that method definition. If this seems like a lot to take in, don't worry. I'll cover this aspect in detail in Chapter 10 of this book.

The instructions themselves may also not make a lot of sense to you yet. In the following chapters, I'll talk more about what these instructions mean. In any case, you see that creating a simple iOS app already entails a lot more than a simple command line tool. There are other kinds of applications that you can also develop in Swift, such as an OS X application with windows, buttons, and so on. This application requires yet another approach to setting up the classes and methods that you need (but that's beyond the scope of this book).

You may also have noticed that it is no longer that clear in which order instructions or methods are executed. When you look at the most simple command line tool, there is a single instruction that prints "Hello, World!" to the console. When executed, the program simply executes that single instruction. When you have a program containing many classes that group methods together that in turn group instructions, it's no longer so straightforward to determine what instructions will be executed and in what order. In the case of the iOS example in this book, a lot happens behind the scenes to ensure that at some point, the method `didMoveToView` is called. However, there is no clear way to see that in the code itself. In this case, you have to rely on the Apple SpriteKit documentation, which states somewhere that the `didMoveToView` method will be called, and that you can put your own game initialization code in it. As a game developer, you will not always understand all the code of your game application. Often, you will use code written by other developers, and when you do, hopefully there are not too many mistakes in it. The other option is to develop everything yourself, from scratch. But in a fast-moving industry such as the game industry, that's not advisable. To quote the famous writer Carl Sagan: "If you wish to make an apple pie from scratch, you must first invent the universe."

# What You Have Learned

In this chapter, you have learned the following:

- How computers work, and that they consist of processors to compute things and memory to store things

- How programming languages have evolved from Assembler languages to modern programming languages such as Swift

- How to create a simple application using the Swift language

# Chapter 2

# Game Programming Basics

This chapter covers the basic elements of programming games and provides a starting point for the chapters that follow. First, you will learn about the basic skeleton of any game, consisting of a *game world* and a *game loop*. You will see how to create this skeleton in Swift by looking at various examples such as a simple application that changes the background color. Finally, I will talk about clarifying your code by using comments, layout, and whitespace in the right places.

## Building Blocks of a Game

This section talks about the building blocks of a game. I discuss the game world in general and then show you the process of changing it using a game loop, which continuously updates the game world before drawing it on the screen.

## The Game World

What makes games such a nice form of entertainment is that you can explore an imaginary world and do things there that you would never do in real life. You can ride on the back of a dragon, destroy entire solar systems, or create a complex civilization of characters who speak in an imaginary language. This imaginary realm in which you play the game is called the *game world*. Game worlds can range from very simple domains such as the Tetris world to complicated virtual worlds in games such as Grand Theft Auto and World of Warcraft.

When a game is running on a computer or a smartphone, the device maintains an internal representation of the game world. This representation doesn't look anything like what you see on the screen when you play the game. It consists mostly of numbers describing the location of objects, how many hit points an enemy can take from the player, how many items the player has in inventory, and so on. Fortunately, the program also knows how to create a visually pleasing representation of this world that it displays on the screen. Otherwise, playing computer games would probably be incredibly boring, with players having to sift through pages of numbers to find out whether they saved the princess or died a horrible death. Players never see the internal representation of the game world, but game developers do. When you want to develop a game, you also need to design how to represent your game world internally. And part of the fun of programming your own games is that you have complete control over this.

Another important thing to realize is that just like the real world, the game world is changing all the time. Monsters move to different locations, the weather changes, a car runs out of gas, enemies get killed, and so on. Furthermore, the player actually influences how the game world is changing! So simply storing a representation of the game world in the memory of a computer isn't enough. A game also needs to constantly register what the player is doing and, as a result, *update* this representation. In addition, the game needs to *show* the game world to the player by displaying it on the monitor of a computer, on a TV, or on the screen of a smartphone. The process that deals with all this is called the *game loop*.

## The Game Loop

The game loop deals with the dynamic aspects of a game. Lots of things happen while a game is running. The players press buttons on the gamepad or touch the screen of their device, and a constantly changing game world consisting of levels, monsters, and other characters needs to be kept up to date. There are also special effects such as explosions, sounds, and much more. All these different tasks that need to be handled by the game loop can be organized into two categories:

- Tasks related to updating and maintaining the game world
- Tasks related to displaying the game world to the player

The game loop continuously performs these tasks, one after the other (see Figure 2-1). As an example, let's look at how you could handle user navigation in a simple game like Pac-Man. The game world mainly consists of a labyrinth with a few nasty ghosts moving around. Pac-Man is located somewhere in this labyrinth and is moving in a certain direction. In the first task (updating and maintaining the game world), you check whether the player is pressing an arrow key. If so, you need to update the position of Pac-Man according to the direction the player wants Pac-Man to go. Also, because of that move, Pac-Man may have eaten a white dot, which increases the score. You need to check whether it was the last dot in the level because that would mean the player has finished the level. If it was a larger white dot, the ghosts need to be rendered inactive. Then you need to update the rest of the game world. The position of the ghosts needs to be updated, you have to decide whether fruit should be displayed somewhere for bonus points, you need to check whether Pac-Man collides with one of the ghosts (if the ghost isn't inactive), and so on. You can see that even in a simple game like Pac-Man, a lot of work needs to be done in this first task. From now on, I'll call this collection of different tasks related to updating and maintaining the game world the *Update* action.

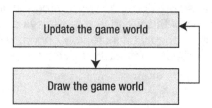

*Figure 2-1. The game loop, which continuously updates and then draws the game world*

The second collection of tasks is related to displaying the game world to the player. In the case of the Pac-Man game, this means drawing the labyrinth, the ghosts, Pac-Man, and information about the game that is important for the player to know, such as how many points they've scored, how many lives they have left, and so on. This information can be displayed in different areas of the game screen, such as at the top or the bottom. This part of the display is also called the *heads-up display* (HUD). Modern 3D games have a much more complicated set of drawing tasks. These games need to deal with lighting and shadows, reflections, culling, visual effects like explosions, and much more. I'll call the part of the game loop that deals with all the tasks related to displaying the game world to the player the *Draw* action.

## The Game Loop in Swift

The previous chapter showed how to create a simple Swift iOS game application. In that application, you saw that instructions are grouped into a method, which in turn is part of a class, as follows:

```
class GameScene: SKScene {
    override func didMoveToView(view: SKView) {
        /* Setup your scene here */
        let myLabel = SKLabelNode(fontNamed:"Chalkduster")
        myLabel.text = "Hello, World!"
        myLabel.fontSize = 65
        myLabel.position = CGPoint(x:CGRectGetMidX(self.frame),
            y:CGRectGetMidY(self.frame))

        self.addChild(myLabel)
    }
    ...
}
```

Basically, the `didMoveToView` method does one job here: create a game world. This game world is very simple since it consists of a text label. So how does the game loop come into play in this example? In fact, the drawing part of the game loop is already taken care of by the SpriteKit engine. The last instruction in the `didMoveToView` method makes sure that the drawing code inside the SpriteKit engine knows that it should draw the text label. If you want to create a more complicated game world, you can simply add more instructions to `didMoveToView`, which creates the objects in the game world. So, creating and drawing the game world seems doable. But how do you change the game world? This is what the *Update* action is for. Take a look at the following example program (see also the BackgroundColor project belonging to this chapter):

```
import SpriteKit

class GameScene: SKScene {

    override func didMoveToView(view: SKView) {
        let myLabel = SKLabelNode(fontNamed:"Chalkduster")
        myLabel.text = "Hello, World!"
        myLabel.fontSize = 65
        myLabel.position = CGPoint(x:CGRectGetMidX(self.frame),
```

```
        y:CGRectGetMidY(self.frame))
    addChild(myLabel)
}

override func update(currentTime: NSTimeInterval) {
    backgroundColor = UIColor.blueColor()
}
}
```

As you can see, a big difference between this program and the previous example is that the GameScene class now groups the following two methods: one called didMoveToView, and one called update. The latter is the method that is going to be executed as a part of the game loop. Because the GameScene class is a special version of the SKScene class, the SpriteKit framework that we use in this book already takes care of creating the game loop and calling the update method. In this example, there is one instruction in the update method:

```
backgroundColor = UIColor.blueColor()
```

This instruction changes the background color of the app to the color blue. Run the BackgroundColor example belonging to this chapter to see what the program does. Now see if you can change the background color to something else. Can you change it to red? Or yellow?

When you run the program, you can't really see that the update method is called many times per second. Add the following instruction between the braces enclosing the instructions grouped in the update method:

```
print(currentTime)
```

When you run the program now, you'll see that a slowly increasing number is printed to the console. This number represents the current system time, measured in seconds passed since the device was last restarted. Every time the update method is called, the system time is printed to the console.

If you want to know how often the update method is called per second, there is an easy way to find out. Click the file called GameViewController.swift. Add the following instruction to the viewWillLayoutSubviews method, just before the closing brace:

```
skView.showsFPS = true
```

When you now run the program, you'll see that a number is printed on the screen. This number, also called the *frame rate*, indicates how many times per second the game world is updated and drawn on the screen. In order to allow for a smooth playing experience, the game world needs to be continuously updated and drawn: update, draw, update, draw, update, draw, update, draw, update, draw, and so on. Furthermore, this happens at a very high speed. Apple devices such as the iPad or the iPhone can deal with frame rates with a maximum of 60 frames per second (or 60 Hz). Higher than that is not possible because the device screen refresh rate is 60 Hz. It is possible, though, that the frame rate drops because the computations in the update method are taking a lot of time. In Chapter 6, I talk more about this issue and what you can do to ensure your games run smoothly both on older and newer Apple devices.

This book shows you many different ways to fill the update method with the tasks you need to perform in your game. During this process, I also introduce many programming techniques that are useful for games (and other applications). The following section looks into the basic game application in more detail. Then, you fill this basic skeleton of a game with additional instructions.

# The Structure of a Program

This section talks about the structure of a program in more detail. In the early days, many computer programs only wrote text to the screen and didn't use graphics. Such a text-based application is called a *console* application. In addition to printing text to the screen, these applications could also read text that a user entered on the keyboard. So, any communication with the user was done in the form of question/answer sequences (Do you want to format the hard drive (Y/N)? Are you sure (Y/N)? and so on). Before windows-based OSes became popular, this text-based interface was very common for text-editing programs, spreadsheets, math applications, and even games. These games were called *text-based adventures*, and they described the game world in text form. The player could then enter commands to interact with the game world, such as go west, pick up matches, or Xyzzy. Examples of such early games are Zork and Adventure. Although they might seem dated now, they're still fun to play!

It's still possible to write console applications, also in a language such as Swift, as you saw in the previous chapter. Although it's interesting to see how to write such applications, this book focuses on programming modern games with graphics.

## Types of Applications

The console application is only one example of a type of application. Another very common type is the *windows* application. Such an application shows a screen containing windows, buttons, and other parts of a *graphical user interface* (GUI). This type of application is often *event-driven*: it reacts to events such as clicking a button or selecting a menu item.

Another type of application is the *app*, run on a mobile phone or a tablet. Screen space is generally limited in these types of applications, but new interaction possibilities are available, such as GPS to find out the location of the device, sensors that detect the orientation of the device, and a touch screen.

When developing applications, it's quite a challenge to write a program that works on all the different platforms. Creating a windows application is very different from creating an app. And reusing the code between different types of applications is difficult. For that reason, *web-based applications* are becoming more popular. In this case, the application is stored on a server, and the user runs the program in a web browser. There are many examples of such applications: think of web-based e-mail programs or social network sites. However, creating a purely web-based application may not always result in the fastest code. A native app generally is much faster. Furthermore, making money with web-based applications is more difficult than with apps. Once you've created your own game app, publishing it in the App Store is easy. After reading this book, you will be able to create such game apps by yourself.

> **Note**    Not all programs fall squarely in one application type. Some Windows applications might
> have a console component, such as a script interface in a game engine. Games often also have a
> window component, such as an inventory screen, a configuration menu, and so on. And nowadays
> the limit of what a program actually *is* has become less clear. Think about a multiplayer game that
> has tens of thousands of players, each running an app on a tablet or an application on a desktop
> computer, while these programs communicate with a complex program running simultaneously on
> many servers. What constitutes the *program* in this case? And what type of program is it?

## Functions

Remember that in an imperative program, the *instructions* are doing the actual job of the
program: they're executed one after the other. This changes the memory and/or the screen
so the user notices that the program is doing something. In the BackgroundColor program,
not all lines in the program are instructions. For example, the following line is not an
instruction, but the start of a function definition:

```
override func didMoveToView(view: SKView) {
```

An example of an instruction is the line print(currentTime), which prints the current
system time to the console. Because Swift is a procedural language, the instructions can be
grouped in functions or methods. In Swift it isn't obligatory that an instruction be part of a
function or method. Look at the following program:

```
import SpriteKit

class GameScene: SKScene {

    let myLabel = SKLabelNode(text:"Hello, World!")

    override func didMoveToView(view: SKView) {
        myLabel.position = CGPoint(x: 100, y: 100)
        addChild(myLabel)
    }

    override func update(currentTime: NSTimeInterval) {
        backgroundColor = UIColor.blueColor()
    }
}
```

As you can see, I moved one instruction out of the didMoveToView method and placed it at
the class level. Although you cannot always do that, it is allowed in this case. In the following
chapter, I will discuss this in more detail.

Functions and methods are very useful. They prevent duplication of code because the
instructions are only in one place, and they allow the programmer to execute those
instructions easily by calling one name. Grouping instructions in a function is done with
braces ({and }). Such a block of instructions grouped together is called the *body* of a

function. Above the body, you write the *header* of the function. An example of a function header is as follows:

```
func printData()
```

The header contains, among other things, the *name* of the function (in this case `printData`). As a programmer, you may choose any name for a function. In some cases, the name of the function is already chosen for you. Look at the following function header:

```
override func update(currentTime: NSTimeInterval)
```

You cannot change the name (`update`) to something else because this method replaces the original method defined in `SKScene` (hence the word `override` in front of the method header). You replace that function because you want to do something other than the standard behavior for updating the game world in `SKScene` (which is doing nothing), namely you want to change the background color.

The name of a function or method is always preceded by the word `func`, and after the name is a pair of parentheses. These serve to provide information to the instructions that are executed inside the function. For example, take another look at the header of `update`. In this header, you see the text `currentTime: NSTimeInterval` between parentheses. This means that the `update` method requires the current system time. This makes sense because if you want to calculate velocities of game objects (typically something you do when you update the game world), you need to know how much time has passed.

## Syntax Diagrams

Programming in a language such as Swift can be difficult if you don't know the language's rules. This book uses so-called *syntax diagrams* to explain how the language is structured. The *syntax* of a programming language refers to the formal rules that define what is a valid program (in other words, a program that a compiler or interpreter can read). By contrast, the *semantics* of a program refer to the actual *meaning* of it. To illustrate the difference between syntax and semantics, look at the phrase "all your base are belong to us." Syntactically, this phrase isn't valid (an interpreter of the English language would definitely complain about it). However, the *meaning* of this phrase is clear: you apparently lost all of your bases to an alien race speaking bad English.

> **Note**   The phrase "all your base are belong to us" comes from the opening cut-scene of the video game Zero Wing (1991, Sega Mega Drive) as a poor translation of the original Japanese version. Since then, the phrase has appeared in my articles, television series, movies, web sites, and books (such as this one!).

A compiler can check the syntax of a program: any program that violates the rules is rejected. Unfortunately, a compiler can't check whether the semantics of the program correspond to what the programmer had in mind. So if a program is syntactically correct, this is no guarantee that it's semantically correct. But if it isn't even syntactically correct, it can't run at all. Syntax diagrams help you to visualize the rules of a programming language such as Swift. For example, Figure 2-2 is a simplified syntax diagram that shows how to define a function in Swift.

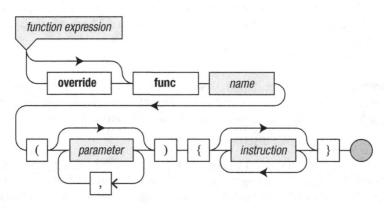

*Figure 2-2. The syntax diagram for a function expression*

You can use syntax diagrams to construct Swift code by starting at the top left of the diagram, in this case at the words *function expression*, and following the arrows. When you reach the gray dot, your piece of code is complete. Here you can clearly see that a function definition starts with the func keyword, optionally preceded by the word override; then you write the name of the function. After that, you write parentheses. Between these parentheses, you can (optionally) write any number of *parameters*, separated by commas. Next, you write a number of instructions, all between braces. After that, you're done because you've reached the gray dot. Throughout this book, I use syntax diagrams to show how to structure your code according to the syntactical rules of the Swift language.

## Calling a Function

When an instruction like print("Hello, World!") is executed, you *call* the print function. In other words, you want the program to execute the instructions grouped in the function print. This group of instructions does exactly what you need for this example: namely, write text to the console. You need to give some extra information to this function because it needs to know what should be written to the console. The (in this case single) parameter provides this extra information. A function can have more than one parameter, as you saw in the syntax diagram. When a function is called, you always write parentheses behind it, and within the parentheses are the parameters (if required).

Do you need to know which instructions are grouped together in the print function in order to use it? No, you don't! This is one of the nice things about grouping instructions in functions. You (or other programmers) can use the function without knowing how it works. By smartly grouping instructions in functions, it's possible to write reusable program pieces that can be used in many different contexts. The print function is a good example of this. It can be used for various applications, and you don't need to know how the function works in order to use it. The only thing you need to know is that you need to provide text as a parameter when you call the function.

# Program Layout

This section deals with the layout of a program's source code. You first see how to add clarifying comments to your code. Then you learn how to write instructions as clearly as possible by using single or multiple lines, whitespace, and indentation.

## Comments

For the human reader of a program (another programmer, or yourself in a couple of months, when you've forgotten the details of how your program worked), it can be very useful to add some clarifying comments to a program. These comments are completely ignored by the compiler, but they make for a more understandable program. There are two ways in Swift to mark comments in your code:

- Everything between the symbol combinations /* and */ is ignored (there can be multiple lines of comments).

- Everything between the symbol combination // and the end of the line is ignored.

It's useful to place comments in your code to explain groups of instructions belonging together, the meaning of parameters, or complete classes. If you use comments, do it to *clarify* the code, not to write the code again in words: you can assume the reader of your code knows Swift. To illustrate this, the following comment line adds to the clarity of the instruction:

```
// Write the current system time to the console
print(currentTime)
```

The following is also a comment, but it doesn't clarify what the instruction does:

```
/* Pass the currentTime value to the print function and execute that function */
print(currentTime)
```

While testing your program, you can also use comment symbols to temporarily remove instructions from the program. Don't forget to remove the parts of your code that are *commented out* once you finish the program because they can lead to confusion when other developers look at your source code.

## Instructions vs. Lines

There are no strict rules about how to distribute the text of a Swift program over the lines in a text file. Usually you write every instruction on a separate line. Swift allows you to write multiple instructions on a single line as long as you separate them by semicolons.

Sometimes, if it makes a program clearer, the programmer writes multiple instructions on a single line. Also, sometimes a single instruction that is very long (containing function/method calls and many different parameters) can be distributed over multiple lines (you'll see this later in this book). Consider the following example:

```
let myLabel = SKLabelNode(fontNamed:"Chalkduster")
myLabel.text = "Hello, World!"; myLabel.fontSize = 65
myLabel.position = CGPoint(x:CGRectGetMidX(self.frame),
    y:CGRectGetMidY(self.frame))
```

Here, the second line contains two instructions: one that changes the text on the label, and one that changes the font size. In this case, writing these two instructions on a single line is not such a bad idea. Both instructions are rather short, and they both change some property of the label. But avoid grouping too many instructions on a single line because it can result in unreadable code, like the following:

```
let myLabel = SKLabelNode(fontNamed:"Chalkduster"); myLabel.text = "Hello, World!"; myLabel.
fontSize = 65; myLabel.position = CGPoint(x:CGRectGetMidX(self.frame), y:CGRectGetMidY(self.
frame))
```

## Whitespace and Indentation

As you can see, the BackgroundColor example uses whitespace liberally. There is an empty line between each method, as well as spaces between each equals sign and the expressions on either side of it. Spacing can help to clarify the code for the programmer. For the compiler, spaces have no meaning. The only place where a space is really important is between separate words: you aren't allowed to write `func update()` as `funcupdate()`. And similarly, you aren't allowed to write an extra space in the middle of a word. In text that is interpreted literally, spaces are also taken literally. There is a difference between

```
print("blue")
```

and

```
print("b l u e")
```

But apart from this, extra spaces are allowed everywhere. The following are good places to put extra whitespace:

- Behind every comma and semicolon (but not before)
- Left and right of the equals sign (=), as in the following:

    ```
    backgroundColor = UIColor.blueColor()
    ```

- At the beginning of lines, so the bodies of methods and classes are indented (usually four spaces) with respect to the braces enclosing the body

You will notice that as soon as you start editing code, Xcode will do some code formatting for you automatically, such as correctly indenting code or placing the opening and closing braces at standard positions.

# What You Have Learned

In this chapter, you have learned the following:

- That the skeleton of a game consists of the game loop and the game world the loop acts on

- How to structure a game program consisting of a few different methods that initialize and update the game world

- The basic layout rules of a Swift program, including how to place comments in your code and where to put extra whitespace to improve readability of the code

# Chapter 3

# Creating a Game World

This chapter will show you how to create a game world by storing information in memory. I will introduce basic types and variables and how they can be used to store or change information. Next, you will see how to store more complicated information in objects that consist of member variables and methods.

## Basic Types and Variables

The previous chapters discussed memory a couple of times. You have seen how to execute a simple instruction like `backgroundColor = UIColor.blueColor()` to set the background color of the app screen to a certain value. In this chapter's example, you will use *memory* to store information temporarily, in order to remember the results of a few simple calculations.

## Types

Types, or *data types*, represent different kinds of structured information. The previous examples used different kinds of information that were passed as parameters to functions. For example, the function `print` requires text, the `update` method in the BasicGame example needs the current system time, and the `printData` function from the example in Chapter 1 doesn't need any information at all in order to perform its task. The compiler can distinguish between all these different kinds of information and, in some cases, even convert information of one type to another. For example, look again at the following Swift instruction:

```
print(currentTime)
```

The `print` function wants text, but what is provided is a time value in seconds, which isn't text but a number. In this case, the Swift compiler is able to automatically translate this number into printable text. However, in general, Swift is a rather strict language, so automatic conversion between different types of information is generally not allowed. Most of the time, you have to explicitly tell the compiler that a conversion between types needs to be done. Such a type conversion is also called a *cast*.

What is the reason for having a strict policy with regard to type conversions? For one thing, clearly defining which type a function or method expects as a parameter makes it easier for other programmers to understand how to use the function. Look at the following header as an example:

```
func playAudio(audioFileId)
```

By only looking at this header, you can't be sure if `audioFileId` is a number or text. That why in Swift, you have to indicate what kind of parameter is expected:

```
func playAudio(audioFileId: Int)
```

You can see that in this header, not only a name is provided, but also a *type* that belongs to this name. The type in this case is `Int`, which in Swift means an integer number.

# Declaration and Assignment of Variables

It's easy to store information in Swift and use it later. What you need to do is provide a name to use when you refer to this information. This name is called a *variable*. A variable is a place in memory with a name. When you want to use a variable in your program, you need to *declare* it before you can actually use it. This is how you declare a variable:

```
var red: Int
```

In this example, the `var` word means that you are declaring a variable. The name of the variable is red. And finally, the `Int` behind the colon means that this variable can store integer numbers. After declaring a variable, you can use it in your program to store information and access it when you need it.

In Swift, you can declare more than a single variable at once. For example,

```
var red: Int, green: Int, fridge: Int, grandMa: Int, applePie: Int
```

Here you declare five different variables that you can now use in your program. When you declare these variables, they will contain arbitrary values. Swift does not allow you to access a variable directly after declaring it. You need to first initialize the variable by assigning a value to it. You can assign a value to a variable by using an *assignment instruction*. For example, let's assign a value to the variable red, as follows:

```
red = 3
```

The assignment instruction consists of the following parts:

- The name of the variable that should be assigned a value
- The = sign
- The new value of the variable

You can recognize the assignment instruction by the equals sign in the middle. However, it's better to think of this sign as "becomes" rather than "equals" in Swift. After all, the variable isn't yet equal to the value to the right of the equals sign—it *becomes* that value after the instruction is executed. The syntax diagram describing the assignment instruction is given in Figure 3-1.

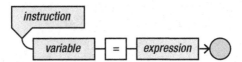

**Figure 3-1.** *Syntax diagram of an assignment instruction*

So now you have seen one instruction for declaring a variable and another instruction to store a value in it. But if you already know which value you want to store in a variable when you declare it, you can combine the declaration of a variable and the first assignment to it:

```
var red: Int = 3
```

When this instruction is executed, the memory will contain the value 3, as shown in Figure 3-2.

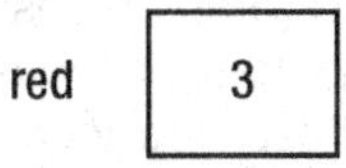

red    | 3 |

**Figure 3-2.** *Memory after a declaration and assignment of a variable*

When you combine the declaration with the initialization of a variable, you don't need to provide the type of information since that's already clear from the value you're assigning. So the instruction

```
var x = 12
```

is the same as

```
var x: Int = 12
```

The process of automatically defining the type of a variable by looking at the value that you assign to the variable is called *type inference*. Once a variable's type is defined (either explicitly or inferred) it cannot be changed. Some languages (such as JavaScript) do allow changing the type of a variable at any point. This is why these languages, as opposed to Swift, are called *loosely typed* languages. Next to variables, Swift also allows you to declare and initialize *constants*. Constants are useful for defining things such as gravity (which will not change, unless your game takes place on different planets), a fixed number of levels that your game consists of, or a mathematical constant such as pi. You declare a constant by replacing var with let, such as

```
let numberOfLevels = 50
```

or with an explicit type indication, such as

```
let numberOfLevels: Int = 50
```

Here are a few more examples of declarations and assignments of numeric variables:

```
let age = 16
var numberOfBananas: Int
numberOfBananas = 2
var a: Int, b: Int
a = 4
var c = 4, d = 15, e = -3
c = d
numberOfBananas = age + 12
```

In the fourth line of this example, you see that it's possible to declare multiple variables in one declaration. You can even perform multiple declarations with assignments in a single declaration, as shown in the sixth line of the example code. On the right side of the assignment, you can put other variables or mathematical expressions, as you can see in the last two lines. The instruction c = d results in the value stored in variable d being stored in variable c as well. Because the variable d contains the value 15, after this instruction is executed, the variable c also contains the value 15. The last instruction takes the value stored in the variable age (16), adds 12 to it, and stores the result in the variable numberOfBananas (which now has the value 28—a lot of bananas!). In summary, the memory looks something like what is depicted in Figure 3-3 after these instructions have been executed.

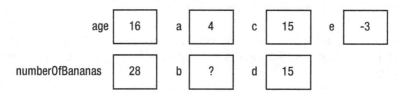

*Figure 3-3. Overview of the memory after declaration and assignment of multiple variables. The variable b contains an arbitrary integer value*

The syntax of declaring variables (with an optional initialization) is expressed in the diagram shown in Figure 3-4. In Figure 3-5, you see the syntax diagram for a constant declaration. Note that the only two differences between the two diagrams are the keyword that is used and the optional or obligatory initialisation of the variable/constant.

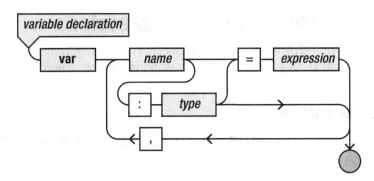

*Figure 3-4.  Syntax diagram of variable declaration with an optional initialization*

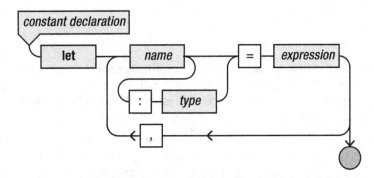

*Figure 3-5.  Syntax diagram of constant declaration and initialization*

## Instructions and Expressions

If you look at the elements in the syntax diagrams, you probably notice that the value or program fragment on the right side of an assignment is called an *expression*. So what is the difference between an expression and an *instruction*? The difference between the two is that an *instruction* changes the memory in some way, whereas an *expression* has a value. Examples of instructions are method calls and assignments, as you saw in the previous section. Instructions often use expressions. Here are some examples of expressions:

```
16
numberOfBananas
2
a + 4
numberOfBananas + 12 - a
-3
"Hello, World!"
```

All these expressions represent a value of a certain type. Except for the last line, all the expressions are numbers. The last expression is a string (of characters). In addition to numbers and strings, there are other kinds of expressions, such as expressions that use operators.

# Operators and More Complex Expressions

This section talks about the different operators that Swift knows. You must learn the priority of each operator so you know in which order calculations are performed.

## Arithmetic Operators

In expressions that are numbers, you can use the following arithmetic operators:

- + (addition)
- - (subtraction)
- * (multiplication)
- / (division)
- % (remainder, or "modulus")

Multiplication uses an asterisk because the signs normally used in mathematics ($\cdot$ and $\times$) aren't found on a computer keyboard. Completely omitting this operator, as is also done in mathematics (for example, in the formula $f(x)=3x$), isn't allowed in Swift because it introduces confusion with variables consisting of more than one character.

The remainder operator, %, gives the division remainder. For instance, the result of 14%3 is 2, and the result of 456%10 is 6. The result always lies between 0 and the value to the right of the operator. The result is 0 if the result of the division is an integer.

## Priority of Operators

When multiple operators are used in an expression, the regular arithmetic rules of precedence apply: multiplication before addition. The result of the expression 1+2*3 therefore is 7, not 9. Addition and subtraction have the same priority, and multiplication and division as well.

If an expression contains multiple operators of the same priority, then the expression is computed from left to right. So, the result of 10-5-2 is 3, not 7. When you want to deviate from these standard precedence rules, you can use parentheses: for example, (1+2)*3 and 3+(6-5). In practice, such expressions generally also contain variables; otherwise you could calculate the results (9 and 4) yourself.

Using more parentheses than needed isn't forbidden: for example, 1+(2*3). You can go completely crazy with this if you want: ((1)+(((2)*3))). However, your program will be much harder to read if you do.

In summary, an expression can be a constant value (such as 12), it can be a variable, it can be another expression in parentheses, or it can be an expression followed by an operator followed by another expression. Figure 3-6 shows the (partial) syntax diagram representing an expression.

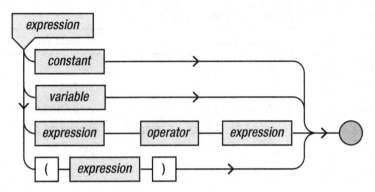

**Figure 3-6.** *Partial syntax diagram of an expression*

# Other Numeric Types

In addition to integer numbers, Swift knows other types of numbers. For example, Swift has a type called Double. Variables of that type can contain numbers with decimals. After the declaration

```
var d: Double
```

you give the variable a value with the assignment operation:

```
d = 2.18
```

Variables of type Double can also contain integer numbers:

```
d = 10
```

Behind the scenes, the compiler will automatically place a zero behind the decimal point. Other than with the Int type, dividing Double variables results in only small rounding errors:

```
d = d / 3
```

The variable d now contains the number 3.33333333.

Apart from Int and Double, there are 10 other types in Swift for numeric variables. Eight of the 10 numeric types can be used for integer numbers. The difference between the types is the range of values that can be represented by a type. Some types allow for a bigger range of values to be represented, but the downside is that these types require more memory. Memory is limited, especially when you're developing games for smartphones. So when you have to store a number, think beforehand which type is best suited. For example, if you want to store the current level index, it makes no sense to use a Double type, since level indices are integer numbers. In that case, a type that only holds positive integer numbers would be more suited. There are types that can contain both negative and positive values; other types only contain positive values. Table 3-1 gives an overview of the various integer types used in Swift.

*Table 3-1. Overview of Available Integer Numeric Types in Swift*

| Type | Space | Lowest Value | Highest Value |
| --- | --- | --- | --- |
| Int8 | 8 bits/1 byte | -128 | 127 |
| Int16 | 16 bits/2 bytes | -32,768 | 32,767 |
| Int32 | 32 bits/4 bytes | -2,147,483,648 | 2,147,483,647 |
| Int64 | 64 bits/8 bytes | -9,223,372,036,854,775,808 | 9,223,372,036,854,775,807 |
| UInt8 | 8 bits/1 byte | 0 | 255 |
| UInt16 | 16 bits/2 bytes | 0 | 65,535 |
| UInt32 | 32 bits/4 bytes | 0 | 4,294,967,295 |
| UInt64 | 64 bits/8 bytes | 0 | 18,446,744,073,709,551,615 |

The Int64 type is only needed if you're planning to use extremely high or low (negative) values. The Int8 type is used if the range of the values is limited. In general, the memory that this saves is only relevant if a lot of these variables (thousands, or even millions) are required. Each integer type also has an unsigned version, and its name begins with a U. Unsigned types can only contain values greater than or equal to 0. Finally, Int holds 32 bits on 32-bit platforms and 64 bits on 64 bit platforms.

For real numbers, there are three different types available. They not only differ in the maximum value that can be stored, but also in precision after the decimal point. You've already seen the Double type. This type has a precision of at least 15 digits. The precision of the Float type can be as little as 6 decimal digits, but a variable of type Float also only takes half the space of Double. Finally, there is a high-precision type called Float80, which can handle up to 19 digits of precision.

Every type has its own target application. For example, the Float80 type could be useful for games that require very precise physical calculations. The Double type is used for many mathematical calculations. Float is used if precision is not that important, but saving memory usage is.

When you convert an expression of a certain type into an expression of another type, it's called a *type conversion*. You can convert a value to another type by writing the type that you want to convert to in front of the expression, and write the expression between parentheses. For example, here is how you convert a Double to a Float:

```
let pi: Double = 3.141592653589793
var smallPi: Float = Float(pi) // contains the value 3.1415927
```

As you can see in the example above, if you convert a Double to a Float, you lose precision. This is why you have to indicate explicitly to the compiler when you want to convert one type into another. If you want to convert a Float to a Double, you will not lose precision, but you still have to explicitly indicate that you want the compiler to convert the value, like so:

```
var myDouble: Double = 12.34
var myFloat: Float = 56.78
var anotherDouble: Double = myFloat // error
```

```
var yetAnotherDouble: Double = Double(myFloat) // OK
var anotherFloat: Float = myDouble             // error
var yetAnotherFloat: Float = Float(myDouble)   // OK
```

# The DiscoWorld Game

In the previous sections, I talked about different variable types and how to declare and assign them. I've given several examples of how to declare and assign variables of types such as Int and Double. Next to the numeric types, there are many other types in Swift. For example, NSTimeInterval is also a type and it represents a time interval in seconds. This is used in the update part of the game loop to determine how much time has passed. You can then use that information to change game object positions or take other actions.

The example in the previous chapter had an update method that looked like this:

```
override func update(currentTime: NSTimeInterval) {
    backgroundColor = UIColor.blueColor()
}
```

As you can see, the update method has a parameter called currentTime, which contains the current system time. Inside the method body, you can use currentTime like a variable. The type of the currentTime variable is NSTimeInterval, which is actually a *type alias* for Double. This means that you can perform calculations with currentTime, and store the result of those calculations in another variable:

```
var time: Double = currentTime % 1
```

The outcome of the expression currentTime % 1 is a number between 0 and 1 since it is the remainder after dividing currentTime by 1. For example, if currentTime contains the value 512.34, then currentTime / 1 = 512, and the remainder currentTime % 1 = 0.34.

Let's now use the variable time to change the background color dynamically. In the example of the previous chapter, you did this:

```
backgroundColor = UIColor.blueColor()
```

In this instruction, you assign a value to something called backgroundColor. That value has a type called UIColor. UIColor is a new type provided by the UIKit framework, which is contained within the SpriteKit framework. Creating a value of that type can be done in a few different ways. The first way is shown above. blueColor is a method that belongs to UIColor, and it creates a value: the color blue. You can also create colors yourself by providing color values between 0 and 1:

```
backgroundColor = UIColor(red: 0, green: 0, blue: 1, alpha: 1)
```

If you construct a UIColor variable in this way, you need to provide four different values: red, green, blue, and alph. The red, green, and blue values determine the *color*, the alpha value determines the *transparency*. The example above creates a blue color. Here are a few examples of other colors:

```
var greenColor: UIColor = UIColor(red: 0, green: 1, blue: 0, alpha: 1)
var redColor: UIColor = UIColor(red: 1, green: 0, blue: 0, alpha: 1)
var grayColor: UIColor = UIColor(red: 0.7, green: 0.7, blue: 0.7, alpha: 1)
var whiteColor: UIColor = UIColor(red: 1, green: 1, blue: 1, alpha: 1)
```

As you can see in these examples, the color intensity values range between 0 and 1, where 1 is the highest color intensity. By setting the red value to 1 and the other two values to 0, you create the color red. You get the color white by setting all intensity values to 1. Similarly, a black color is achieved by setting all values to 0. Using these RGB values, it is possible to create a wide range of colors.

In the DiscoWorld example, you will use the passed game time to vary the color. You already stored a time value varying between 0 and 1 in a variable, as follows:

```
var time: Double = currentTime % 1
```

You can now use this variable to change the background color as follows:

```
backgroundColor = UIColor(red: CGFloat(time), green: 0, blue: 0, alpha: 1)
```

When you create a UIColor value, it expects parameters of a type called CGFloat. The CGFloat type is mainly targeted to graphics applications (the letters "CG" in the type stand for Core Graphics). All of the Apple classes and libraries related to graphics use this type, including UIColor. If an App is compiled for a 64-bit platform, the CGFloat type is an alias for Double. For a 32-bit platform, CGFloat is an alias for Float. This is why you sometimes have to convert expressions to CGFloat. In this case, time is a Double value, so you need to convert it to a CGFloat value first. For the other parameters, conversion is not necessary since numeric constants such as 0 or 1 are automatically translated into Float or Double values.

The nice thing in this example is that you can see how the game loop works to dynamically change the game world. When you run the DiscoWorld example, you'll see the color changing from black to red every second. As an exercise, can you make the color change from red to black every second? Can you change into a different color? And how about going from red to blue? Can you change the code in such a way that the color transition takes two seconds instead of one? Try out a few different things with this example.

To finalize this example, add the following instruction to the update method:

```
myLabel.position = CGPoint(x: 100, y: CGFloat(time * 200))
```

This instruction changes the position of the text label depending on the value of the time variable. CGPoint is another type that you are going to use quite a lot. It represents a two-dimensional point in space. If you create a value of type CGPoint, you need to provide parameters of type CGFloat, similar to UIColor. The difference is that in order to create a CGPoint value you need *x* and *y* coordinates in pixel space. If you run the program, you'll see that the text label moves up 200 pixels every second and then resets itself to the bottom of the screen. This is because the time variable is always a value between 0 and 1, and you multiply this value by 200. Figure 3-7 shows a screenshot of the DiscoWorld example. Try to play around with a few different values. Can you make the label move down instead of up? Or can you make it move to the right? How about moving it diagonally?

*Figure 3-7. A screenshot of the DiscoWorld example*

# Scope of Variables

The place where you declare a variable has consequences for where you're allowed to use the variable. Look at the variable time in the DiscoWorld example. This variable is declared (and assigned a value) in the update method. Because it's declared in the update method, you're only allowed to use it in this method. For example, you aren't allowed to use this variable in the didMoveToView method. Of course, you could declare another variable called time in the didMoveToView method, but it's important to realize that the time variable declared in update would in that case not be the same time variable declared in the didMoveToView method.

Alternatively, if you declare a variable at the *class* level, you can use it anywhere in the class. The myLabel variable has been declared at the class level, and it's accessed by two methods in the class, didMoveToView and update. The didMoveToView method needs to access it because the label needs to be added to the game world. The update method needs to access it in order to change its position. Therefore, it's logical that this variable needs to be declared at the class level so that all methods belonging to the class can use the variable.

The places where a variable can be used are together called the variable's *scope*. In this example, the scope of the variable time is the update method, and the scope of the variable myLabel is the class scope.

# What You Have Learned

In this chapter, you have learned the following:

- How to store basic information in memory using variables

- How to create numeric values as well as values of more complicated types such as UIColor or CGPoint

- How to use the update method to change the game world by manipulating variables

# Chapter 4

# Game Assets

The previous chapters showed you how to make a very basic game application in Swift. You saw how to create a game project in Xcode, and then write a few lines of code to change the background color of an app or to display a text label. You were also introduced to the game loop, and you used the update part of the game loop to vary the background color over time. This chapter will show you how to draw images on the screen, which is the first step toward making nice-looking games. In computer graphics, these images are also called *sprites*. Sprites are generally loaded from a file. This means any program that draws sprites is no longer simply an isolated set of instructions, but relies on *game assets* that are stored somewhere. This immediately introduces a number of things that you need to think about:

- Where are sprites located?
- How do you load and draw a sprite on the screen?
- How do you deal with the resolutions and aspect ratios of the various iDevices?

This chapter answers these questions.

Sound is another type of game asset. And at the end of this chapter, you will also learn how to play music and sound effects in your game.

> **Note** The name *sprite* comes from *spriting*, which is the process of creating two-dimensional, partially transparent raster graphics that are used for video games. In the early days, creating these two-dimensional images was a lot of manual work, but it resulted in a particular style of imagery that inspired people to create similar images of their own, resulting in an artistic technique called *pixel art* or *sprite art*.

# Locating Sprites

Before a program can use any kind of assets, it needs to know where to look for those assets. By default, a game project in Xcode has a folder called *Images.xcassets*. Look at the SpriteDrawing example belonging to this chapter. When you open this project in Xcode and left-click Images.xcassets, you will see that it lists two files: one that represents the app icon, and another one called spr_balloon. The latter refers to an image of a balloon that you can draw on the screen. If you left-click the balloon, you'll see that the image contains several sub-images at different resolutions (see Figure 4-1). These different resolutions are necessary because of the different technical specs of various iOS devices (an iPad Air with its Retina screen has a much higher resolution than an iPhone 4). I'll talk more about this issue later in this chapter.

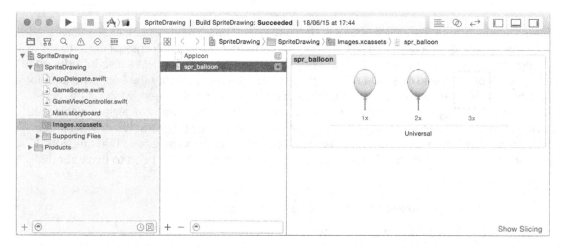

*Figure 4-1.* *Images used in the SpriteDrawing example*

# Loading and Drawing Sprites

Any image part of the Images.xcassets folder can be loaded and drawn on the screen. This is done in a way very similar to drawing a text label on the screen. The following is the GameScene class from the SpriteDrawing example belonging to this chapter:

```
class GameScene: SKScene {
    var balloonSprite = SKSpriteNode(imageNamed: "spr_balloon")

    override func didMoveToView(view: SKView) {
        backgroundColor = UIColor.lightGrayColor()
        balloonSprite.position = CGPoint(x: 200, y: 200)
        addChild(balloonSprite)
    }
}
```

You can see that a variable called balloonSprite is created. This variable refers to a value of type SKSpriteNode. In order to create this value, you have to pass along a parameter: the *name* of the sprite that should be loaded. In the didMoveToView method, you assign a position to the balloonSprite variable, and finally, you add it to the scene. Figure 4-2 shows the output of the SpriteDrawing program.

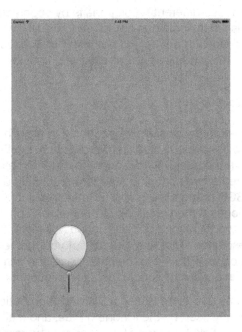

*Figure 4-2. The output of the SpriteDrawing program*

# Resolutions and Aspect Ratios

A big challenge when you're developing games for iOS is making sure that your game looks nice on different iOS devices. It's not enough to design nice sprites; you have to make sure that the size and resolution matches the requirement of the platform. There is a very big difference in the required sprite quality between an iPad 2 with a screen resolution of 1024x768 pixels versus an iPad Air that has a 2048x1536 resolution due to its Retina screen. Not only are the resolutions different, the *aspect ratios* differ between devices as well. An iPad has a much more square screen with its 4:3 aspect ratio versus the widescreen 16:9 aspect ratio of the iPhone 6. So how do you deal with these differences between iOS devices?

Of course, a possible solution is to create your game such that it only works on a single device. That way, you don't have to deal with differences between iOS devices at all. However, you will lose a lot of players that way. In the following paragraphs, I'll show you a way to make sure your sprites work well on several devices, without having to change the code. The main thing you need to watch out for is making sure that the internal game world size doesn't change too much. For example, consider that the iPhone 4 resolution is 960x640 and the iPad Air is 2048x1536. One way to deal with these two very different resolutions is that the iPad Air simply shows a bigger part of the game world than the iPhone 4 (since more fits on its screen). However, that's not a good idea. When you design a game that should always show a single screen, such as most of the example games in this book, you can't apply this trick. And showing a much larger part of the game world on some devices influences the gameplay. If you create a strategy game, you don't want iPhone 4 players to have a disadvantage compared to iPad Air players because they cannot see oncoming attacks as well.

The other way to deal with these different resolutions is by separating the game world size from the screen size. This is what Apple has opted for. Internally, when you write the code for your game, you are working with points and not with pixels directly. However, in some cases, points and pixels correspond directly. For example, consider the following change to the SpriteDrawing example:

```
balloonSprite.position = CGPoint(x: 201, y: 200)
```

The sprite is moved one point in the positive *x* direction. On the iPhone 3GS or the iPad 2, this means that the sprite will move *one pixel* in that direction. On the iPad Air however, the sprite will move *two pixels* in the positive *x* direction. In order to have more or less the same size visuals, you need to create two sprites: a standard resolution one (called "1x" by Apple) that works on the iPhone 3GS or the iPad 2, and a Retina resolution one (called "2x") for the iPad Air and the newer iPhones. When you look at the balloon sprite, you'll see that there are sprites for both the 1x and 2x resolution. The Retina (2x) resolution sprites are double the size of the standard (1x) resolution. That way, the size of your game stays the same whether you play it on an iPad 2 or on an iPad Air. In the latter case, the game will look a lot better since you can provide higher quality artwork in the 2x resolution format.

Since the iPhone 6 Plus came out, there is also a 3x resolution option, also called Retina HD. This resolution is currently only used by the iPhone 6 Plus, and it allows you to create art at a yet higher resolution, namely triple the size of the standard (1x) resolution.

The games in this book use art that has been optimized for all the iDevices, except the iPhone 6 Plus. If you open any of the examples, you'll see that all the sprites are provided in the 1x and 2x resolutions. Note that the example games will run just fine on an iPhone 6 Plus, even though the images are not optimized for it; however, the graphics would be crisper if images at 3x resolution were used.

Apart from the resolution that is used, you need to think about the aspect ratio. One thing you can do in your code is make sure that overlays such as buttons or a health bar are always placed relative to the size of the screen. The only area where you need to be careful is when designing *background images*. If your background images are not large enough, you will see black space on some devices.

In this book, I use a background image of 2668x1536 pixels at Retina (2x) resolution. The standard resolution (1x) is then 1334x768 pixels. A background image of this size is large enough such that none of the devices show any black space. Because the iPhone screens are much smaller than the iPad screens, an iPhone will show only a small part of the background. For example, the iPhone 6 in landscape mode has a width of 667 points and uses a 2x resolution of 1334. This is only half of the total background image at Retina resolution (which is 2668 pixels). In order to more closely match the iPhone and iPad points, I add these lines of code to each of the example games used in this book:

```
var viewSize = skView.bounds.size
if UIDevice.currentDevice().userInterfaceIdiom == .Phone {
    viewSize.height *= 2
    viewSize.width *= 2
}
```

Without going into too much detail, this code doubles the point resolution in case the app is running on an iPhone. The result of this is that a background of 2668x1536 will now show almost completely on an iPhone 6, and when creating apps that should work on both iPads and iPhones, you don't have to think that carefully anymore about which device your game is running on.

Most of the devices will only be able to show a part of the background image. On an iPad, the sides of the background will not be visible. On an iPhone 6, a strip on the top and bottom will not be shown (if the trick of doubling the point resolution explained above is applied). After taking into account all the different devices, you end up with a playable area: an area of the background that is always visible on all devices, regardless of the aspect ratio and resolution. Figure 4-3 shows an overview of the playable area for the standard (1x) and Retina (2x) resolutions.

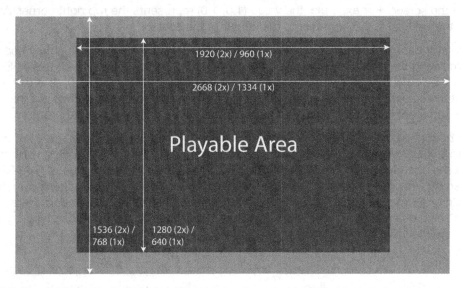

Figure 4-3. The playable area of a background image

You can use this information to design your backgrounds correctly. If you want an element of the background to be visible on all devices, make sure that it is located inside the playable area. Again, this is only an issue for background design. Other elements of the game (such as a menu, overlays, the player character, and so on) can be dealt with differently. If you add these elements, simply determine their position according to the size of the screen. You will see a few examples of this approach in the games that you'll develop while reading this book.

> **Note**    The backgrounds and sprites for the games in this book are designed in such a way that they work for most iDevices. There are a few tradeoffs involved when doing this. For example, on some devices only a part of the background will be shown. Also, game objects may look quite small on small screens such as the iPhone 4 or 5. If you design a game, you may consider using different assets altogether for specific devices, and perhaps even design different levels for the iPhone and iPad versions separately. It's better to design a game that works really well on a limited set of devices than a game that doesn't work all that well on any device.

The ScreenSizeTest example belonging to this chapter shows you what part of the game world each device shows by displaying Figure 4-3 as a background image. Try it on different devices in the iOS simulator to see what it looks like. Here is one interesting line of code in this example, which you can find in the didMoveToView method within the GameScene.swift file:

```
anchorPoint = CGPoint(x: 0.5, y: 0.5)
```

Remember that the origin of the coordinate system in a scene is in the *bottom left* of the screen. The code above changes that so that the origin is in the *center* of the screen. The value set as the origin of the coordinate system is specified in terms of the total width and height of the screen. For example, the value (1.0, 1.0) represents the top right corner. And as a result, the value (0.5, 0.5) represents the center of the screen.

Especially for backgrounds, setting the origin to the center of the screen is useful because then calculating the background position for different devices becomes much easier. Since sprites are by default drawn with their center at the position, and position (0, 0) is now the center of the screen, sprites are now by default centered on the screen. Leave out this line of code (or comment it out), and see what happens when you run the example program.

The line of code above is an assignment instruction. The variable called anchorPoint is assigned a value. The value that is assigned is CGPoint(x: 0.5, y:0.5). You can also say that this line of code assigns a value of *type* CGPoint to anchorPoint. A value of type CGPoint is created by writing the name of the type and then, between parentheses, the parameters needed in order to create that value. In this case, an *x* and a *y* value are needed. Here you can also see a difference between simple, built-in types such as Int. For those types, you simply write the value that you want to assign:

```
var age: Int = 12
```

For more complex types (such as CGPoint), you need to write the type name and then, between parentheses, the parameters needed to create the value. Another example of a more complex type is UIColor. Here is an example of an assignment that uses the UIColor type:

```
backgroundColor = UIColor(red: CGFloat(time), green: 0, blue: 0, alpha: 1)
```

Here you see the same syntax. Write the type name and then, between parentheses, the required parameters. One of these parameters is red. And that parameter is assigned a value that's also created by a non-builtin type called CGFloat. Also, you can see that you write the name of the type (CGFloat) and, between parentheses, the required parameter (time). Whenever you create a value using a complex type such as UIColor or CGPoint, this value is also called an *object*, or an *instance* of that type.

Types are very useful. They provide a kind of blueprint that describes what a value should look like. For example, the CGPoint type describes a data structure for two-dimensional points. You don't have to think about how to create such a data structure; CGPoint does that for you. You only need to provide the right parameter values when you create a CGPoint instance.

# Moving Sprites

Now that you're able to draw a sprite on the screen, you can use the game loop to make it move, just like you did with the text label in the DiscoWorld example in Chapter 3. In the SpriteDrawing program, you drew a balloon on the screen. Let's make a small extension of this program that changes the balloon's position based on the passed time. First, you need to add the update method to the GameScene class, so that it becomes a part of the game loop. In the DiscoWorld example, you retrieved and stored the current time as follows:

```
var time: Double = currentTime % 1
```

Let's try to change the position of the balloon so that it flies from the left side of the screen to the right side. A simple way to do this is by changing the position using the time variable. In order to avoid too many conversions between types, you store the time not as a Double, but as a CGFloat, which is the main type used in SpriteKit to represent floating point values:

```
var time = CGFloat(currentTime % 1)
```

Now, you can change the position of the balloon by using the time variable, as follows:

```
balloonSprite.position = CGPoint(x: time * 200, y: 200)
```

Since the time variable always has a value between 0 and 1, the *x* value will have a range from 0 to 200 (since you multiply time by 200). However, the width of the viewing area on your iDevice probably is not 200 points, but something else. Moreover, the width also depends on whether you hold the device horizontally or vertically. Fortunately, the GameScene class has a variable called size, which contains two other variables, width and height. Have a look at the following line of code:

```
balloonSprite.position = CGPoint(x: time * size.width), y: 200)
```

Instead of multiplying the time by a fixed value, this instruction multiplies the time by the current width of the screen. As a result, the balloon will move from the left side of the screen to the right side. The MovingSprite example belonging to this chapter shows the result of changing the balloon position in this way. If you rotate the device (in the iOS simulator, choose Hardware ➤ Rotate left, for example), you'll see that the balloon still moves from the left side to the right side of the device regardless of the device orientation and screen width. Try a few different things to see how you can modify this program. Can you make the sprite move from the right to the left? Can you make the sprite move faster or slower?

# Loading and Drawing Multiple Sprites

Building games that can only display a single sprite is somewhat boring. You can make your game a bit more visually appealing by displaying a background sprite. This means you have to load and position two sprites instead of one. The MovingSpriteWithBackground example shows you how to do this. In this example, you can see that there are now two variables referring to a sprite:

```
var backgroundSprite = SKSpriteNode(imageNamed: "spr_background")
var balloonSprite = SKSpriteNode(imageNamed: "spr_balloon")
```

When you're dealing with multiple sprites, you need to think about which sprite should be drawn on top. In this example, you want the balloon to be drawn on top of the background and not vice versa. How to do this? Until now, you've seen that the game world has an *x* and a *y* axis, with the default origin at the bottom left of the screen. In fact, the game world also has a *z* axis, which is sticking out of the screen toward you. You can change the position of a sprite on this *z* axis. Since it sticks out of the screen, a higher *z* position value means that the sprite is closer to you. So if you choose a higher *z* position for the balloon than for the background, the balloon will be drawn closer to you and therefore it will be visible on top of the background. Here are the two assignment instructions that achieve this:

```
backgroundSprite.zPosition = 0
balloonSprite.zPosition = 1
```

When the correct *z* positions of the sprites are set, you add them to the scene (see Figure 4-4):

```
addChild(backgroundSprite)
addChild(balloonSprite)
```

*Figure 4-4. The MovingSpriteWithBackground example*

In order to make the balloon move correctly from the left to the right, you need to modify the code in the update method that calculates its position. This is necessary because you changed the origin of the coordinate system to the center of the screen. The only thing you need to do is subtract half the width of the screen from the *x* position, as follows:

```
balloonSprite.position = CGPoint(x: time * size.width - size.width/2, y: 200)
```

Here you see that you can use `size` to retrieve the size of the screen. Although it may look like `size` is a variable, it is something else: a *property*. Properties belong to a class, just like methods. The difference is that properties do not need parameters between parentheses; they simply represent a value of some sort. In this case, that value is the size of the screen. This value, in turn, has two parts: a *width* and a *height*. Each represents a `CGFloat` number value. Since `time` is also of type `CGFloat`, you can use these values in combination with each other, without having to do any type conversions.

You've used properties before. For example, you used `anchorPoint` to change the origin of the coordinate system, which is also a property. You have even defined your own properties already. If a variable is defined at the class level (`backgroundSprite` or `balloonSprite` are examples of this), then this variable is called a property of the class. Later on, I'll discuss properties in more detail.

Every time you want to draw a sprite on the screen, you can define an `SKSpriteNode` property and add it to the scene. For instance, if you want to draw a few balloons at different positions over the background, you simply define a property for every balloon you want to add to the scene:

```
var balloonSprite2 = SKSpriteNode(imageNamed: "spr_balloon")
var balloonSprite3 = SKSpriteNode(imageNamed: "spr_balloon")
var balloonSprite4 = SKSpriteNode(imageNamed: "spr_balloon")
```

You need to make sure that each sprite is added to the scene in the `didMoveToView` method, as follows:

```
override func didMoveToView(view: SKView) {
    anchorPoint = CGPoint(x: 0.5, y: 0.5)
    backgroundSprite.zPosition = 0
    balloonSprite.zPosition = 1
    balloonSprite2.zPosition = 1
    balloonSprite3.zPosition = 1
    balloonSprite4.zPosition = 1
    addChild(backgroundSprite)
    addChild(balloonSprite)
    addChild(balloonSprite2)
    addChild(balloonSprite3)
    addChild(balloonSprite4)
}
```

Here you can also see that all the balloon sprites are being drawn in front of the background. You can also draw multiple moving sprites at the same time. For each balloon, you need to change its position in the update method:

```
override func update(currentTime: NSTimeInterval) {
    var time = CGFloat(currentTime % 1)
    balloonSprite.position = CGPoint(x: time * size.width - size.width/2, y: 200)
    balloonSprite2.position = CGPoint(x: time * size.width - size.width/2 - 100, y: 200)
    balloonSprite3.position = CGPoint(x: time * size.width - size.width/2, y: 0)
    balloonSprite4.position = CGPoint(x: time * size.width - size.width/2 - 100, y: 0)
}
```

Play around with the example. Think of different ways to draw moving balloons on the screen. Try a few different position values. Can you make some balloons move faster or slower than others?

# Configuring the Device Orientation

Especially when developing games, it's important to think about the orientation of the device. Are you going to create a game that is supposed to be played in portrait mode or in landscape mode? Some games work better in portrait mode, others in landscape mode. This also depends on the way the player interacts with the game world. For example, a portrait mode game is designed in such a way that you hold the phone like you always hold it, and operate the screen with your other hand. This is a good approach for games where you swipe over the screen such as Temple Run. Side-scrolling games, on the other hand, are generally better in landscape, since you want to show as much width of a level as possible to avoid too much scrolling. In this book, you'll develop both portrait and landscape games.

By default, a project in Xcode allows for any device orientation, and it will rotate the graphics accordingly. For most games, this is not desirable because you generally create a layout that works well in either portrait mode or landscape mode–not both. There is an easy way to change the allowed device orientations in the project settings of Xcode. Click the project in the top left of the screen, and then select the target (for example, MovingSpriteWithBackground). Under Deployment Info, you can select the allowed orientations. In the Devices selection box, choose whether you want to change the allowed orientations of the iPad version, the iPhone version, or the Universal version of the app (which is the option you choose if you want to create an app that works for both iPhones and iPad). Figure 4-5 shows the orientation selection screen in Xcode. Run the program and see how the app responds in the iOS simulator when you simulate a device rotation. You can rotate the device by going to the Hardware menu in the simulator and then choose whether you want to rotate left or right.

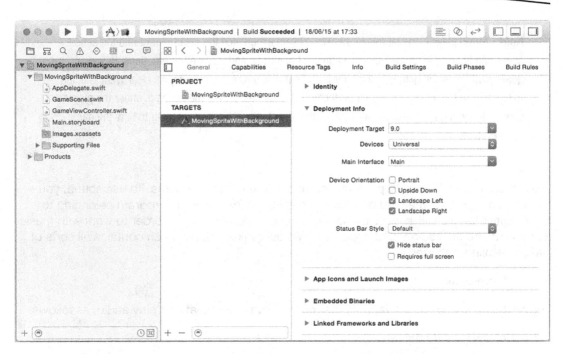

*Figure 4-5.* *Choosing the device orientations that the app supports. If the projects and targets list is not visible, click the icon left of the menu item General to open the panel*

# Music and Sounds

Most games contain sound effects and background music. These are important for various reasons. Sound effects give important cues to indicate to the user that something has happened. For example, playing a click sound when the user clicks a button provides feedback to the user that the button was indeed pressed. Hearing footsteps indicates that enemies might be nearby, even though the player may not see them yet. And hearing a bell ringing in the distance can give an indication that something is about to happen. The old game Myst was a classic in this respect because many cues about how to progress were passed to the player through sounds.

Atmospheric sound effects like dripping water, wind in the trees, and the sound of cars in the distance enhance the experience and give a feeling of being present in the game world. They make the environment more alive, even when nothing is actually happening on the screen.

> **Note**   Music plays a crucial role in the way players experience the environment and the action.
> Music can be used to create tension, sadness, happiness, and many other emotions. However,
> dealing with music in games is a lot harder than it is in movies. In movies, it's clear what is going
> to happen, so the music can match perfectly. But in games, part of the action is under the player's
> control. Modern games use adaptive music that constantly changes according to how the game
> story evolves.

In Swift, it's relatively easy to play background music or sound effects. To use sound, you
first need a sound file that you can play. In the SoundTest example program belonging to
this chapter, the file snd_music.mp3 serves as background music. In order to work with music
and sound effects, you need to import the AVFoundation library, which contains all sorts of
classes dealing with media:

```
import AVFoundation
```

The next step is declaring a variable that refers to an object that can play audio, as follows:

```
var audioPlayer = AVAudioPlayer()
```

Now you can initialize the audio player to start playing a certain audio file in the
didMoveToView method. This happens in three steps. The first step is to construct a so-called
URL that represents the location of the sound file. This URL needs to be constructed in such
a way that it works across all iDevices. This is the line of code that achieves it:

```
let soundURL = NSBundle.mainBundle().URLForResource("snd_music", withExtension: "mp3")
```

This looks like a complicated instruction. An NSBundle object is a location in the file system
that groups code and resources that can be used in a program. The mainBundle method
returns an NSBundle object corresponding to the location of the app executable. Finally, the
URLForResource method constructs a file location (URL) within the bundle location. So in the
end, all you're doing is creating a representation of where a file is located that can be easily
interpreted by the computer.

Now that you have constructed this file URL, you can initialize the audio player with a
reference to that file:

```
audioPlayer = try! AVAudioPlayer(contentsOfURL: soundURL!)
```

Finally, you can start playing the audio by calling the play method, as follows:

```
audioPlayer.play()
```

You may want to reduce the volume of the background music so you can play (louder) sound
effects over it later. Setting the volume is done with the following instruction:

```
audioPlayer.volume = 0.4
```

The volume property is a value between 0 and 1, where 0 means no sound and 1 plays back the sound at full volume.

Technically, there is no difference between background music and sound effects. Normally, background music is played at a lower volume; and many games loop the background music so that when the song ends, the audio is played from the beginning again. For that you can use the numberOfLoops property:

```
audioPlayer.numberOfLoops = 0 // default behavior: audio plays only once
audioPlayer.numberOfLoops = 1 // audio is repeated once (= audio played twice)
audioPlayer.numberOfLoops = -1 /* a negative value means the number of loops is
    infinite, so the audio will always keep playing */
```

All the games you develop in this book use both types of sound (background music and sound effects) to make the games more exciting. For every sound effect or background music object, you need to create a separate audio player object. Play around with the example. Can you add a few loops to the music? Also try to change the volume of the sound.

> **Note**   You need to watch out for a few things when using sounds and music in your game. Sound can be annoying to some players, so if you do use sound effects or music, make sure there is a way for the player to turn them off. Also, don't force players to wait until a sound has finished playing before they can continue. You might have composed a great song that you want to play while the introduction screen is shown, but players don't launch your game to listen to your music—they want to play! The same principle holds for in-game video sequences. Always provide a way for the user to skip those (even if you got your favorite family member to provide the zombie sounds). Finally, some players may have limited disk space on their iPhone or iPad, so try to use small sound files whenever possible.

# What You Have Learned

In this chapter, you have learned the following:

- How to load game assets such as sprites and sounds into memory
- How to draw multiple sprites on the screen and move them around
- How to play background music and sound effects in your game

Part **II**

# Painter

In this part, you will develop a game called *Painter* (see Figure II-1). While you're developing this game, I will also introduce a few new techniques that are very useful when programming games, such as organizing instructions in classes and methods, conditional instructions, iteration, and much more.

*Figure II-1. The Painter game*

The goal of the Painter game is to collect three different colors of paint: red, green, and blue. The paint falls from the sky in cans that are kept floating by balloons, and you must make sure each can has the right color before it falls through the bottom of the screen. You can change the color of the paint by shooting a paint ball of the desired color at the falling can. You can select the color that you shoot by using the R, G, and B keys on your keyboard. You can shoot a paint ball by left-clicking in the game screen. If you click further away from the paint cannon, you give the ball a higher velocity. The place where you click also determines the direction in which the cannon shoots. For each can that lands in the correct bin, you get 10 points. For each wrongly colored can, you lose a life (indicated by the yellow balloons at top left of the screen). You can run the final version of this game by downloading the example code and running the PainterFinal example from Chapter 11.

# Chapter 5

# Reacting to Player Input

An important element of a game is that it reacts to what the player is doing. On iPhones or iPads, games mainly respond to touch input by the player, which also holds true for the games you develop while reading this book. Some games also use other input data such as the built-in accelerometer, which I'll briefly discuss in this chapter. In order to deal with input data, you're going to need a few new programming concepts, such as the `if` instruction, which will be introduced in this chapter.

## Dealing With Touch Input

Any Apple device using a touch screen can track multiple fingers and how they move over the screen. The finger movements that a user makes can be interpreted as *gestures* (such as swiping to move to another page, or a pinching motion to zoom in or out), or the finger locations can be used directly to control elements of the game. In order to deal with touch input, there are three important events that you need to handle in your program:

- The player starts touching the screen somewhere with their finger(s).
- The player moves their finger(s) over the screen.
- The player stops touching the screen with their finger(s).

Since a touch screen can handle multiple touches at the same time, these events sometimes refer to one finger, and sometimes to multiple fingers. For each of these three events, you can add a method to the `GameScene` class that handles the event. Inside these methods, you have access to the various finger locations that were detected by the touch screen. For now, let's create a very simple touch-handling program that only remembers a single touch location regardless of how many fingers the player has on the screen. If you open the `GameScene.swift` file in the Painter1 example belonging to this chapter, you can take a look at the code.

You need to store the touch location somewhere, so let's add a property of type `CGPoint` to the `GameScene` class for that purpose:

```
var touchLocation = CGPoint(x: 0, y: 0)
```

To see how touching with multiple fingers works, let's also add a property in which you keep track of how many fingers the player has touching the screen (which initially is assumed to be zero):

```
var nrTouches = 0
```

You now need to change the values of the touchLocation and nrTouches properties whenever the player interacts with the touch screen. Once you've done that, you can make corresponding changes to the game world, such as moving a sprite, or handling the player touching a button.

In order to deal with touch input, you need to add three methods to the GameScene class that correspond to the three types of events mentioned earlier. These methods are named touchesBegan, touchesMoved, and touchesEnded. Here is the touchesBegan method:

```
override func touchesBegan(touches: Set<UITouch>, withEvent event: UIEvent?) {
    let touch = touches.first!
    touchLocation = touch.locationInNode(self)
    nrTouches = nrTouches + touches.count
}
```

This method gets two parameters. The first is a variable called touches. This variable is of type Set<UITouch> and it represents one or more touch locations. Set is a so-called *generic type*, because it can represent various kinds of sets. The brackets behind the type name indicate what kind of set it is. For example, the type Set<Int> represents a set of integer number. In this case, Set<UITouch> represents a set of UITouch objects. A UITouch object represents all the combined information pertaining to a touch, such as its location, at what time the user started this touch, and so on. The second parameter (which is not used in the method body) contains other information about the event, such as the exact time when the event occurred. You can also see that this second parameter has two names. The first name (withEvent) is used when this method is called, and the second name (event) is used when you want to access the event object inside the method body. There are many other features and options when writing a method or a function in Swift. Chapter 6 contains a more detailed discussion of methods and functions.

The body of the method consists of three instructions. The first instruction declares a constant called touch and assigns the result of the expression touches.first! to it. The first part of the expression is touches, which is the set of locations where the player is touching the screen. Then, there is a dot and a property name first. You have seen the usage of the dot before, as in

```
background.zPosition = 0
```

In Swift, the dot generally means that you retrieve information from an object or change the object in some way. The object that you are manipulating at the moment is written before the dot. Behind the dot, you indicate how you want to manipulate the object. In the example above, the background object has a piece of information (or: a property) called zPosition, and you change the object by assigning a value of 0 to zPosition. Here is another example of how you can use the dot:

```
var myVariable: Int = background.position.x
```

In this example, you retrieve the position from the background sprite, and then from that position its x value. Instead of directly accessing information, you can also call a *method* that manipulates an object, such as

```
background.removeFromParent()
```

The removeFromParent method manipulates the background object by removing it from the game scene. Basically, it undoes the following instruction:

```
addChild(background)
```

Going back to the touch input example, first is a property of the Set<UITouch> type, and it returns the first element in the set of touches. The whole expression ends with an *exclamation mark*. This has something to do with the fact that it is possible that the touches object is empty, meaning that the first property cannot retrieve a location, since there aren't any locations. The exclamation mark means that the programmer knows about it and guarantees that touches will never be empty–which is reasonable, since the touchesBegan method would never be called if the player has not started touching the screen. Chapter 12 discusses the usage of the exclamation mark, also called *unwrapping*, in more detail.

The second instruction in the touchesBegan method assigns a value to the touchLocation property. The value is the result of calling the methodlocationInNode from the touch variable with one parameter, self. This calculates the position of the touch location with respect to the game scene. The word self refers to the game scene object. The exact meaning of self will be discussed later in more detail.

So, to summarize, the first two instructions retrieve a touch information object from a set of touches, calculates its location in the game scene, and then assigns that location to the touchLocation property. The third, final instruction is much simpler; it adds the number of touches in the set (retrieved using the count property) to the nrTouches property, like so:

```
nrTouches = nrTouches + touches.count
```

This instruction illustrates once more that you should never read the = symbol as "equals" in Swift but always as "becomes." So, the right-hand side of this assignment is the sum of the current value of nrTouches and the number of new touches that have begun. There is a shorthand version for this assignment, and it looks like this:

```
nrTouches += touches.count
```

You can read this instruction as "add touches.count to nrTouches". Similarly, Swift also knows shorthand notations for subtraction (-=), multiplication (*=) and division (/=), among others.

You can see that the shorthand notation for subtraction is used in the touchesEnded method, which contains only a single instruction:

```
override func touchesEnded(touches: Set<UITouch>, withEvent event: UIEvent?) {
    nrTouches -= touches.count
}
```

In this method, you simply subtract the number of touches that have ended from the nrTouches variable. As a result, the nrTouches variable now keeps track of how many fingers the player currently has placed on the touch screen.

The final method you need to define is touchesMoved. This takes care of any finger movement by the player. Since the number of touches doesn't change, the method contains two instructions: one to retrieve the touch information, and one to update the touch location:

```swift
override func touchesMoved(touches: Set<UITouch>, withEvent event: UIEvent?) {
    let touch = touches.first!
    touchLocation = touch.locationInNode(self)
}
```

Again, realize that this approach is not compatible with the player touching the screen in multiple places, since you are retrieving only a single touch location from the set. In Chapter 12, I will show you a more elegant solution that properly deals with multiple touches and touch movements.

# Using the Touch Location to Change the Game World

In the previous section, you've seen how to read touch input and store a touch location in a property. You can use that touch location to make changes to the game world. For example, you could draw a sprite at the touch location. One of the features of the Painter game is that it contains a cannon barrel that rotates according to the location where the player touches the screen. This cannon is controlled by the player in order to shoot paint balls. In this section, you will learn how to add such a rotating cannon barrel to the game.

You have to declare a few properties to make this possible. In any case, you will need properties for storing the background and the cannon-barrel sprites. As you can see, the following properties have been declared and initialized in the code:

```swift
var background = SKSpriteNode(imageNamed: "spr_background")
var cannonBarrel = SKSpriteNode(imageNamed: "spr_cannon_barrel")
```

In the didMoveToView method, you need to place these objects at their correct position, make sure that the cannon barrel is drawn on top of the background, and add the objects to the game scene. You also need to choose the correct origin (anchor point) for the cannon barrel because when you rotate a sprite, it will rotate around its origin. Here are the instructions that do this:

```swift
background.zPosition = 0
cannonBarrel.zPosition = 1
cannonBarrel.position = CGPoint(x:-412, y:-220)
cannonBarrel.anchorPoint = CGPoint(x:0.24, y:0.5)
addChild(background)
addChild(cannonBarrel)
```

The position of the barrel is chosen such that it fits nicely on the cannon base that is already drawn on the background. The barrel image contains a circular part with the actual barrel attached to it. You want the barrel to rotate around the center of the circular part.

That means you have to set this center as the origin. Because the circle part is at left on the sprite and the radius of this circle is half the height of the cannon-barrel sprite, you set the barrel origin to (0.24, 0.5), as you can see in the code. Try changing these values in the Painter1 example to see what is happening when you rotate the sprite.

The next step is calculating the rotation that the cannon barrel should have depending on the touch location. Since this has to happen every time the player moves, the best place to do this is in the update method. So how do you calculate the angle? Have a look at Figure 5-1.

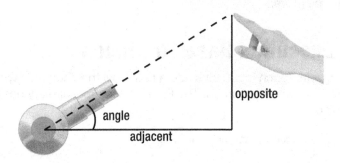

**Figure 5-1.** *Calculating the angle of the barrel based on the touch location*

If you remember your math classes, you may recall that angles in triangles can be calculated with *trigonometric functions*. In this case, you can calculate the angle using the *tangent* function, which is given as follows:

$$tan(angle) = \frac{opposite}{adjacent}$$

In other words, the angle is given by

$$angle = arctan\left(\frac{opposite}{adjacent}\right)$$

You can calculate the length of the opposite and adjacent sides by calculating the difference between the touch location and the position of the cannon barrel, as follows:

```
let opposite = touchLocation.y - cannonBarrel.position.y
let adjacent = touchLocation.x - cannonBarrel.position.x
```

Now you have to calculate the arctangent using these values. How do you do this? Fortunately, Swift knows a number of useful mathematical functions, including trigonometric functions such as sine, cosine, and tangent, and their inverses (arcsine, arccosine, and arctangent). There are two functions that can calculate the arctangent. The first version takes a single value as a parameter. You can't use this version in this case: when the touch location is directly over the barrel, a division by zero will occur because adjacent is zero.

For situations where the arctangent needs to be calculated while taking into account possible singularities such as this, there is an alternative arctangent function. The `atan2` function takes opposite and adjacent lengths as separate parameters and returns the equivalent in radians of 90 degrees in this situation. You can use this function to calculate the angle as follows:

```
cannonBarrel.zRotation = atan2(opposite, adjacent)
```

As you can see, you rotate the cannon barrel about the z axis, which is the axis sticking out of the screen toward the player.

# Conditional Execution Based on Touch

To further test dealing with touch input, let's add a text label that indicates whether or not the player is currently touching the screen. The Painter1 example already has a property declared for that purpose:

```
var touchingLabel = SKLabelNode(text:"not touching")
```

As you can see, the label is initialized with the text "not touching". What you need to do is check in the `update` method whether the `nrTouches` property contains a value larger than zero. If that is the case, the text should be changed to "touching". If `nrTouches` equals zero, the text should be "not touching". So, you need to somehow execute instructions only if some condition is met. You can do that with a *conditional instruction*, and it uses a new keyword, `if`.

With the `if` instruction, you can provide a condition and execute a block of instructions if this condition is true (in total, this is sometimes also referred to as a *branch*). Here are some examples of conditions:

- The player has touched the screen.
- The number of seconds that have passed since the start of the game is larger than 1,000.
- The cannon barrel has a rotation between 0 and 90 degrees.
- The monster has eaten your character.

These conditions can either be *true* or *false*. A condition is an *expression* because it has a value (it's either *true* or *false*). This value is also called a *Boolean* value. With an `if` instruction, you can execute a block of instructions if a condition is true. Take a look at this example `if` instruction:

```
if nrTouches > 0 {
    touchingLabel.text = "touching"
}
```

The condition is written right after the `if` keyword. A block of instructions follows, enclosed by braces. In this example, the text of the label is changed to "touching" as soon as the number of recorded touches is larger than 0. You can place multiple instructions between the braces if you want:

```
if nrTouches > 0 {
    touchingLabel.text = "touching"
    let opposite = touchLocation.y - cannonBarrel.position.y
    let adjacent = touchLocation.x - cannonBarrel.position.x
    cannonBarrel.zRotation = atan2(opposite, adjacent)
}
```

In this example, you change the cannon rotation only if the player is actually touching the screen. Here is another example of an `if` instruction:

```
if nrTouches == 0 {
    touchingLabel.text = "not touching"
}
```

This instruction changes the text of the touching label to "not touching" if the player is not touching the screen. You can also define an alternative when you write an if instruction:

```
if nrTouches > 0 {
    touchingLabel.text = "touching"
    let opposite = touchLocation.y - cannonBarrel.position.y
    let adjacent = touchLocation.x - cannonBarrel.position.x
    cannonBarrel.zRotation = atan2(opposite, adjacent)
} else {
    touchingLabel.text = "not touching"
}
```

In this example, if the number of touches is larger than zero, the label text is set to "touching" and the cannon rotation is calculated. In all other cases (if nrTouches is zero or smaller), the touching label text is set to "not touching".

# Testing for Alternatives

When there are multiple categories of values, you can find out with `if` instructions which case you're dealing with. The second test is placed after the `else` of the first `if` instruction so that the second test is executed only when the first test fails. A third test could be placed after the `else` of the second `if` instruction, and so forth.

The following fragment determines how well the player scored, so that you can display different messages to the player:

```
if score < 100 {
    print("Ouch, you definitely need to play more!")
} else if score < 500 {
        print("Good job, well done.")
      } else if score < 1000 {
            print("Very nice score!")
          } else {
            print("Awesome, you are indestructible!")
          }
```

After every else (except the last one) is another if instruction. If the player scored very low (less than 100 points), a message ("Ouch…") is displayed and the rest of the instructions are ignored (they're after the else, after all). Better players, on the other hand, go through all the tests (less than 500? less than 1000?) before you conclude that the player got a very high score.

I used indentation in this fragment to indicate which else belongs to which if. When there are many different categories, the text of the program becomes less and less readable. Therefore, as an exception to the usual rule that instructions after the else should be indented, you can use a simpler layout with such complicated if instructions:

```
if score < 100 {
    print("Ouch, you definitely need to play more!")
} else if score < 500 {
    print("Good job, well done.")
} else if score < 1000 {
    print("Very nice score!")
} else {
    print("Awesome, you are indestructible!")
}
```

The additional advantage here is that using this layout, it's a lot easier to see which cases are handled by the instructions. In addition to the if instruction, there is an instruction called switch that is better suited for dealing with many different alternatives. See Chapter 19 for more information about how to use switch.

The syntax of the if instruction with an alternative is represented by the syntax diagram in Figure 5-2. The body of an if instruction consists of one or more instructions between braces because the body is a *block* of instructions, as defined in the syntax diagram in Figure 5-3. After the else keyword, an arrow goes back to the if keyword to allow defining a chain of alternatives, as explained previously in this section.

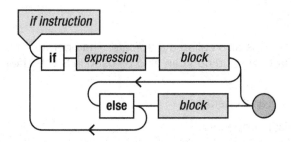

*Figure 5-2. Syntax diagram of the if instruction*

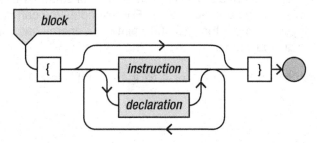

*Figure 5-3. Syntax diagram of a block of instructions*

# Comparison Operators

The condition in the header of an if instruction is an expression that returns a truth value: *true* or *false*. When the outcome of the expression is *true*, the body of the if instruction is executed. In these conditions, you're allowed to use comparison operators. The following operators are available:

- < (less than)
- <= (less than or equal to)
- > (greater than)
- >= (greater than or equal to)
- == (equal to)
- != (not equal to)

These operators may be used between any two values. On the left side and the right side of these operators, you may put constant values, variables, or complete expressions with addition, multiplication, or whatever you want. You test the equality of two values using a double equals sign (==). This is very different from a single equals sign, which denotes an assignment. The difference between these two operators is very important:

x = 5 means *Assign* the value 5 to x.

x == 5 means *Is* x equal to 5?

# Logic Operators

In logical terms, a condition is also called a *predicate*. The operators that are used in logic to connect predicates (*and*, *or*, and *not*) can also be used in Swift. They have a special notation:

- &&  is the logical *and* operator.

- ||  is the logical *or* operator.

- !  is the logical *not* operator.

You can use these operators to check for complicated logical statements so that you can execute instructions only in very particular cases. For example, you can display a "You win!" message only if the player has more than 10,000 points, the enemy has a life force of 0, and the player's life force is greater than 0:

```
if playerPoints > 10000 && enemyLifeForce == 0 && playerLifeForce > 0 {
    print("You win!")
}
```

# The Boolean Type

Expressions that use comparison operators or that connect other expressions with logical operators also have a type, just like expressions that use arithmetic operators. After all, the result of such an expression is a value, one of the two truth values of *true* or *false*. In Swift, these truth values are represented by the true and false keywords.

In addition to being used to express a condition in an if instruction, logical expressions can be applied in a lot of different situations. A logical expression is similar to an arithmetic expression, except that it has a different type. For example, you can store the result of a logical expression in a variable, pass it as a parameter, or use that result again in another expression.

The type of truth values is Bool (or *Boolean*), named after the English mathematician and philosopher George Boole (1815–1864). Here is an example of a declaration and an assignment of a Boolean variable:

```
var test: Bool
test = x > 3 && y < 5
```

In this case, if x contains, for example, the value 6 and y contains the value 3, the Boolean expression x > 3 && y < 5 will evaluate to true and this value will be stored in the variable test. You can also store the Boolean values true and false directly in a variable:

```
var isAlive: Bool = false
```

Boolean variables are extremely handy for storing the status of different objects in a game. For example, you can use a Boolean variable to store whether the player is still alive, whether the player is currently jumping, whether a level is finished, and so on. You can use Boolean variables as an expression in an if instruction, like so:

```
if isAlive {
    // do something
}
```

In this case, if the expression isAlive evaluates to true, the body of the if instruction is executed. You might think this code would generate a compiler error and you need to do a comparison of the Boolean variable, like this:

```
if isAlive == true {
    // do something
}
```

However, this extra comparison isn't necessary. A conditional expression as in the if instruction *must evaluate to* true or false. Because a Boolean variable already represents one of these two values, you don't need to perform the comparison.

You can use the Boolean type to store complex expressions that are either true or false. Let's look at a few additional examples:

```
var a = 12 > 5
var b = a && 3 + 4 == 8
var c = a || b
if !c {
    a = false
}
```

Before you read on, try to determine the value of the variables a, b, and c after these instructions have been executed. In the first line, you declare and initialize a Boolean a. The truth value that is stored in this Boolean is evaluated from the expression 12 > 5, which evaluates to true. This value is then assigned to variable a. In the second line, you declare and initialize a new variable b, in which you store the result of a more complex expression. The first part of this expression is the variable a, which contains the value true. The second part of the expression is a comparison expression 3 + 4 == 8. This comparison is not true (3 + 4 doesn't equal 8), so this evaluates to false, and therefore the logical *and* also results in false. Therefore, the variable b contains the value false after this instruction executes.

The third instruction stores the result of the logical *or* operation on variables a and b in variable c. Because a contains the value true, the outcome of this operation is also true, and this outcome is assigned to c. Finally, there is an if instruction, which assigns the value false to variable a, but only if !c evaluates to true. In this case, c is true, so !c is false, which means the body of the if instruction is not executed. Therefore, after all the instructions are executed, a and c both contain the value true, and b contains the value false.

Doing these kinds of exercises shows that it's very easy to make logical mistakes. This process is similar to what you do when you debug your code. Step by step, you move through the instructions and determine the values of the variables at various stages. A single mix-up can cause something you assume to be true to evaluate to false!

# Changing the Color of the Cannon

In the previous sections, you saw how to use the `if` instruction to check whether the player has touched the screen. Now, let's extend the program so that tapping in the center of the cannon barrel changes the color of the paint ball that the cannon can shoot. You can see this behavior by running the Painter2 example belonging to this chapter.

To program this behavior, you are going to need three extra sprites, one for each color. If you open the `Images.xcassets` folder in the Painter2 project in Xcode, you see these three extra sprites appearing in the list. In the `GameScene` class, you add properties to refer to these sprites, as follows:

```
var cannonRed = SKSpriteNode(imageNamed: "spr_cannon_red")
var cannonGreen = SKSpriteNode(imageNamed: "spr_cannon_green")
var cannonBlue = SKSpriteNode(imageNamed: "spr_cannon_blue")
```

These sprites should be at the same position as the cannon barrel (which has its origin set to the center of the rotating disc):

```
cannonRed.position = cannonBarrel.position
cannonGreen.position = cannonBarrel.position
cannonBlue.position = cannonBarrel.position
```

You also have to make sure that these sprites are drawn on top of the barrel, and not behind it. To achieve this, you set their z position to a value higher than that of the cannon barrel (which has a z position of 1):

```
cannonRed.zPosition = 2
cannonGreen.zPosition = 2
cannonBlue.zPosition = 2
```

The issue is that you don't want to draw all three of these sprites but just one of them, depending on the current paint color that the cannon will be shooting. For that, you can use the `hidden` property that each (sprite) node has in the SpriteKit framework. Initially, you hide the `cannonGreen` and `cannonBlue` sprites:

```
cannonGreen.hidden = true
cannonBlue.hidden = true
```

Now, only the `cannonRed` sprite is going to be drawn on the screen. Of course, the sprites need to be added to the scene in order for this to work correctly:

```
addChild(cannonRed)
addChild(cannonGreen)
addChild(cannonBlue)
```

The next step is dealing with the player tapping in the center of the cannon barrel disc to change the color that the cannon should shoot. One challenge that you have to address is how to detect a tap. Until now, the program only stores a touch location. There is no way to know whether the player has just placed his/her finger on the screen or whether he/she has been touching that same spot on the screen for multiple seconds. A very simply solution is to add an extra variable that maintains whether the player has just tapped or not. This variable is of type Bool, and you initially set it to false:

```
var hasTapped: Bool = false
```

Now whenever the player starts touching the screen, you set this property to true. This is done in the touchesBegan method:

```
override func touchesBegan(touches: Set<UITouch>, withEvent event: UIEvent?) {
    let touch = touches.first!
    touchLocation = touch.locationInNode(self)
    nrTouches = nrTouches + touches.count
    hasTapped = true
}
```

In order to process only a single tap, you need to reset this property to false again at the end of the update method. That way, when the player starts touching the screen, the hasTapped property becomes true and you can deal with it in the update method, after which the property immediately becomes false again.

If the player is touching the screen, you need to handle two different cases. The first case is that the player is touching the screen outside of the center of the cannon barrel disc. In this case, you need to calculate the angle of the cannon barrel. The second case is that the player has tapped in the center of the cannon barrel. In this case, you need to change the color of the cannon center by hiding or showing the colored sprites you added to the game scene. How do you detect whether the player has tapped in the center of the cannon barrel? You can do this by determining if the touch location is within the *bounds* of one of the color sprites. Each sprite node has a property that calculates a rectangle surrounding the sprite (also called the *bounding box*). Here is how you retrieve the bounding box of the cannonRed sprite:

```
let rect = cannonRed.frame
```

The rect variable is of type CGRect. The CGRect type has a few useful methods and properties. For example, it has a method called contains, which indicates if a point falls inside a rectangle. Here is how you can use it:

```
if rect.contains(touchLocation) {
    // the player is touching the screen inside the cannonRed bounding box!
}
```

So, let's use this method to handle the various cases in the Painter game. The first case is that the player touches the screen outside of the cannon barrel disc:

```
if !cannonRed.frame.contains(touchLocation) {
    let opposite = touchLocation.y - cannonBarrel.position.y
    let adjacent = touchLocation.x - cannonBarrel.position.x
    cannonBarrel.zRotation = atan2(opposite, adjacent)
}
```

Note how you use the logical *not* operator to construct the condition of the if instruction. In the alternative case (the player is touching inside the bounding box of cannonRed), you only need to do something when the player has also tapped, like so:

```
if !cannonRed.frame.contains(touchLocation) {
    // update the cannon barrel angle
}
else if cannonRed.frame.contains(touchLocation) && hasTapped {
    // change the color of the cannon barrel disc
}
```

Because the alternative case is only executed if the condition in the if instruction is not true (in other words, the cannonRed frame contains the touch location), you can write a shorter if instruction that accomplishes the same thing:

```
if !cannonRed.frame.contains(touchLocation) {
    // update the cannon barrel angle
}
else if hasTapped {
    // change the color of the cannon barrel disc
}
```

Inside the alternative case, you need to change the color of the cannon barrel disc. If it is currently red, it needs to become green. If it's green, it needs to become blue. Finally, if it's blue, it needs to become red again. This way, the player can switch between colors by tapping multiple times on the cannon barrel disc. The way to change the color is by changing the hidden properties of the three cannon barrel disc sprites. One of them should always be false, and the other two should be true. Take a look at the following lines of code:

```
let tmp = cannonBlue.hidden
cannonBlue.hidden = cannonGreen.hidden
cannonGreen.hidden = cannonRed.hidden
cannonRed.hidden = tmp
```

In the first line of this code, you store the hidden status of cannonBlue in a temporary variable. Then, the hidden status of cannonGreen is copied to cannonBlue. So, if the green disc was visible, now the blue disc will be visible as well. Then, the cannonRed.hidden status is assigned to the cannonGreen.hidden status. Finally, the cannonRed.hidden status is set to the hidden status stored in the tmp variable, which was the old cannonBlue.hidden status. The result of moving around the hidden values between the variables in this way is exactly the behavior that is needed. Try it out yourself. Suppose that the red, green, blue hidden statuses are true, false, true (in other words, green is visible). Determine the outcome of executing the instructions above. You will see that the outcome is true, true, false (blue is visible). Run that again through the instructions, and you will get false, true, true (red is visible). And so on. Run the Painter2 program to see the final result (see Figure 5-4 for a screenshot).

*Figure 5-4. The Painter2 example*

# A Few Final Remarks

Now that you have written the code to achieve the behavior that is needed for this game, you probably noticed that it resulted in a rather complicated piece of code inside the update method:

```
if nrTouches > 0 {
    touchingLabel.text = "touching"
    if !cannonRed.frame.contains(touchLocation) {
        let opposite = touchLocation.y - cannonBarrel.position.y
        let adjacent = touchLocation.x - cannonBarrel.position.x
        cannonBarrel.zRotation = atan2(opposite, adjacent)
    } else if hasTapped {
        let tmp = cannonBlue.hidden
        cannonBlue.hidden = cannonGreen.hidden
        cannonGreen.hidden = cannonRed.hidden
        cannonRed.hidden = tmp
    }
} else {
    touchingLabel.text = "not touching"
}
hasTapped = false
```

What makes this code look complicated is that there is an if instruction that contains another if instruction inside its body. If you look at the total number of possibilities of what code will be executed, it's not that bad. If the player is touching the screen, then the touch label text will be changed and either the cannon will be rotated or (if the player has also tapped) the cannon barrel disc color will be changed. If the player is not touching the screen, only the touching label text is changed. So in total there are three so-called *control paths*. Figure 5-5 depicts these three control paths in a diagram. These diagrams are called *flow charts*, and they provide developers with visual feedback about what a piece of a program is doing. You can draw these charts yourself if you want to clarify how a piece of code is working, or if you want to map out the different cases that your program should handle. Another way to clarify such pieces of code is by adding comments, as is done in the Painter2 example.

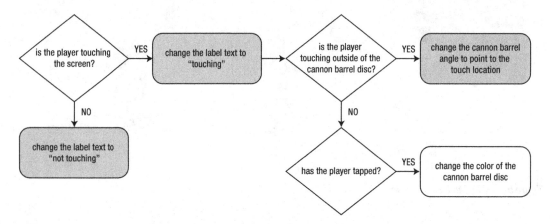

*Figure 5-5. A flow chart depicting the various ways in which touch input is dealt with in Painter2*

As your programs become more complex, it will also become more difficult to understand which cases a piece of code handles. This often leads to bugs. A programmer may think that his code handles all the different cases, but of course, programmers are also human, and humans make mistakes. Testing code is a lot of work, which means that not all bugs are going to be found. This is the reason why many game companies release patches of already released games to fix bugs that became apparent only after many people played the game.

# What You Have Learned

In this chapter, you have learned the following:

- How to react to touch input such as a tap or a moving finger using `if` instructions

- How to formulate conditions for these instructions using Boolean values

- How to use `if` instructions with different alternatives

# Chapter 6

# A Flying Ball

In this chapter, you will start organizing the source code of the Painter game a bit more. This is necessary because as you start adding more and more things to the game, the source code will become more complicated. You will explore using methods to structure the code more logically. You'll conclude this chapter by adding a moving ball to the game.

## Methods

You've already seen and used quite a few different kinds of methods and functions. For example, there is a clear difference between the `UIColor.blackColor()` method and the `print()` function: the latter one expects a parameter (a string), whereas the first one doesn't. The `blackColor` method belongs to `UIColor`, as opposed to `print`, which is a standalone function. Additionally, some functions/methods can have a *result value* that can be used in the instruction that does the method call, such as storing the result in a variable, like so:

```
var myColor = UIColor.blackColor()
```

Here, you call the `blackColor` method that is defined as a part of `UIColor`, and you store its result in the variable `myColor`. Apparently, `blackColor` provides a result value that can be stored. The `print` function, on the other hand, doesn't provide a result that you can store in a variable. Of course, it does have an effect of some sort because it prints text to the console, which could also be considered a result of the function call. However, when I talk about the *result* of a function, I don't mean that the function has some effect on the screen. I mean the *function call* returns a value that can be stored in a variable. This is also called the *return value* of a method or function. In mathematics, it's common that a function has a result. The mathematical function $f(x)=x^2$ takes as a parameter an $x$ value and it returns its square as a result. You could write this mathematical function in Swift like so:

```
func square(x : Int) -> Int {
    return x*x
}
```

If you look at the header of this method, you see that it takes one parameter called x. After the closing parenthesis, you see an arrow and the word Int. This means that this method returns an integer value that can be stored in a variable, like so:

```
var sx = square(10)
```

After this instruction is executed, the variable sx will contain the value 100. In the function body, you indicate using the keyword return the actual value that the function returns. In the case of square, the function returns the outcome of the expression x*x. Note that executing the return instruction also terminates execution of the rest of the instructions in a function. Any instructions placed *after* the return instruction are not executed. For example, consider the following function:

```
func square(x : Int) -> Int {
    return 12
    var tmp = 45
}
```

In this example, the second instruction (var tmp = 45) will never be executed because the instruction before it ends the function. This is a very handy feature of the return instruction, and you can use it to your advantage, as in the following code:

```
func squareRoot(x : Int) -> Int {
    if x < 0 {
        print("Error: cannot compute square root of a negative number!")
        return 0
    }
    // Calculate the square root, we are now sure that x >=0.
    return ...
}
```

In this example, you use the return instruction as a safeguard against wrong input by the user of the method. You can't calculate the square root of a negative number, so you handle the case where x is negative before you do any calculations or raise any annoying, potentially hard-to-debug errors. Note that a function that returns a value must return a value through all of the possible logic paths. So if you write a function that contains an if instruction that handles a few alternative cases, you have to make sure that the function returns a value in each of those cases. In the example above, there are two cases, and in each of the two cases a value is returned.

The atan2 function is another example of a function that has parameters and returns a value that you can store in a variable, as you did in the Painter2 example:

```
cannonBarrel.zRotation = atan2(opposite, adjacent)
```

An example of a method that doesn't have a return value is the update method in the GameScene class:

```
override func update(currentTime: NSTimeInterval) {
    if nrTouches > 0 {
        touchingLabel.text = "touching"
        if !cannonRed.frame.contains(touchLocation) {
            let opposite = touchLocation.y - cannonBarrel.position.y
            let adjacent = touchLocation.x - cannonBarrel.position.x
            cannonBarrel.zRotation = atan2(opposite, adjacent)
        } else if hasTapped {
            let tmp = cannonBlue.hidden
            cannonBlue.hidden = cannonGreen.hidden
            cannonGreen.hidden = cannonRed.hidden
            cannonRed.hidden = tmp
        }
    } else {
        touchingLabel.text = "not touching"
    }
    hasTapped = false
}
```

Because this method doesn't have a return value, you don't need to use the return keyword in the body of the method, although doing so can sometimes still be useful. For example, you could use the return keyword here to increase code readability by removing the nested if instruction, as follows:

```
override func update(currentTime: NSTimeInterval) {
    if nrTouches <= 0 {
        hasTapped = false
        touchingLabel.text = "not touching"
        return
    }
    touchingLabel.text = "touching"
    if !cannonRed.frame.contains(touchLocation) {
        let opposite = touchLocation.y - cannonBarrel.position.y
        let adjacent = touchLocation.x - cannonBarrel.position.x
        cannonBarrel.zRotation = atan2(opposite, adjacent)
    } else if hasTapped {
        let tmp = cannonBlue.hidden
        cannonBlue.hidden = cannonGreen.hidden
        cannonGreen.hidden = cannonRed.hidden
        cannonRed.hidden = tmp
    }
    hasTapped = false
}
```

In this method, you first check if the player touches the screen. If that is not the case, you reset the hasTapped flag, change the text label, and return from the method. Any instructions after that will then no longer be executed.

Notice that whenever a method with no return value is called, it has no result that can be stored in a variable. For example, in

```
var what = print("hello!")
```

print doesn't have a return value, so the compiler will raise a warning if you write such an instruction in your program.

If a method or function has a return value, this value doesn't necessarily have to be stored in a variable. You can also directly use it in an if instruction, as you do in the update method:

```
if !cannonRed.frame.contains(touchLocation) {
    // do something
}
```

Here, the contains method returns a Boolean value, and if this value is false, the body of the if instruction will be executed (due to the exclamation mark meaning "not"). The difference between things that have a value and things that don't have a value is something you've seen before: it's the same difference you saw between *instructions* (which don't have a value) and *expressions* (which do have a value). So, this means !cannonRed.frame. contains(touchLocation) is an *expression*, whereas print("hello") is an *instruction*.

In summary, there are methods/functions with or without parameters, and methods/functions can have a return value or not. You can use functions and methods to organize code into logical blocks of instructions that belong together. For example, it makes sense to have a function called atan2 that groups all the instructions needed to compute the arctangent of two sides of a triangle. This way, you only have to write those instructions once, and then later you don't have to think about how to calculate it; you simply call the function you wrote earlier. Games often have many of these useful functions and methods. For example, wouldn't it be useful to have a method that checks whether or not an image is positioned outside of the screen? This could be useful in a game where objects are flying in and out of the screen, or games where you have a player that could fall through the bottom of the screen and die (which is the case in many platform games). Depending on what you need, you as the programmer decide if you're going to write a method with or without parameters and whether that method has a return value.

## Parameter Names and Labels

Let's look a bit more in detail at parameters, how you declare them, and how you call them. Take a look at the following function:

```
func sign(val: Int) -> Int {
    if val < 0 {
        return -1
    } else if val > 0 {
        return 1
    } else {
        return 0
    }
}
```

This function calculates the sign of an integer value. If the value passed as a parameter is greater than 0, the function returns 1. If the value is negative, the function returns -1. If the value is 0, the result of the function call is also 0, like so:

```
var someVariable = sign(3) // someVariable will contain the value 1
someVariable = sign(-12)    // someVariable will now contain the value -1
someVariable = sign(0)      // someVariable now contains the value 0
```

When you look at the function header, you see that the parameter has a name (val). Inside the function body, you refer to the parameter by that name. When the function is called, you simply write the value that you need the parameter to be inside the parentheses. If a function has more than one parameter, you simply write the parameter values between parentheses. For example, this is the header of the atan2 function:

```
func atan2(lhs: CGFloat, rhs: CGFloat) -> CGFloat
```

This function has two parameters, and you call it as follows:

```
cannonBarrel.zRotation = atan2(opposite, adjacent)
```

Next to functions, Swift also knows methods. Recall that a method groups instructions, just like a function. But as opposed to a function, a method is also part of a class. Swift has different rules for methods that define the way that parameters are dealt with. Methods that have a single parameter generally work in the same way as a function: you simply write the parameter value between parentheses when you call the method. If a method has more than one parameter, things change. Suppose that you define the following method inside the GameScene class:

```
func max(val1: Int, val2: Int) -> Int {
    if val1 < val2 {
        return val2
    } else {
        return val1
    }
}
```

This method expects two parameters and it returns the highest number of the two. Because there are two parameters, you need to be specific about which parameter value maps to which parameter name when you call the method, as follows:

```
var maxValue = max(3, val2: 12)
```

In the Swift language, you generally don't write the label in front of the first parameter, but you do write one for the second, third, and so on parameters in a method. This is the case for all methods, except for methods that create an object. In that case, you also need to explicitly write the label for the first parameter. The following is an example:

```
var background = SKSpriteNode(imageNamed: "spr_background")
```

Here you create an *object* of type SKSpriteNode and store it in a variable. Swift then requires the parameter label imageNamed.

Swift makes a distinction between internal and external parameter labels. Let's slightly rewrite the max method as follows:

```
func max(val1: Int, b val2: Int) -> Int {
    if val1 < val2 {
        return val2
    } else {
        return val1
    }
}
```

As you can see, the second parameter now has two labels. The first label, (b), is the *external* parameter label name. If you call the method, you should use that label instead of val2 to refer to the second parameter, like so:

```
var result = max(12, b: 3)
```

The labels val1 and val2 are the *internal* label names. These are the label names that should be used inside the method body. You can use external label names to force users to also provide a label for the first parameter, by modifying the header of the max method as follows:

```
func max(firstValue val1: Int, secondValue val2: Int) -> Int
```

Now you need to provide both labels when calling the max method:

```
result = max(firstValue: 12, secondValue: 3)
```

If you decide that labels are not necessary at all, you can indicate that by using an underscore for the external label name in the header, as follows:

```
func max(val1: Int, _ val2: Int) -> Int
```

You can now call the max method without providing any labels whatsoever:

```
result = max(12, 3)
```

Note that you only need to write an underscore before the second label since the first label name is already omitted by default. As you can see, Swift provides you with many options for defining parameter names and many ways to refer to parameters inside and outside of the function or method body. Also, with all these different rules for functions and methods, it can sometimes be hard to know whether or not you should write a label name when you call a method or function. Fortunately, the Xcode development environment will automatically detect errors for you and propose a fix. Try it yourself by adding labels to the atan2 call in the Painter2 program. You'll see that Xcode proposes that the labels be removed to fix the compiler error.

It is a good idea to think about what kind of parameter labels you want to use in different situations. Explicit parameter labels help make the meaning of the parameters clearer. For example, the firstValue and secondValue labels in the max function earlier in this chapter help to clarify the meaning of the parameters: they represent the values of which the function returns the maximum. As another example, consider the following function:

```
func calculateAgeInMonths(years y: Int, months m: Int) {
    return y * 12 + m
}
```

If you call this function, it is useful to know which of the two parameters is what. The explicit year and month labels help to clarify this:

```
var myAgeInMonths = calculateAgeInMonths(years: 18, months: 3)
```

On the other hand, sometimes parameter labels make your instructions longer than necessary. For instance, the max method doesn't really need explicit labels for its parameters. It doesn't matter what the parameters are called; the method simply returns the largest value. By carefully deciding which parameters need labels and which don't, your code become much cleaner and it will be easier to understand by others.

---

**DECLARATIONS VS PARAMETERS**

Declarations of variables have a lot in common with parameters that are written in the method header. In fact, those parameters also are declarations, but there are a few differences:

- Variables are declared in the body of the method; parameters are declared between the parentheses in the method header.

- Variables get a value by using an assignment instruction; parameters automatically get a value when the method is called.

- Variable declarations start with the word var; parameter declarations don't.

---

# Default Parameter Values

In a method or function body, you can also specify default values for certain parameters. This can be useful because it provides a convenient, shorter way to call the method/function for the commonly used case. For instance, consider method jump that makes a player character jump up. Its header could look like this:

```
func jump(speed: Int = 200, animate: Bool = true)
```

In this header, you see that the method has two parameters: the speed at which the character should jump up, and whether or not the character should be animated while it's jumping. Each of these parameters has a default value. In this case, the programmer who wrote this method expects that most often the player will jump with a speed of 200, and the character should be animated. Now because of those default values, you can call this method as follows:

```
jump()
```

This is exactly the same as calling the method as follows:

```
jump(speed: 200, animate: true)
```

Whenever a parameter has a default value, you always need to write the label in front of it when you call the method with a different value for that parameter, as you can see in the method call above. Here is another example:

```
jump(animate: false)
```

This calls the jump method using the default speed of 200, but with the animation off. Using default parameter values makes calling your methods easier, but they are not always needed. For example, you could rewrite the header of the max method defined earlier in this chapter as follows:

```
func max(val1: Int = 12, b val2: Int = 34) -> Int
```

In this header, you defined default values for both the parameters, but they do not make sense since there is no set of values that the max method will often be called with. If a default value for a parameter does make sense (as in the case of the jump method), it's highly recommended to write it in the header. Not only will it result in shorter code when calling the method, it will also give the users of the method an idea of how the programmer envisions that the method will be used. The latter argument is especially important if a method has many, very low-level parameters and the user has no idea what value to choose. Default parameter values in this case provide the user with a good baseline for using the method without knowing all the details about the meaning of all the parameters.

# Reorganizing Instructions into Methods

The Painter2 example from the previous chapter was still relatively short because it only displayed a background and a rotating cannon. Commercial games obviously are much more complex than that. They contain many different objects that can have complex behaviors and interactions. This is where methods are useful. Take a look at the Painter3 example belonging to this chapter. You will see that the instructions that belong together are now grouped in methods. For example, the method called initCannon contains all the instructions for initializing the cannon game object:

```
func initCannon() {
    cannonRed.zPosition = 1
    cannonGreen.zPosition = 1
    cannonBlue.zPosition = 1
    cannonBarrel.anchorPoint = CGPoint(x:0.233, y:0.5)
    cannon.position = CGPoint(x:-430, y:-280)
    cannon.zPosition = 1
```

```
    cannonGreen.hidden = true
    cannonBlue.hidden = true
    cannon.addChild(cannonRed)
    cannon.addChild(cannonGreen)
    cannon.addChild(cannonBlue)
    cannon.addChild(cannonBarrel)
}
```

You can see that there is now an object referred to as cannon, which is a property stored in the GameScene class:

```
var cannon = SKNode()
```

All the parts of the cannon (the barrel, and the three color indicators) are now part of this object. The cannon object, in turn, is part of the gameWorld object. This is done by the following line of code in the didMoveToView method:

```
gameWorld.addChild(cannon)
```

You can also see this in Figure 6-1, which displays the complete hierarchy of game objects in this example. It's useful to group objects that belong together because it makes it easier to manipulate those objects as a whole. For example, positioning the cannon (including its barrel and the three color indicators) can now be done with a single instruction in the initCannon method, like so:

```
cannon.position = CGPoint(x:-430, y:-280)
```

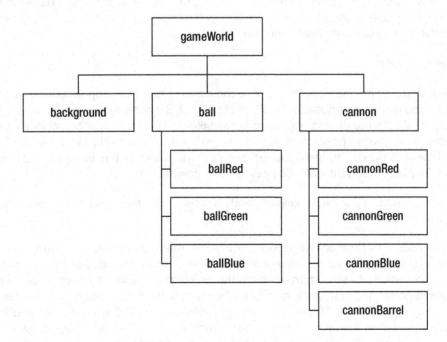

*Figure 6-1. The game object hierarchy of the Painter3 example*

Because you initialize the cannon object in a separate method, the method that initializes the game scene (didMoveToView) has now also become much easier to read:

```
override func didMoveToView(view: SKView) {
    anchorPoint = CGPoint(x: 0.5, y: 0.5)

    background.zPosition = 0
    gameWorld.addChild(background)

    initCannon()
    gameWorld.addChild(cannon)

    initBall()
    gameWorld.addChild(ball)

    addChild(gameWorld)

    delta = NSTimeInterval(view.frameInterval) / 60
}
```

In Painter3, game objects have their own initialization method, except for the background because that is a very basic object. And as you can see, the Painter3 example contains not only a cannon, but also a ball (which will be dealt with later in this chapter).

# Moving Between Local and World Coordinates

One side effect is that you need to take into account that game objects now have different *local coordinate systems*. Add the following line to the Painter3 program at the end of the didMoveToView method in the GameScene.swift file:

```
print(cannonRed.position)
```

You will see that it prints the position (0, 0) to the console once the app is run. However, the cannonRed node is drawn at position (-430, -280). Why? Because that is the position of the cannon object. Within the cannon object, the cannonRed node has a *local position* of (0, 0). So how do you get the world position of the cannonRed node? You can do this by converting the local position of cannonRed to the node representing the world. In this example, that node is gameWorld. Replace the print call above with the following two lines:

```
let worldCannonRedPos = gameWorld.convertPoint(cannonRed.position, fromNode: cannonRed)
print(worldCannonRedPos)
```

The first line calls a method called convertPoint. This method converts a point from a local coordinate system to another coordinate system. The point that is converted is cannonRed.position. The coordinate system from which the point is converted is the one belonging to the cannonRed node. And finally, the coordinate system to which the point is converted is the one belonging to gameWorld. The result of this conversion is stored in a variable, and then printed to the screen in the second instruction. When you run this code, you will see that now the world coordinates of the cannonRed object are printed.

There are two versions of the convertPoint method, one that converts *from* a coordinate system, and another that converts *to* a coordinate system. Sometimes converting to a coordinate system can be useful, such as when you want to handle touch input. Touch input is expressed in world coordinates. If you want to check if the player has tapped on the cannon color indicator, you need to convert the touch location to the local coordinate frame of the cannon color indicator object. Here is how you do that with the convertPoint method:

```
let localTouch: CGPoint = gameWorld.convertPoint(touchLocation, toNode: cannonRed)
```

You can then compare this local touch location with the cannon color indicator to find out whether the player has tapped on it or not:

```
if !cannonRed.frame.contains(localTouch) {
    // rotate the cannon toward the player touch location
} else if hasTapped {
    // change the cannon color
}
```

You can see the complete code for handling the cannon input by looking at the handleInputCannon method in the GameScene.swift file of the Painter3 example.

# Adding a Ball to the Game World

In the Painter game, the cannon is aimed by following the moving finger position of the player. When the player removes her finger from the screen, the cannon should shoot a ball matching the current color of the cannon. For that reason, you will need three different sprites for the ball: red, green, and blue. In the Painter3 example, these sprites are stored as properties of the GameScene class, as follows:

```
var ballRed = SKSpriteNode(imageNamed: "spr_ball_red")
var ballGreen = SKSpriteNode(imageNamed: "spr_ball_green")
var ballBlue = SKSpriteNode(imageNamed: "spr_ball_blue")
```

These three sprite nodes are stored as a part of a node called ball. In the initBall method, you can see the instructions that initialize the ball:

```
func initBall() {
    ball.zPosition = 1
    ball.addChild(ballRed)
    ball.addChild(ballGreen)
    ball.addChild(ballBlue)
    ball.hidden = true
}
```

Initially the ball is hidden. As soon as the player shoots the ball, it will become visible. Because the ball moves, you also need to store its *velocity*. This velocity is a vector that defines how the position of the ball changes over time. For example, if the ball has a velocity of (0,1), then every second the y-position of the ball increases by 1 point (meaning the ball flies upward). In Painter3, the velocity is represented by the ballVelocity property.

When the player wants to shoot the ball, she needs to take two steps. First, the player aims the cannon by moving her finger over the screen. Then, after removing her finger from the screen, the ball is shot. In order to keep track of when the ball is ready to be shot, you add a Boolean property readyToShoot:

```
var readyToShoot = false
```

In the games you develop in this book, most of the objects have a position and a velocity. Because the book is only concerned with 2D games, both the position and the velocity are always variables that consist of an x and a y variable. When you update these game objects, you need to calculate the new position based on the velocity vector and the time that has passed. Later in this chapter, you will see how to do this.

Although you will not use it for this particular game, the SpriteKit framework has a built-in physics engine. This makes it really easy and fun to put physics in your game. In the second game developed in this book, you'll learn how to use this physics engine to create a game that relies on physical interaction, in the same vein as games like Cut the Rope or Crayon Physics.

# Shooting the Ball

When the player removes his finger from the screen, the ball is shot. The speed of the ball and the direction in which it's moving are determined by the position where the player placed his finger last. The ball should move in the direction of that position; and the further away from the cannon the player touched the screen, the higher the speed of the ball. This is an intuitive way for the user to control the speed of the ball. Whenever you design a game, think carefully about how instructions from the user are received, and the most natural or efficient way to process them.

In order to handle input, you add a handleInputBall method to the GameScene class. Inside this method, the first step is to check whether the player is currently touching the screen. If that is the case, and the player isn't touching the cannon color indicator, you know that the player is aiming the cannon. The player can only start shooting the ball if it is not already shooting; in order words, the ball should also be hidden. If all these things are true, set the readyToShoot property to true:

```
let localTouch: CGPoint = gameWorld.convertPoint(touchLocation, toNode: cannonRed)
if nrTouches > 0 && !cannonRed.frame.contains(localTouch) && ball.hidden {
    readyToShoot = true
}
```

A second if instruction checks if the player has removed her finger from the screen. This is the case if nrTouches equals zero, and the readyToShoot property is true:

```
if (nrTouches <= 0 && readyToShoot && ball.hidden) {
    // shoot the ball!
}
```

Inside the if instruction, you need to do a couple of things. You know the player has touched somewhere and that the ball has to be shot from the cannon. The first thing you do is change the hidden status of the ball, since when you shoot the ball, it should be visible:

```
ball.hidden = false
```

Next, you reset the readyToShoot property to false as well, since the ball is currently being shot:

```
readyToShoot = false
```

Because the ball is now moving, you need to give it a *velocity*. This velocity is a vector in the direction of the place where the player last touched the screen. You can calculate this direction by subtracting the ball position from the touch location. Because the velocity has an x component and a y component, you need to do this for both dimensions:

```
ballVelocity.x = touchLocation.x - cannon.position.x
ballVelocity.y = touchLocation.y - cannon.position.y
```

Calculating the velocity in this way also gives the desired effect that when the player touches further from the cannon, the velocity is greater, because then the difference between the touch location and the ball position is also greater. However, if you were to play the game now, the ball would move a bit slowly. Therefore, you multiply this velocity with a constant value that gives the ball a velocity that is usable in the context of this game:

```
let velocityMultiplier = CGFloat(1.4)
ballVelocity.x = (touchLocation.x - cannon.position.x) * velocityMultiplier
ballVelocity.y = (touchLocation.y - cannon.position.y) * velocityMultiplier
```

I chose the constant value of 1.4 after testing the gameplay with different values. Each game will have a number of these *gameplay parameters* that you'll need to tweak while play-testing the game to determine their optimal value. Finding the right values for these parameters is crucial for a balanced game that plays well, and you need to make sure the values you choose don't make the game overly easy or difficult. For example, if you chose a constant value of 0.3 instead of 1.4, the ball would move a lot slower. This would make the game much more difficult, and it might even make the game unplayable because the ball might never be able to reach the far end of the screen.

## Updating the Ball Position

In this section, you are going to start defining the behavior of the ball. There are basically two possibilities: either the ball is waiting to be shot, or the ball is currently flying through the air. In order to translate this behavior into instructions that update the ball's velocity and subsequently its position, let's write a method called updateBall in which you group these instructions. This is the complete method:

```
func updateBall() {
    if !ball.hidden {
        ballVelocity.x *= 0.99
        ballVelocity.y -= 15
```

```
        ball.position.x += ballVelocity.x * CGFloat(delta)
        ball.position.y += ballVelocity.y * CGFloat(delta)
    }
    else {
        // calculate the ball position
        let opposite = sin(cannonBarrel.zRotation) * cannonBarrel.size.width * 0.6
        let adjacent = cos(cannonBarrel.zRotation) * cannonBarrel.size.width * 0.6
        ball.position = CGPoint(x: cannon.position.x + adjacent,
            y: cannon.position.y + opposite)

        // set the ball color
        ballRed.hidden = cannonRed.hidden
        ballGreen.hidden = cannonGreen.hidden
        ballBlue.hidden = cannonBlue.hidden
    }
    if isOutsideWorld(ball.position) {
        ball.hidden = true
        readyToShoot = false
    }
}
```

As you can see, this method uses an `if` instruction to distinguish between the two possible *states* that the ball is in. If the ball is not hidden, then it must be flying through the air. In that case, the body of the `if` instruction is executed. This body consists of four instructions. The first two instructions update the velocity, and the last two update the position. The first instruction updates the x direction of the velocity. You multiply the velocity with a value of 0.99, the effect of which is that the velocity slowly decreases. This is done to simulate air friction. The second instruction increases the y velocity in each update. This is done to simulate the effect that *gravity* has on the ball. Together, the velocity changes in the x and y directions result in plausible ball behavior. Of course, in the real world, the gravity is not 15. But then again, your real world doesn't consist of pixels, either. Physics in game worlds doesn't always accurately represent physics in the real world. When you want to incorporate some form of physics in your game (be it very simple or extremely complex), the most important part isn't that the physics is realistic, but that the *game is playable*. This is why in a strategy game, an airplane will move as fast as a soldier walking on the ground. If the game used realistic speeds for those two objects, it would result in an unplayable game.

The current position of the ball is updated by adding the velocity to its x and y components. Here are the instructions that do this:

```
ball.position.x += ballVelocity.x * CGFloat(delta)
ball.position.y += ballVelocity.y * CGFloat(delta)
```

As you can see, the velocity is multiplied by a factor `delta`. Why is this?

# Fixed Timestep vs. Variable Timestep

The delta factor is a property that's defined in GameScene, as follows:

```
var delta: NSTimeInterval = 1/60
```

It represents a time interval of 1/60 seconds. This corresponds to the default frame rate set in SpriteKit, which is 60 frames per seconds. So, in fact, delta represents the amount of time that passes between game loop cycles.

By multiplying the velocity by this factor delta, you are in fact taking into account the frame rate of the game engine in your calculations. The frame rate is closely linked to the frequency at which iOS devices refresh their screen. This frequency is fixed to 60Hz (in other words, just like the frame rate, which is 60 times per second). It's possible in SpriteKit to change the frame rate to some other value by changing the frameInterval property in the SKView class. For example, in the didMoveToView method, you could set the frame interval to 2, which means the frame rate will drop to 30 frames per second, as follows:

```
view.frameInterval = 2
```

Obviously, you will then also need to update the delta factor so that it matches the new frame rate:

```
delta = NSTimeInterval(view.frameInterval) / 60
```

But what happens when you run your game on a very slow device, and the engine is not able to perform the game loop 60 times per second, but actually runs at 50 frames per second? Well, since delta is in no way related to the real time that has passed, it means that your entire game will slow down, since the game logic still thinks that the fixed amount of time set in the delta variable (1/60 seconds) has passed since the last time update was called. Because the delta value is fixed, this kind of game loop is also called a *fixed timestep* approach.

Having your game slow down a bit sometimes is not a bad thing per se. You have to watch out, though, that the game doesn't structurally run too slow. It may have negative side effects. For one, the player could lose interest in the game because the objects are not moving realistically anymore, and playing the game takes too long. Another side effect could be that the game becomes too easy to play and this would put players with older devices at an unfair advantage.

One way to deal with this is to keep track of how much time actually has passed since the last update. That's why the update method in GameScene has a parameter called currentTime. This parameter gives you the current system time. You can perform a few calculations to find out how much time has passed since the last update cycle. First, add a property in which you store the time at the last update:

```
var lastUpdateTimeInterval: NSTimeInterval = 0
```

In the update method, you can then calculate how much time has passed, as follows:

```
let timePassed: NSTimeInterval = currentTime - lastUpdateTimeInterval
lastUpdateTimeInterval = currentTime
```

What you can now do is calculate the difference between the delta value and the actual time passed. If that value is too big, you can decide to increase the frame interval and calculate a new delta value so that the game play better matches the device. If you want, you can write a much more advanced version that calculates an average difference with delta over the last few frames and then, based on that difference, decides if the frame rate needs to be slowed down or sped up.

A completely different approach to using a fixed delta value is to simply calculate the delta value every time the update method is called, and then use that delta value in the game. This is referred to as the *variable timestep* approach.

```
delta = currentTime - lastUpdateTimeInterval
lastUpdateTimeInterval = currentTime
```

Variable timestep has a few advantages over the previous method. For one, you don't have to worry about frame rates anymore. The delta value will always correspond to the time that has actually passed. This means that your game world will automatically run at the same speed, regardless of the actual frame rate. If the frame rate drops, the game world speed is automatically adapted. Variable timestep is especially useful in games where high frame rates are desirable, such as in first-person shooters where camera motions can be quite fast because the camera is controlled directly by the player. In those cases, a variable timestep can result in smoother motions and a more pleasurable gaming experience.

A disadvantage of using a variable timestep is that your game logic needs to be robust enough to deal with large fluctuations in delta values. For instance, suppose that you have an arrow that is shooting through the air. Now suppose that at some point, the delta value is very big due to a hiccup in the system, and you simply calculate the new arrow position by multiplying the velocity by delta and adding that to the current position. You may have inadvertently moved the arrow through an object that it shouldn't have moved through (such as an opponent), without handling the collision. It may also lead to the player being able to enter parts of the game world that shouldn't be accessible to him/her. So, watch out when you use the delta value in this way. It can lead to unexpected behavior.

Another disadvantage of variable timestep is that the time continues even if the player is temporarily doing something different (like opening a menu in the game or saving the game). Generally, players won't be very happy if they discover that while they were browsing their inventory, their character was killed in the game world. A similar thing happens when the player temporarily switches to another app. The system time continues, and so does the game world. When using a fixed timestep, the game simply continues where it was paused when the player reactivates the app because the game objects don't care about the real time that has passed, only about the fixed delta value.

> **Note**  In the old days, computers were so slow that the concept of a fixed timestep didn't exist. Game developers assumed that everyone would be playing their game on an equally slow machine, so they called the game-loop methods as often as possible and simply updated the position of an object with a constant velocity factor. As a result, when computers became faster, these games became more and more difficult to play! Players don't like this. Therefore, always take the elapsed time into account when calculating things like velocities and positions, and make sure that your game properly matches its frame rate to the capabilities of the device it is being played on.

## Updating the Ball Color

If the ball isn't currently shooting, the player is allowed to change its color. You do that by retrieving the current color of the cannon and changing the color of the ball accordingly. That way, you're sure the color of the ball always matches the color of the cannon. The easiest solution is simply mapping the hidden statuses of the cannon color indicator objects to the different colored balls:

```
ballRed.hidden = cannonRed.hidden
ballGreen.hidden = cannonGreen.hidden
ballBlue.hidden = cannonBlue.hidden
```

You also need to update the position of the ball. This is necessary because when the ball isn't in the air, the player can modify its shooting position by rotating the barrel of the cannon. Therefore, you need to calculate the correct ball position here to ensure that it matches the current orientation of the cannon barrel. Using the sine and cosine functions, you calculate the new position as follows:

```
let opposite = sin(cannonBarrel.zRotation) * cannonBarrel.size.width * 0.6
let adjacent = cos(cannonBarrel.zRotation) * cannonBarrel.size.width * 0.6
ball.position = CGPoint(x: cannon.position.x + adjacent, y: cannon.position.y + opposite)
```

As you can see, you multiply the opposite and adjacent sides with a value of 0.6 so the ball is drawn a bit more than halfway up the rotated barrel.

The second part of the updateBall method also is an if instruction:

```
if isOutsideWorld(ball.position) {
    ball.hidden = true
    readyToShoot = false
}
```

This part of the method deals with the event that occurs when the ball goes outside the game world. In order to calculate if this is true, you add a method called isOutsideWorld to GameScene. The goal of this method is to check whether a given position is outside the game world. You define the boundaries of the game world using a few simple rules. Remember that SpriteKit's origin is in the bottom left corner of the screen. In the games developed in this book, the origin (or anchor point) of the game scene is set to the center of the screen to more easily adapt to different devices. In this setting, an object is outside the game world if its x-position is smaller than minus half the width of the screen or larger than half the width of the screen. An object is also outside the game world if its y-position is less than the minus half the height of the screen. Note that I don't say an object is outside the game world if its y-position very large. Why not? I chose to do this so it's possible for a player to shoot a ball in the air and let the ball be momentarily above the screen before falling down again. Often you see a similar effect in platform games, where a character can jump up and disappear partly outside the screen as opposed to falling through the bottom of the screen (which generally means instant death of the character).

If you look at the header of this method, you see that it expects one parameter, a position:

```
func isOutsideWorld(pos: CGPoint) -> Bool
```

The return value of this method is a Boolean. If you want to check whether a position is outside the screen, you need to know the width and height of the screen. Painter3 adds a property called gameSize to the GameScene class. This property is given a value in the init method in GameScene:

```
override init(size: CGSize) {
    super.init(size: size)
    gameSize = size
}
```

Later, I will discuss the meaning of this method in more detail. For now, let's assume this method is called when the app is started.

In the isOutsideWorld method, you use the gameSize property to determine whether a position is outside the game world. The body of the method consists of a single instruction using the keyword return to calculate a Boolean value. The logical *or* operation is used to cover the different cases in which the position is outside the game world:

```
return pos.x < -gameSize.width/2 || pos.x > gameSize.width/2 || pos.y < -gameSize.height/2
```

As you can see, you don't mind if the y coordinate is greater than gameSize.height/2. This allows you to have the ball end up above the screen and fall back in again.

Let's return to the updateBall method. The second if instruction calls the isOutsideWorld method in its condition; if this method returns the value true, then the ball is hidden again, and the readyToShoot property is reset to false (so that the ball can be shot again by the player).

Methods such as isOutsideWorld can be *reused* in different parts of the program, which saves development time and results in shorter, more readable programs. For example, isOutsideWorld will probably also be useful for the paint cans later in the game, to test whether they have fallen out of the screen.

When you run the Painter3 example, you can see that it's now possible to aim the cannon, choose a color, and shoot a ball (see Figure 6-2). In the next chapter, you add paint cans to this game.

*Figure 6-2. The Painter3 example*

# What You Have Learned

In this chapter, you have learned the following:

- The different kinds of methods/functions (with/without parameters, and with/without a return value)
- The difference between fixed and variable timesteps
- How to add a flying ball to the game world

# 7

# Game Object Types

In the previous chapters, you saw how to create a game world that contains a few different game objects, such as a cannon and a ball. You also saw how to let game objects interact with each other. For example, the ball object updates its color according to the color of the cannon. In this chapter, you will add falling paint cans to the game world. However, before you can do that, you have to reexamine how to create and manage objects in Swift. I will introduce the class concept as a means to create multiple game objects of a certain type. Then, you will apply the class concept to other parts of the Painter game application. Furthermore, you will learn how to incorporate randomness in your games.

## Creating Multiple Objects of the Same Type

Until now, you only needed one instance of each game object in Painter. There is only one cannon and there is only one ball. In the Painter examples you've seen so far, these objects were represented by a number of properties in the GameScene class. For example, the following properties encompass the cannon object:

```
var cannon = SKNode()
var cannonBarrel = SKSpriteNode(imageNamed:"spr_cannon_barrel")
var cannonRed = SKSpriteNode(imageNamed: "spr_cannon_red")
var cannonGreen = SKSpriteNode(imageNamed: "spr_cannon_green")
var cannonBlue = SKSpriteNode(imageNamed: "spr_cannon_blue")
```

Similarly, the ball object also has a few properties associated with it:

```
var ball = SKNode()
var ballRed = SKSpriteNode(imageNamed: "spr_ball_red")
var ballGreen = SKSpriteNode(imageNamed: "spr_ball_green")
var ballBlue = SKSpriteNode(imageNamed: "spr_ball_blue")
var ballVelocity = CGPoint.zeroPoint
var readyToShoot = false
```

Suppose you want to be able to shoot multiple balls at the same time in the Painter game. If you did this the way you dealt with objects until now, you would need to create a copy of the properties above for every ball you want to add to the game. As a result, the GameScene class would start to become very big, and thus harder to understand. Furthermore, copying code generally is not a good idea. If in the future you want to extend the ball with a fourth color, you would need to update the property list for every ball you added to the game.

# Classes as Types

In Swift, it's possible to group properties into a new type, by using a *class*. The Painter4 example shows you how to use classes to group properties that belong together logically. Take a look at the following class definition:

```
class Cannon {
    var node = SKNode()
    var barrel = SKSpriteNode(imageNamed:"spr_cannon_barrel")
    var red = SKSpriteNode(imageNamed: "spr_cannon_red")
    var green = SKSpriteNode(imageNamed: "spr_cannon_green")
    var blue = SKSpriteNode(imageNamed: "spr_cannon_blue")
}
```

A class creates a new *type*. So, after you have defined a class Cannon, you can create *an instance of the type* Cannon. The definition of the Cannon class establishes that a cannon contains a node (which represents the object in the scene graph), a barrel sprite, and three sprites, each representing a cannon color. In Painter4, this class definition is written above the GameScene class. Inside GameScene, you no longer have to write all those properties that encompass a cannon; you can simply create a property of type Cannon, as follows:

```
var cannon = Cannon()
```

The cannon property now contains the data as defined in the class Cannon. You can access that data by using a dot. For example, this is the new version of the initCannon method that now initializes the cannon property:

```
func initCannon() {
    cannon.red.zPosition = 1
    cannon.green.zPosition = 1
    cannon.blue.zPosition = 1
    cannon.barrel.anchorPoint = CGPoint(x:0.233, y:0.5)
    cannon.node.position = CGPoint(x:-430, y:-280)
    cannon.node.zPosition = 1
    cannon.green.hidden = true
    cannon.blue.hidden = true
    cannon.node.addChild(cannon.red)
    cannon.node.addChild(cannon.green)
    cannon.node.addChild(cannon.blue)
    cannon.node.addChild(cannon.barrel)
}
```

So, instead of accessing the properties directly as you did in Painter3, you are now accessing them as a part of the cannon *object*. In a similar way, you can also define a class Ball:

```
class Ball {
    var node = SKNode()
    var red = SKSpriteNode(imageNamed: "spr_ball_red")
    var green = SKSpriteNode(imageNamed: "spr_ball_green")
    var blue = SKSpriteNode(imageNamed: "spr_ball_blue")
    var velocity = CGPoint.zeroPoint
    var readyToShoot = false
}
```

Again, you now only have to define a single property in GameScene:

```
var ball = Ball()
```

And accessing the data in the ball object is done exactly like with the cannon object. Here is an excerpt of the new updateBall method:

```
if !ball.node.hidden {
    ball.velocity.x *= 0.99
    ball.velocity.y -= 15
    ball.node.position.x += ball.velocity.x * CGFloat(delta)
    ball.node.position.y += ball.velocity.y * CGFloat(delta)
}
```

The nice part of this approach is that it's easy to add more balls to the game:

```
var ball2 = Ball()
var ball3 = Ball()
var ball4 = Ball()
```

Instead of having to define all the properties for each ball, you simply create an instance of the Ball class. The only issue is that currently the updateBall method only updates the object referred to by ball. If you add a ball2, ball3, and ball4, these will not be updated automatically. A naïve way of solving this problem is to simply copy the code written in updateBall three times, and replace ball for ball2, ball3, and ball4 in each copy. This is not an ideal solution. For one, copying code means you have to deal with version management problems. For example, what if you find a bug in the updateBall method code? You have to make sure you copy the improved code to the other Ball objects. If you forget one copy, the bug is still there when you thought you solved it. Another problem is that this approach simply doesn't scale up very well. What happens if you want to extend the game such that the player can shoot 20 balls at the same time? Do you copy the code 20 times? Also, that the bigger your Swift files become, the longer it takes for the compiler to translate them into machine code. Finally, duplicated code looks ugly, clutters up your source code files, and makes it hard to find other sections of the code that you need, leading to excessive scrolling and a general reduction of your coding efficiency.

A slightly less naïve way of addressing this problem is by supplying the Ball object as a parameter to the updateBall method:

```
func updateBall(aBall: Ball) {
    if !aBall.node.hidden {
        aBall.velocity.x *= 0.99
        aBall.velocity.y -= 15
        aBall.node.position.x += aBall.velocity.x * CGFloat(delta)
        aBall.node.position.y += aBall.velocity.y * CGFloat(delta)
    }
    else {
        // more code manipulating the aBall object
    }
}
```

Then, in the update method, you can simply call this method, passing each ball as a parameter:

```
override func update(currentTime: NSTimeInterval) {
    ...
    updateBall(ball)
    updateBall(ball2)
    updateBall(ball3)
    updateBall(ball4)
    ...
}
```

You need to do the same thing for initializing each ball as well as for ball input handing. Although this is an acceptable solution, it doesn't really scale in the long run, either. In the Painter game, only a few different game objects exist: a cannon, a ball, and three paint cans. Commercial games may have hundreds of different game objects. If you have to add initialization, input handling, and updating methods to the GameScene class for each object type, that class would become huge, which in turn would make it really cumbersome to edit the code.

A better way to deal with this is to make the initBall, handleInputBall, and updateBall methods a part of the Ball class instead of the GameScene class. Take a look at the Painter5 example belonging to this chapter. A few things have changed with respect to the previous example. First, the Ball and Cannon classes are now defined in separate files. This is a good thing because it will make your source code much easier to browse. Another thing that has changed is that the methods for initializing the ball, handling ball input, and updating the ball are now a part of the Ball class. Similarly, the Cannon class also has its own methods now. From now on, I will use handleInput and updateDelta as the default names for the game loop methods that deal with handling input and updating the game world.

# Input Handling in a Separate Class

When you put methods for handling input into the Ball and Cannon classes, you need some way to access the location where the player is touching the screen. One way to do this is by also defining a separate class for dealing with input. Let's call this class InputHelper.

Inside this class, you put the properties for keeping track of the player touch input. You also add a method for checking whether the player is touching somewhere on the screen. This is the complete class:

```
class InputHelper {
    var touchLocation = CGPoint(x: 0, y: 0)
    var nrTouches = 0
    var hasTapped: Bool = false

    func isTouching() -> Bool {
        return nrTouches > 0
    }
}
```

In the GameScene class, you add a property of type InputHelper, as follows:

```
var inputHelper = InputHelper()
```

You can then pass along the InputHelper object as a parameter when you call the handleInput methods of the ball and the cannon, as follows:

```
cannon.handleInput(inputHelper)
ball.handleInput(inputHelper)
```

As a result, you have access to the touch information in each game object class. For example, in the Cannon class, you use the isTouching method of the InputHelper class to determine whether the cannon should be rotated. If the player is not touching, you don't have to do anything but return from the handleInput method:

```
if !inputHelper.isTouching() {
    return
}
```

# Initializing Objects

Whenever you create an instance of a class (such as Ball or Cannon), the object that is created needs to be initialized somehow. For example, when you create a ball, you need to load a few sprites, set an initial velocity, make sure the ball is hidden, and so on. In Swift, each class has its own *initializers* that do this job. You can recognize that a method is an initializer by its name. Initializers are always called init. Furthermore, when you define an initializer, you omit the word func. Here is the initializer of the Ball class:

```
init() {
    node.zPosition = 1
    node.addChild(red)
    node.addChild(green)
    node.addChild(blue)
    node.hidden = true
}
```

In the initializer body, you see that the node property is manipulated. Its z position is changed (so that balls always appear before the background); the red, green, and blue ball sprites are added; and the node is set to *hidden*. This init method is called automatically when you create an instance of Ball:

```
var b = Ball()
```

An instruction like this does a few things:

- Memory is reserved for storing an instance of Ball.
- The stored properties inside Ball are assigned a value, and these values are stored in memory.
- The Ball initializer is called.
- A reference to the newly created instance is assigned to the variable b.

Since an initializer is very similar to a method, you can also add parameters to it. For example, consider the following initializer:

```
init(position: CGPoint) {
    node.zPosition = 1
    node.addChild(red)
    node.addChild(green)
    node.addChild(blue)
    node.hidden = true
    node.position = position
}
```

This initializer accepts a position and you use it as follows to create a Ball instance:

```
var ballPosition = CGPoint(x: 10, y: -50)
var anotherBall = Ball(position: ballPosition)
```

Note that initializer parameters always need to be given a label when the initializer is called. Of course, you can specify not to use a label explicitly, just like you can do in a method:

```
init(_ position: CGPoint) {
    // initializer code here
}
```

A class can have many different initializers, each having different parameters used for creating instances of your class. It is also possible to define a class without explicitly adding an init method to it. In that case, Swift uses a built-in default initializer that simply sets the default values defined for the properties. This is actually what happened in the Painter4 example, where the Ball class was defined as follows:

```
class Ball {
    var node = SKNode()
    var red = SKSpriteNode(imageNamed: "spr_ball_red")
    var green = SKSpriteNode(imageNamed: "spr_ball_green")
```

```
    var blue = SKSpriteNode(imageNamed: "spr_ball_blue")
    var velocity = CGPoint.zeroPoint
    var readyToShoot = false
}
```

Each of the properties in this Ball class has a default value. For example, the default value for readyToShoot is false, and the default value for the ball velocity is zero. When an instance of this Ball class is created, the default initializer is called, which assigns the default values to the properties. The Swift compiler requires that every property part of a class is initialized when the instance of the class is created. This requirement forces developers to make sure all the data in an instance has been properly assigned, leading to less bugs related to uninitialized data.

Finally, it's good to know that initializers can call other initializers. Swift makes a distinction between *designated* initializers and *convenience* initializers. A designated initializer completely initializes an instance, including all its properties. The init method in Ball is a good example of such an initializer. A convenience initializer has a slightly different syntax:

```
convenience init(position: CGPoint) {
    self.init()
    node.position = position
}
```

As you can see, it uses the convenience keyword to indicate that this is not a designated initializer. The purpose of convenience initializers is to provide a layer over the designated initializers to make creating instances of your class easier. A convenience initializer must call another initializer in its body, and it must do this before it can assign any values to properties. In this example, the first line calls the designated initializer. It uses the keyword self, which I'll cover in more detail later. Instead of calling a designated initializer, you can also call another convenience initializer (which, in turn, calls another initializer). This results in a chain of convenience initializer calls. The only important thing to remember is that in the end, a designated initializer should be called. It's useful that a convenience initializer calls another initializer. It allows you to write shorter code. The convenience initializer only contains two lines of code, which is one-third of this designated initializer:

```
init(position: CGPoint) {
    node.zPosition = 1
    node.addChild(red)
    node.addChild(green)
    node.addChild(blue)
    node.hidden = true
    node.position = position
}
```

Furthermore, basic object initialization code is now written in a single spot in your class: in the designated initializer. This means that if there is a bug in that code, and you solve it for that initializer, it is automatically solved for any convenience initializer that relies on the designated initializer.

> **Note**    Another name for an initializer is a *constructor*. The latter is the term commonly used in languages such as C# and Java.

# The Self Keyword

Now that you've defined a class for a few types of objects in Painter, let's reexamine the code that describes what objects can do. For example, in Painter4, the cannon input handling was defined in the `handleInputCannon` method, part of the `GameScene` class. Here is an excerpt of the body of that method:

```
let opposite = touchLocation.y - cannon.node.position.y
let adjacent = touchLocation.x - cannon.node.position.x
cannon.barrel.zRotation = atan2(opposite, adjacent)
```

By looking at this code, it's very easy to see which objects are being manipulated. In the first line, you retrieve the y-position from the node that is a part of the `cannon` object, and use that to calculate the opposite side of a triangle. In the last line of code, you're setting the rotation around the z axis of the barrel sprite belonging to the cannon to a certain value, calculated using the opposite and adjacent sides of the same triangle. The reason why it's easy to see what objects are being manipulated is because in this simple situation, each object has a unique name that you use to refer to it.

Now let's look at what that same code fragment looks like in the `Cannon` class:

```
let opposite = touchLocation.y - node.position.y
let adjacent = touchLocation.x - node.position.x
barrel.zRotation = atan2(opposite, adjacent)
```

The code looks almost the same, except there no longer is a reference to a `cannon` object. That's because in the methods of the `Cannon` class, you don't know the name of the object. For all you know, a developer could have written the following lines of code in the `GameScene` class:

```
var cannon = Cannon()
var anotherCannon = Cannon()
var chrisTheCrazyCannon = Cannon()
var aVariableNameWayTooLongForSuchASimpleThingAsACannon = Cannon()
cannon.handleInput()
anotherCannon.handleInput()
chrisTheCrazyCannon.handleInput()
aVariableNameWayTooLongForSuchASimpleThingAsACannon.handleInput()
```

The `handleInput` method is called four times, each time on a different object. This means that inside the body of `handleInput`, sometimes `barrel` may refer to `anotherCannon.barrel`, sometimes it refers to `cannon.barrel`, and sometimes it refers to a `barrel` object belonging to yet another Cannon instance. In other words, in the body of `handleInput`, you never know the name of the object that the method is manipulating.

Now let's take another look at this line of code in the body of handleInput:

```
let opposite = touchLocation.y - node.position.y
```

What does node refer to? If cannon.handleInput is called, it refers to cannon.node. If anotherCannon.handleInput is called, it refers to anotherCannon.node. When you call a method on an object, the compiler makes a binding between that object and the method, and it makes sure that references to properties are properly resolved when the method is executed.

Even if you don't know the name of the object you are manipulating inside a method, you can still refer to that object, using the keyword self. In other words, self refers to the object you are currently manipulating. So instead of the instruction above, you could have written this:

```
let opposite = touchLocation.y - self.node.position.y
```

So, for example, if cannon.handleInput is called, you use self in the body of handleInput to refer to the instance that cannon refers to. So why not simply avoid the use of self altogether and write the following?

```
let opposite = touchLocation.y - cannon.node.position.y
```

This code will fail for several reasons. First, it means that your code will now only be suitable to work with a single Cannon instance, called cannon. That's not desirable. The whole point of using a class to define a type is that you can create as many instances of the class that you need. Second, this is never going to work since cannon is actually part of the GameScene class. So if you refer to that object using the name cannon, you need to indicate where it belongs. In Painter4, it is part of the object that is an instance of GameScene, so you need to know the name of that instance as well. Where is this instance created? Have a look at the GameViewController class, and you'll see this line:

```
let scene = GameScene(size: viewSize)
```

Okay, so can you then write scene.cannon in the handleInput method of the Cannon class? Unfortunately, no, you can't. The scene variable is a *local variable* in the viewWillLayoutSubviews of the GameViewController class, so there is no way to access it outside that method.

And this is why the self keyword is useful. It allows you to easily refer to the object you are manipulating in a method, without putting any restriction on the users of the class you have written. They can name the instance any way they like, and they can make as many instances of the class as they like.

However, one thing you may realize now is that as soon as you introduce multiple classes in your game, it can be challenging to make sure that you have access to the objects you need. For example, take a look at the following instruction in the updateBall method of Painter4:

```
ball.red.hidden = cannon.red.hidden
```

This complicates things. It seems that the ball requires access to the cannon object. So, how do you get that object in the updateDelta method of the Ball class? Let's redesign the code in order to properly solve this.

# Accessing Other Objects Using Static Variables

One of the main issues of splitting code between classes is that somehow you are going to need access to other objects in the game. These objects (such as a ball or a paint can) are stored as properties in a class. In order to access those properties, you need an instance of the class, which in turn is stored somewhere else. This leads to a large chain of objects belonging to other objects belonging to other objects. Somehow, you need to write your code in such a way that there is a root object, from which you access everything else.

Let's first start by creating an object that represents the game world. In the Painter5 example, you can see that there is a class called GameWorld. This class contains all the properties related to the game world, and it makes sure that any game loop methods are called on the objects as needed. If you can somehow make an instance of GameWorld that can be accessed anywhere, then the problem of the endless chain of objects is solved.

There are several ways in Swift to do this. One way is to create a so-called *class property* (sometimes called *type property*). A class property is different from a regular property in that it is not attached to an object, but to a class. Take a look at the following simple example:

```
class Car {
    static var nrOfCars: Int = 0
    var nrOfSeats: Int = 4

    init() {
        Car.nrOfCars++
    }
}
```

As you can see, one property (nrOfCars) has the keyword static in front of it. Now look at the following instruction:

```
Car.nrOfCars++
```

In order to access the variable, you do not need an actual instance of Car. The property is bound to the class itself. This also means that it doesn't t matter how many cars you create; there will always be a single place in memory that Car.nrOfCars refers to. In the init method, the class property nrOfCars is incremented. As a result, you can now use this property to keep track of how many Car objects have been created.

You can apply the class property principle to create an instance of GameWorld inside the GameScene class:

```
static var world = GameWorld()
```

Since world is a class property of GameScene, you access it by writing GameScene.world. Then, once you have the instance, you can access its properties. For example, you could write the following instruction in the updateDelta method of Ball:

```
red.hidden = GameScene.world.cannon.red.hidden
```

Another name for class property is *static variable*, which is the term used in programming languages such as Java or C# (which explains the use of the static keyword to define a class property in Swift).

# The Double Role of Classes

There are two roles of classes in a program. The first is that a class groups methods that belong together. The second role is that a class represents a type. One could also say that a class is a *blueprint* for an object, and as such it describes two things:

■ The data that is contained within an object. In the case of balls, this data consists of a node, a velocity, sprites that represent each color, and a variable indicating whether the ball is shooting. An *initializer* sets up an instance of the class.

■ The methods that *manipulate* the data. In the Ball class, these methods are the game-loop methods (handleInput and updateDelta).

The concept of classes and objects is extremely powerful. It forms the basis of the *object-oriented programming paradigm*. Swift is a very flexible language, in that it doesn't oblige you to use classes. You could write code using only functions and global variables if you wanted to. But because classes are such a powerful programming concept and are widely used in the (game) industry, this book exploits them as much as possible. The SpriteKit framework is heavily built upon the object-oriented paradigm, as are many other libraries or engines targeted towards game development. By learning how to properly use classes, you can design much better software, in *any* object oriented programming language. For an overview of the role of a class, and how it is connected with other programming concepts, see Figure 7-1.

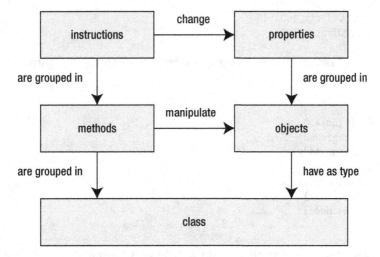

*Figure 7-1. The two roles of the class concept*

> **Note** When programming games, you often have to make a trade-off between how long it takes to do something and how often you do it. In the case of Painter, if you're only ever going to create one or two balls, then it might not be worth going through the trouble of creating a separate class for the balls. However, it's often the case that things scale up slowly. Before you know it, you're copying and pasting dozens of lines of code because you didn't create an easier way to do it once. When you design your classes, consider the long-term gains of a proper design, even if that requires a short-term sacrifice such as having to do some extra programming work to make the class design more generic.

# Writing a Class with Multiple Instances

As the final step in this chapter, let's add a few paint cans to the Painter game. These paint cans should be given a random color, and they should fall down from the top of the screen. Once they have fallen out of the bottom of the screen, you assign a new color to them and move them back to the top. For the player, it seems as though different paint cans are falling each time. Actually, you need only three paint can objects that are reused. In the PaintCan class, you define what a paint can is and its behaviors. Then, you can create multiple instances of this class. In the GameWorld class, you store these instances in three different properties. Here is a complete list of the stored properties in GameWorld:

```
var node = SKNode()
var background = SKSpriteNode(imageNamed: "spr_background")
var cannon = Cannon()
var ball = Ball()
var can1 = PaintCan(pOffset: -10)
var can2 = PaintCan(pOffset: 190)
var can3 = PaintCan(pOffset: 390)
```

In the GameWorld initializer, you set up the game world by adding all the game objects to the node:

```
init() {
    background.zPosition = 0
    node.addChild(background)
    node.addChild(cannon.node)
    node.addChild(ball.node)
    node.addChild(can1.node)
    node.addChild(can2.node)
    node.addChild(can3.node)
}
```

A difference between the PaintCan class and the Ball and Cannon classes is that paint cans have different positions. This is why you pass along a coordinate value as a parameter when the paint cans are created. This value indicates the desired x-position of the paint can. The y-position doesn't have to be provided, because it will be calculated based on the y-velocity of each paint can. In order to make things more interesting, you let the cans fall with different, random velocities. (How you do that is explained later in this chapter.) In order to calculate this velocity, you want to know the minimum velocity a paint can should have, so it doesn't fall too slowly. To do this, you add a property `minVelocity` that contains the value. As a result, these are the properties belonging to the `PaintCan` class:

```
var node = SKNode()
var red = SKSpriteNode(imageNamed: "spr_can_red")
var green = SKSpriteNode(imageNamed: "spr_can_green")
var blue = SKSpriteNode(imageNamed: "spr_can_blue")
var velocity = CGPoint.zeroPoint
var positionOffset = CGFloat(0)
var minVelocity = CGFloat(40)
```

Just like the cannon and the ball, a paint can has a certain color. By default, you choose the red paint can sprite. Initially, you set the y-position of the paint can such that it's drawn just outside the top of the screen, so that later in the game, you can see it fall. In the `GameWorld` initializer, you create three `PaintCan` objects, each with a different x-position.

Because the paint cans don't handle any input (only the ball and the cannon do this), you don't need a `handleInput` method for this class. However, the paint cans do need to be updated. One of the things you want to do is to have the paint cans fall at random moments and at random speeds. But how can you do this?

# Dealing with Randomness in Games

One of the most important parts of the paint can behavior is that some aspects of it should be *unpredictable*. You don't want every can falling at a predictable speed or time. You want to add a factor of *randomness* so that every time the player starts a new game, the game will be different. Of course, you also need to keep this randomness in control. You don't want one can to take three hours to fall from top to bottom while another can takes only one millisecond. The speed should be random, but within a *playable range of speeds*.

What does randomness actually mean? Generally, random events or values in games and other applications are managed by a *random number generator*. In Swift, there is a function called `arc4random()` that returns a random positive integer value each time you call it:

```
var i = arc4random()
/* i now contains a random integer value in the range 0 - Uint32.max
   (= 4294967295) */
```

How does a computer generate a completely random number? Isn't a computer a deterministic device that can only execute programs consisting of predetermined instructions? Indeed, theoretically, in game worlds and computer programs, you can predict precisely what is going to happen because a computer can only do exactly what you tell it to do. Therefore, strictly speaking, a computer isn't capable of producing a completely random number. One way to pretend that you can produce random numbers is by picking a number from a predefined, very large table of numbers. Because you aren't really producing random numbers, this is called a *pseudo-random number generator*. Sometimes random number generators can generate a number in a range, such as between 0 and 1, but they often can also generate an arbitrary number or a number in another range. Every number within the range has an equal chance of being generated. In statistics, such a distribution is called a *uniform distribution*.

Suppose that when you start a game, you begin generating "random" numbers by walking through the table. Because the number table doesn't change, every time you play the game, the same sequence of random numbers is generated. In order to avoid this problem, some random number generators allow you to indicate in the beginning that you want to start at a *different* position in the table. The position where you start in the table is also called the *seed* of the random number generator. Often, you take a value for the seed that is different every time you start the program, such as the current system time. In case of the arc4random function, you don't have to provide a seed value, since the function does it automatically for you.

How do you use a random number generator to create randomness in your game world? Suppose you want to spawn an enemy 75% of the times that a user steps through a door. In that case, you generate a random number between 0 and 1. If the number is less than or equal to 0.75, you spawn an enemy; otherwise, you don't. Because of the uniform distribution, this will lead exactly to the behavior that you require. The following Swift code illustrates this:

```
var spawnEnemyProbability = CGFloat(arc4random()) / CGFloat(UInt32.max)
if spawnEnemyProbability >= 0.75 {
    // spawn an enemy
} else {
    // do something else
}
```

In this example, you first convert the random number to a floating-point value. Then, you divide it by a constant UInt32.max, which represents the maximum value that a 32-bit integer can represent. As a result, the value of spawnEnemyProbability will always be in the range between 0 and 1.

Let's look at another example. Suppose you want to calculate a random speed between 0.5 and 1. To achieve this, you generate a random number between 0 and 1, divide this number by 2, and add 0.5, like so:

```
var randomNr = CGFloat(arc4random()) / CGFloat(UInt32.max)
var newSpeed = randomNr / 2 + 0.5
```

In order to make generating random number easier, Painter5 contains the following function (defined in the PaintCan.swift file):

```
func randomCGFloat() -> CGFloat {
    return CGFloat(arc4random()) / CGFloat(UInt32.max)
}
```

Humans aren't really any better than computers at understanding "true" randomness. This is why your MP3 player in shuffle mode sometimes seems to keep playing the same songs over and over. You perceive naturally occurring streaks to be non-random when in fact they are random. This means programmers sometimes have to create a function that appears random to humans—even though it's not truly random.

In games, you have to deal very carefully with randomness. A wrongly designed mechanism to spawn random units may spawn units of a certain type more often for certain players, giving them an unfair (dis)advantage. Furthermore, when you design your games, make sure random events don't have too much influence over the outcome. For example, don't have the player roll a die after completing 80 levels of your highly challenging platform game and let the outcome of the roll determine whether the player dies.

# Calculating a Random Velocity and Color

Each time a can falls, you want to create a random velocity and color for it. You can use the arc4random and the user-defined randomCGFloat functions to help you do this. Let's first look at creating a random velocity. In order to set a velocity for the can, you want to take into account a minimal velocity such that the can doesn't fall down too slowly. For that, you use the minVelocity property. This property is given an initial value when a PaintCan instance is created:

```
var minVelocity = CGFloat(40)
```

You use this minimum velocity value when you calculate a random velocity, as follows:

```
velocity = CGPoint(x: 0.0, y: randomCGFloat() * -40 - minVelocity)
```

The velocity in the x direction is zero because cans aren't moving horizontally—they only fall down. The y velocity is calculated using the random number generator. You multiply this random value by -40 and subtract the value stored in the property minVelocity in order to get a negative y velocity between -minVelocity and -minVelocity-40. If minVelocity equals 40, this results in a y velocity between -40 and -80.

To calculate a random color, you also use the random number generator, but you want to choose among a few discrete options (red, green, or blue). This is where the original arc4random_uniform function is useful. The function allows for an optional parameter to indicate the range: arc4random_uniform(x) returns a number between 0 and x-1. For example, look at this instruction:

```
let randomval = arc4random_uniform(3)
```

The variable randomval will now contain either 0, 1, or 2. Using some Boolean logic, it is now rather straightforward to set the color of the paint can:

```
red.hidden = randomval != 0
green.hidden = randomval != 1
blue.hidden = randomval != 2
```

Now that you are able to generate random colors and velocities, it's time to define the final behavior of the paint can.

# Updating the Paint Can

The updateDelta method in the PaintCan class should do at least the following things:

- Set a randomly created velocity and color if the can currently is not yet falling

- Update the can position by adding the velocity to it

- Check whether the can has fallen completely, and reset it in that case

For the first task, you can use an if instruction to check whether the can currently is hidden. Furthermore, you want to introduce a bit of unpredictability for when the can appears. In order to achieve that effect, you assign a random velocity and color only if some random number generated by the randomCGFloat function is smaller than a threshold of 0.01. Because of the uniform distribution, only in approximately 1 out of 100 random numbers will the number be smaller than 0.01. Here is the if instruction that achieves this:

```
if node.hidden {
    if randomCGFloat() > 0.01 {
        return
    }
    // the code that comes here will be executed only once in a while
}
```

Next to this can initialization step, you also need to update the can position by adding the current velocity to it, taking into account the elapsed game time, just as you did with the ball:

```
node.position.x += velocity.x * CGFloat(delta)
node.position.y += velocity.y * CGFloat(delta)
```

Now that you've initialized the can and updated its position, you need to handle the special cases. For the paint can, you have to check whether it has fallen outside the game world. If so, you need to reset it. The nice thing is that you already wrote a method to check whether a certain position is outside the game world: the isOutsideWorld method in the GameWorld class. You can now use that method again to check whether the position of the can is outside the game world. If this is the case, you need to reset the can so it's placed at the top, outside the screen again. In order to make sure that the paint can is completely out of the screen before you reset it, you first need to calculate the top of the can:

```
let top = CGPoint(x: node.position.x, y: node.position.y + red.size.height/2)
```

Then, you use an if instruction to check if the can has fallen out of the screen. If that is the case, you hide the can:

```
if GameScene.world.isOutsideWorld(top) {
    node.hidden = true
}
```

Finally, in order to make the game a bit more challenging, you slightly increase the minimum velocity of the can each time you go through the updateDelta method:

minVelocity += 0.02

Because the minimum velocity slowly increases, the game becomes more difficult as time progresses.

All the code for the Painter5 example is available in the example folder belonging to this chapter. Figure 7-2 shows a screenshot of the Painter5 example, which now has three falling paint cans.

*Figure 7-2. The Painter5 example with a cannon, a ball, and three falling paint cans*

# What You Have Learned

In this chapter, you have learned the following:

- How to define and use multiple classes in your game
- How to create multiple instances of a type/class
- How to add randomness to your game to increase replayability

Chapter **8**

# Colors and Collisions

By now, you've implemented quite a large part of the Painter game. You've seen how to define game object classes by using the class mechanism. By using classes, you gain more control over how game objects are structured and how to create game objects of a certain type. Each class is defined in its own Swift file. That way, when you need a cannon or a ball with the same behavior in a future game you're working on, you can simply copy these files and create instances of these game objects in your game.

When you look more closely at the definition of a class, you can see that a class defines the internal structure of an object (which properties it consists of) as well as methods that manipulate this object in some way. These methods can help define more precisely the possibilities and limitations of an object. For example, if someone wanted to reuse the Ball class, they wouldn't need a lot of detailed information about how a ball is structured. Simply creating an instance and calling the game-loop methods suffices to add a flying ball to the game. Generally, when you design a program, whether it's a game or a completely different kind of application, it's important to clearly define what is possible with objects of a certain class. Methods are one way to do that. This chapter shows you another way to define an object's possibilities: by defining *computed properties*. The chapter also introduces a type used for representing colors, and shows how to handle a collision between the ball and a paint can (if that happens, the paint can needs to change color).

## A Different Way to Represent Colors

In the previous versions of Painter, you dealt with colors rather practically. For example, in the Cannon class, you kept track of the current color by using the hidden statuses of the red, green, and blue cannon sprites. You did a similar thing in the Ball class, except you used colored ball sprites instead of cannon color indicator sprites. For example, here are the instructions that update the ball color according to the current cannon color:

```
red.hidden = GameScene.world.cannon.red.hidden
green.hidden = GameScene.world.cannon.green.hidden
blue.hidden = GameScene.world.cannon.blue.hidden
```

Because of the way these instructions work, the Ball class needs to have knowledge about the sprites that the Cannon class uses internally. That's a pity, since classes are supposed to help *separate* code, not introduce dependencies. Another issue is that it's not really easy to understand what the code means. To an outsider looking at the code in the Cannon or Ball class, it could seem like you copy sprite hidden statuses for no particular reason. Of course, you could add comments to your code to explain what you're doing, but that doesn't solve the core of the problem. Ideally, code should be written in such a logical fashion that it almost explains itself.

Wouldn't it be better if you could define colors more uniformly and use that definition in all the game-object classes to represent different colors? Of course it would! Another reason to start unifying the usage of colors in your games now is that the current approach will take much longer to program if you ever decide to increase the number of possible colors in the game (to 4, 6, 10, or more).

The Painter6 example belonging to this chapter is a new version of the Painter game where colors are dealt with in a different way, by using the UIColor type you've seen before. UIColor has a few useful class methods that produce different colors:

```
let redColor = UIColor.redColor()
let greenColor = UIColor.greenColor()
let blueColor = UIColor.blueColor()
```

# Controlled Data Access for Objects

Three game-object classes represent an object of a certain color: Cannon, Ball, and PaintCan. For simplicity, let's start with how you can modify the Cannon class to use the color definitions from the previous section. This is the list of properties in the Cannon class:

```
var node = SKNode()
var barrel = SKSpriteNode(imageNamed:"spr_cannon_barrel")
var red = SKSpriteNode(imageNamed: "spr_cannon_red")
var green = SKSpriteNode(imageNamed: "spr_cannon_green")
var blue = SKSpriteNode(imageNamed: "spr_cannon_blue")
```

What you could do is add another stored property that represents the current color of the cannon:

```
var color = UIColor.redColor()
```

If you want to know the color of the cannon, you can then simply check the value of this property. However, this isn't an ideal solution. You now store redundant data because the color information is represented by both the color property as well as the hidden statuses of the three cannon sprites. You might introduce bugs this way if you forget to change one of these properties when the color of the cannon changes.

Another solution is to define two methods that allow users of the Cannon class to retrieve and set the color information. You can then leave the property list as is but add methods to read and write a color value. For example, you could add the following two methods to the Cannon class:

```
func getColor() -> UIColor {
    if (!red.hidden) {
        return UIColor.redColor()
    } else if (!green.hidden) {
        return UIColor.greenColor()
    } else {
        return UIColor.blueColor()
    }
}

func setColor(col : UIColor) {
    if col != UIColor.redColor() && col != UIColor.greenColor()
        && col != UIColor.blueColor() {
        return
    }
    red.hidden = col != UIColor.redColor()
    green.hidden = col != UIColor.greenColor()
    blue.hidden = col != UIColor.blueColor()
}
```

Now the user of the Cannon class doesn't need to know that internally you use the sprite hidden statuses to determine the current color of the cannon. The user can simply pass along a color definition to read or write the color of the cannon:

```
myCannon.setColor(UIColor.blueColor())
var cannonColor = myCannon.getColor()
```

Note that the code inside these methods contains a safety mechanism. The getColor method will never return anything other than either a red, green, or blue color. Similarly, setColor will not do anything unless the color passed as a parameter is either red, green, or blue. This is a nice approach because it provides some security that objects of type Cannon will maintain a consistent state. For example, setColor makes sure that there is always a single sprite that is not hidden. Of course, at the moment that doesn't mean so much since users of the Cannon class can still change the hidden statuses by simply accessing the sprite properties. In Chapter 16, you'll see a way to protect the data inside your objects more so that this is no longer possible.

Sometimes, the methods that read and write data in an object are called *getters* and *setters* by programmers. In many object-oriented programming languages, methods are the only way to access the data inside an object, so for each property that needs to be accessible outside of the class, programmers added a getter and a setter. Swift provides a feature that is relatively new to object-oriented programming languages: *computed properties*. A computed property is a replacement for a getter and a setter. It defines what happens when you retrieve data from an object and what happens when you assign a value to data inside an object.

# Adding a Computed Property to a Class

In Swift, it is very easy to add a computed property to a class. For example, instead of the two methods above (getColor and setColor), you can add a computed property called color as follows:

```
var color: UIColor {
    get {
        if (!red.hidden) {
            return UIColor.redColor()
        } else if (!green.hidden) {
            return UIColor.greenColor()
        } else {
            return UIColor.blueColor()
        }
    }
    set(col) {
        if col != UIColor.redColor() && col != UIColor.greenColor()
            && col != UIColor.blueColor() {
            return
        }
        red.hidden = col != UIColor.redColor()
        green.hidden = col != UIColor.greenColor()
        blue.hidden = col != UIColor.blueColor()
    }
}
```

A computed property definition consists of a few things:

- The name of the property (for example, color)

- The type of the property (in this case, UIColor)

- A get part and/or a set part

A computed property is quite similar to a stored property: it has both a name and a type. The difference between a stored property and a computed property is that with a computed property, you have control over what happens when a value is written to or read from it. Reading from or writing to the computed property color is done as follows:

```
myCannon.color = UIColor.redColor()
if myCannon.color == UIColor.redColor() {
    // do something
}
```

In the first line of this code example, a value (UIColor.redColor()) is assigned to the property. This means that the instructions in the set part of the property will be executed. The second line contains an if instruction. In the condition of that instruction, the color property value is read out. The get part of the color property determines what happens when a property is read.

Behind the set part, you can indicate between parentheses the parameter name you should use in the body (in the case of the color property, this parameter is called col). If you omit the parameter name, then the name newValue is used by default:

```
var color: UIColor {
    get {
        ...
    }
    set {
        if newValue != UIColor.redColor() && newValue != UIColor.greenColor()
            && newValue != UIColor.blueColor() {
            return
        }
        red.hidden = newValue != UIColor.redColor()
        green.hidden = newValue != UIColor.greenColor()
        blue.hidden = newValue != UIColor.blueColor()
    }
}
```

Not all computed properties have to contain both a get and a set part. For example, have a look at the following property in the Cannon class in the Painter6 example:

```
var ballPosition: CGPoint {
    get {
        let opposite = sin(barrel.zRotation) * barrel.size.width * 0.6
        let adjacent = cos(barrel.zRotation) * barrel.size.width * 0.6
        return CGPoint(x: node.position.x + adjacent, y: node.position.y + opposite)
    }
}
```

This property calculates the position of the ball depending on the orientation of the cannon barrel. It has CGPoint as a type. In the Ball class, the property is used to calculate the ball position:

```
node.position = GameScene.world.cannon.ballPosition
```

The ballPosition property has no set part. In other words, this computed property is *read-only*. The following instruction would lead to a compiler error:

```
GameScene.world.cannon.ballPosition = CGPoint(x: 0, y: 0)
```

Depending on what you need, you can define read-only properties as well as properties that allow both reading and writing. By defining useful properties and methods in your classes, the game code becomes generally shorter and much easier to read. In this book, you will use stored properties, computed properties, and methods to define behavior and data access for objects.

# Handling Collisions Between the Ball and the Cans

The Painter6 example extends the game by handling collisions between the ball and the cans. If two objects collide, you have to handle this collision in the update method of one of the two objects. In this case, you can choose to handle collisions in the Ball class or in the PaintCan class. Painter6 handles the collision in the PaintCan class because if you were to do it in the Ball class, you would need to repeat the same code three times, once for each paint can. By handling collisions in the PaintCan class, you get this behavior automatically because each can checks for itself whether it collides with the ball.

Detecting if there is a collision is very easy in the SpriteKit framework. The SKNode class, which forms the basis for structuring the game world, contains methods and properties for calculating a node's *bounding box* (a box that encloses the node). For representing boxes, there is a type called CGRect. For example, this line of code calculates the bounding box of a node using the frame property:

```
let boundingBox = node.frame
```

Unfortunately, the frame property only looks at the node itself, not its children. This means that if the node contains children (such as a red, green, and blue sprites), those sprites are not taken into account when calculating the bounding box. This is not the behavior you want. Instead of the frame property, SKNode also has a method called calculateAccumulatedFrame, which does take into account the children of a node:

```
let accumulatedBoundingBox = node.calculateAccumulatedFrame()
```

The CGRect type has a method called intersects that indicates whether two boxes intersect. You use that method in the PaintCan class to determine if the paint can collides with the ball, as follows:

```
let paintCanBox = node.calculateAccumulatedFrame()
let ballBox = GameScene.world.ball.node.calculateAccumulatedFrame()
if paintCanBox.intersects(ballBox) {
    // handle the collision
}
```

If there is a collision between the ball and the can, you need to change the color of the can to the color of the ball. Next, you have to reset the ball so it can be shot again. The following two instructions do exactly that:

```
color = GameScene.world.ball.color
GameScene.world.ball.reset()
```

In the reset method of the Ball class, you hide the ball and reset the readyToShoot variable, so that the player can shoot the ball once more:

```
func reset() {
    node.hidden = true
    readyToShoot = false
}
```

You can try out the Painter6 example to see that collisions between the ball and the paint cans are properly handled.

As you've probably noticed, the collision-detection method used here isn't very precise. In Chapter 13, you'll see a better way of dealing with collisions that directly uses the shape of the sprite, although this does make your game run more slowly if you don't watch out.

> **Note**    In the end, simple lines of code like the ones written in this section make all the difference in the player experience. As you build up your game application, you'll find that sometimes the littlest thing to the player took the longest to program, and the biggest changes were achieved with only one or two lines!

# Values and References

Before finishing this chapter, let's have a look at how objects and variables are actually dealt with in memory. When dealing with types such as Int or Float, the variables are directly associated with a place in memory. For example, look at the following instruction:

```
var i: Int = 12
```

After this instruction has been executed, the memory will look as depicted in Figure 8-1.

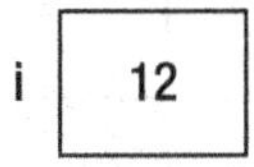

*Figure 8-1. Memory overview after declaring and initializing a single Int variable*

Now, you can create a new variable j, and store the value of variable i in that variable:

```
var j: Int = i
```

Figure 8-2 shows how the memory has changed after this instruction.

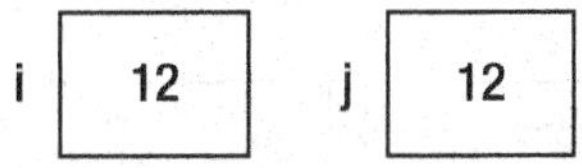

*Figure 8-2. Memory overview after declaring and initializing two variables and assigning the value of one to the other*

You can assign another value to the j variable, for example, by executing the instruction j = 24, and this results in the memory depicted in Figure 8-3.

*Figure 8-3. Memory overview after multiple declarations and assignments*

All of this is pretty straightforward, right? Let's have a look at what happens when you use variables of a more complicated type, such as the Cannon class. Look at the following code:

```
var cannon1 = Cannon()
var cannon2 = cannon1
```

Looking at the example using the Int type, you would expect that there are now two Cannon objects in the memory: one stored in the variable cannon1, and one stored in cannon2. However, this is not the case! Actually, both cannon1 and cannon2 *refer to the same object*. After the first instruction (creating the Cannon object), the memory looks as depicted in Figure 8-4.

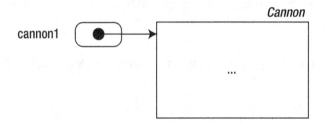

*Figure 8-4. The variable cannon1 contains a reference to a Cannon object*

Here, you see that there is a big difference between how a basic type such as Int or Bool is represented in memory and more complicated types such as the Cannon class. In Swift, all objects of a class type are stored as *references* as opposed to values. This means that a variable such as cannon1 doesn't directly contain the Cannon object, but it contains a *reference* to it. After declaring the cannon2 variable and assigning it the value of cannon1, you can see what the memory looks like in Figure 8-5.

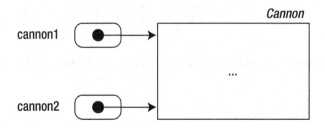

*Figure 8-5. Both cannon1 and cannon2 refer to the same object*

By looking at the code, you can actually see that there is only ever a single object created, since the Cannon initializer is only called once in this instruction:

```
var cannon1 = Cannon()
```

An important reason that objects having a class as a type work this way is because it avoids having to copy a lot of data in memory. An object of type Cannon will contain quite a few stored properties. If this data has to be copied every time the object is passed along to another part of the code, the program would become a lot less efficient.

Since cannon1 and cannon2 refer to the same object, changing things in the object referred to by cannon1 has the same effect as changing them through the cannon2 reference. For example,

```
cannon2.color = UIColor.redColor()
```

Now the expression cannon1.color would be the result of UIColor.redColor(), since both cannon1 and cannon2 refer to the same object! This also has an effect on how objects are passed around in methods and functions. Consider the following function:

```
func square(n : Int) {
    n = n * n
}
```

And now the following instructions:

```
var someNumber = 10
square(someNumber)
```

After executing these instructions, the value of someNumber is still 10 (and not 100). Why is this? It is because when the square function is called, the Int parameter is passed *by value*. The variable n is a local variable inside the function that initially contains the value of the someNumber variable. Inside the function, the local variable n is changed to contain n * n, but this doesn't change the someNumber variable because it is another location in memory. Because class objects are passed by *reference*, the following example will change the object that is passed as a parameter:

```
func changeColor(cannon : Cannon) {
    cannon.color = UIColor.redColor()
}
// ...
var cannon1 = Cannon()
changeColor(cannon1) // The object referred to by cannon1 now has a red color.
```

Note that there is a way to pass a type such as Int by reference, using the inout keyword:

```
func squareWithInout(inout n : Int) {
    n = n * n
}
```

You can now call the function as follows:

```
var someNumber = 10
squareWithInout(&someNumber)
// someNumber now contains the value 100!
```

When you call a function or method with an `inout` parameter, you need to write an & sign in front of the variable that you pass as a parameter. The & sign turns the variable into a reference.

# Structs

In the previous section, you saw that variables and constants are passed by value or by reference depending on their type. Types such as `Int` or `Bool` that are passed by value are also called *structs* in Swift. As opposed to structs, variables that have a class as a type are passed by *reference*.

Structs, which are passed by value, are generally used for more basic kinds of objects. For example, the `CGPoint` type is a struct, as is the `UIColor` type. Consider the following variable declaration and initialization:

```
var position = CGPoint()
```

In Figure 8-6, you can see what the memory looks like. Note that the `position` variable is not a reference but a value. This means that the following instruction makes a complete copy of the `CGPoint` object, as you can also see in Figure 8-7:

```
var position2 = position
```

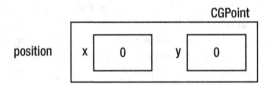

*Figure 8-6. A struct variable*

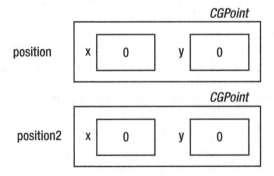

*Figure 8-7. Two struct variables – one is a copy of the other*

Generally, classes can be quite complicated when represented in memory. They can contain properties of other classes or structs. Any of these types may in turn consist of other properties, and so on.

Figure 8-8 shows what the memory could look like when you create a new instance of a Cannon object. You can see the different kinds of objects that are in a Cannon instance. Each object consists of other objects. For example, the SKNode object that node refers to has a CGPoint struct to represent the position, a Boolean value indicating whether the node is hidden, a link to its parent node, its z position, and more. In some cases, references point to the same object, as is the case with parent (in red) and node. When you create your classes, it can sometimes be helpful to draw these kinds of diagrams to get a feeling of which object belongs where and at which places references to these objects are stored.

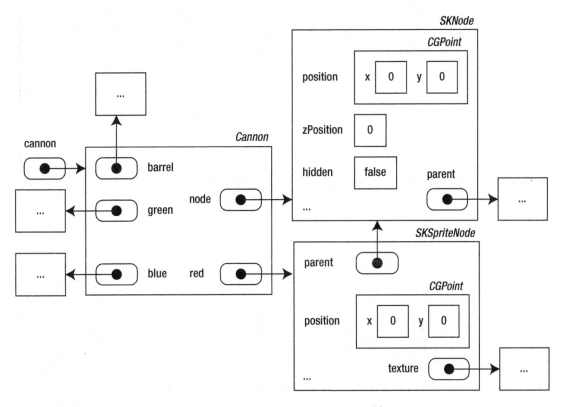

*Figure 8-8. An impression of the memory structure that represents a Cannon object*

Just like you can create your own classes, you can also create your own structs. For example, you could define a struct representing a person with a name and an age as follows:

```
struct Person {
    var name: String = ""
    var age: Int = 0
}
```

# What You Have Learned

In this chapter, you have learned the following:

- How to add properties to your classes
- How to handle basic collisions between game objects
- How to define game objects that have different colors
- The difference between values and references

# Chapter 9

# Limited Lives

In this chapter, you will make the Painter game more interesting by giving the player a limited number of lives. If players miss too many paint cans, the game is over. The chapter discusses how to deal with that and how to display the current number of lives to the player. In order to do the latter, you will learn a few programming constructs for repeating a group of instructions several times.

## Maintaining the Number of Lives

To introduce some danger and incentive to work hard in the game, you would like to limit the number of paint cans of the wrong color that the player can allow to fall through the bottom of the screen. The Painter7 example adds this kind of behavior to the game and uses a limit of five.

The choice of a limit of five paint cans is one of many examples of the decisions you have to make as a game designer and developer. If you give the player only a single life, then the game will be too hard to play. Giving the player hundreds of lives removes the incentive for the player to play well. Determining such parameters often happens by play-testing the game and determining reasonable parameter values. In addition to testing the game yourself, you can also ask your friends or family to play your game to get some idea of what values to choose for these parameters.

In order to store the life limit, you add an extra (stored) property to the GameWorld class:

```
var lives = 5
```

You initially set this value to 5 when you declare the property in the class. Now you can update the value whenever a paint can falls outside the screen. You perform this check in the updateDelta method of the PaintCan class. Therefore, you have to add a few instructions in that method to deal with this. The only thing you need to do is check whether the color of the paint can is the same as its target color when it falls through the bottom of the screen. If that is not the case, you have to decrement the lives counter in the GameWorld class.

Before you can do this, you have to extend the `PaintCan` class so that `PaintCan` objects know that they need to have a target color when they fall out of the bottom of the screen. Painter7 passes along this target color as a parameter when you create the `PaintCan` objects in `GameWorld`:

```
var can1 = PaintCan(positionOffset: -10, targetColor: UIColor.redColor())
var can2 = PaintCan(positionOffset: 190, targetColor: UIColor.greenColor())
var can3 = PaintCan(positionOffset: 390, targetColor: UIColor.blueColor())
```

You store the target color in a variable in each paint can, as you can see in the initializer of `PaintCan`:

```
init(positionOffset: CGFloat, targetColor: UIColor) {
    self.positionOffset = positionOffset
    self.targetColor = targetColor
    node.zPosition = 1
    node.addChild(red)
    node.addChild(green)
    node.addChild(blue)
    node.hidden = true
}
```

You now extend the `updateDelta` method of `PaintCan` so that it handles the situation where the paint can falls outside the bottom of the screen. If that happens, you need to move the paint can back to the top of the screen. If the current color of the paint can doesn't match the target color, you decrease the number of lives by one:

```
let top = CGPoint(x: node.position.x, y: node.position.y + red.size.height/2)
if GameScene.world.isOutsideWorld(top) {
    if color != targetColor {
        GameScene.world.lives = GameScene.world.lives - 1
    }
    node.hidden = true
}
```

You might want to decrease the number of lives by more than one at some point. In order to facilitate this, you can change the penalty into a variable:

```
let penalty = 1
if GameScene.world.isOutsideWorld(top) {
    if color != targetColor {
        GameScene.world.lives = GameScene.world.lives - penalty
    }
    node.hidden = true
}
```

This way, you can introduce steeper penalties if you want to, or dynamic penalties (first miss costs one life, second miss costs two, and so on). You could also introduce a special paint can; if the player shoots that can with a ball of the right color, the penalty for mismatching paint can colors temporarily becomes zero. Can you think of other ways of dealing with penalties in the Painter game?

# Indicating the Number of Lives to the Player

Obviously, players would like to know how they're doing. So, you have to indicate somehow on the screen how many lives the player has left. In the Painter game, you do that by displaying a number of balloons in the upper-left corner of the screen. Using the knowledge you have, you initially add five balloons to be drawn:

```
var livesNode = SKNode()
let livesSpr1 = SKSpriteNode(imageNamed: "spr_lives")
livesSpr1.position = CGPoint(x: 0, y: 0)
livesNode.addChild(livesSpr1)
let livesSpr2 = SKSpriteNode(imageNamed: "spr_lives")
livesSpr2.position = CGPoint(x: Int(livesSpr2.size.width), y: 0)
livesNode.addChild(livesSpr2)
let livesSpr3 = SKSpriteNode(imageNamed: "spr_lives")
livesSpr3.position = CGPoint(x: 2 * Int(livesSpr3.size.width), y: 0)
livesNode.addChild(livesSpr3)
let livesSpr4 = SKSpriteNode(imageNamed: "spr_lives")
livesSpr4.position = CGPoint(x: 3 * Int(livesSpr4.size.width), y: 0)
livesNode.addChild(livesSpr4)
let livesSpr5 = SKSpriteNode(imageNamed: "spr_lives")
livesSpr5.position = CGPoint(x: 4 * Int(livesSpr5.size.width), y: 0)
livesNode.addChild(livesSpr5)
```

By multiplying the width of the sprite by a number and storing that as the x-position of the sprite, you end up with five sprites drawn next to each other. Now you can add a few lines in the update method to change the hidden statuses of these sprites, so that they correctly show the number of lives:

```
livesSpr5.hidden = lives > 4
livesSpr4.hidden = lives > 3
livesSpr3.hidden = lives > 2
livesSpr2.hidden = lives > 1
livesSpr1.hidden = lives > 0
```

Although it works, this isn't a very nice solution. You are writing similar instructions several times. And what happens if you decide that the player should get ten lives initially instead of five? You'd need to write twice as much code. And if you decide to make the maximum number of lives completely dynamic, for example by letting the player win extra lives, this solution won't work at all. Fortunately, there is a better approach: *iteration*.

# Executing Instructions Multiple Times

Iteration in Swift is a way to repeat instructions a number of times. Have a look at the following code fragment:

```
var x = 10
while x >= 3 {
    x = x - 3
}
```

The second instruction is called a while loop. This instruction consists of a kind of header (while x >= 3) and a body (x = x - 3) between braces, which is very similar to the structure of an if instruction. The header consists of the word while followed by a *condition*. The body itself is an instruction. In this case, the instruction subtracts 3 from a variable. However, it could just as well have been another kind of instruction, such as calling a method or accessing a property. Figure 9-1 shows the syntax diagram of the while instruction.

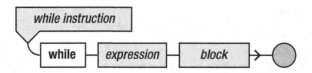

*Figure 9-1. Syntax diagram of the while instruction*

When the while instruction is executed, its body is executed multiple times. In fact, as long as the *condition* in the header yields true, the body will be executed. In this example, the condition is that the x variable contains a value that is 3 or greater. In the beginning, the variable contains the value 10, so it's certainly greater than 3. Therefore, the body of the while instruction is executed, after which the variable x contains the value 7. The condition is then evaluated again. The variable is still greater than 3, so the body is executed once more, after which the variable x contains the value 4. Again, the value is greater than 3, so the body is executed again, and x will contain the value 1. At that point, the condition is evaluated, but it's no longer true. Therefore, the repeating instruction comes to an end. So, after this piece of code is executed, the variable x contains the value 1. In fact, what you've programmed here is integer division using the while instruction. Of course, in this case it's easier to simply use the following single line of code that achieves the same result:

```
var x = 10 % 3
```

If you want to draw the player's number of lives on the screen, you can use a while instruction to create the lives sprites more efficiently:

```
var livesNode = SKNode()
var index = 0
while index < lives {
    let livesSpr = SKSpriteNode(imageNamed: "spr_lives")
    livesSpr.position = CGPoint(x: index * Int(livesSpr.size.width), y: 0)
    livesNode.addChild(livesSpr)
    index = index + 1
}
```

In this while instruction, the body is executed as long as the variable index contains a value less than lives (which is a variable you assume is declared and initialized to a certain value somewhere else). Every time the body is executed, you add a sprite to the game world at a certain position, and then you increment index by 1. The result is that you create a sprite object exactly lives times! So, you're using the variable index here as a *counter*.

> **Note**  You start with index equal to zero and continue until index has reached the same value as lives. This means the body of the while instruction is executed for the values 0, 1, 2, 3, and 4 of index. As a result, the body is executed five times.

As you can see in this example, the body of a while instruction may contain more than a single instruction.

The position at which you draw the sprites depends on the value of index. This way, you can draw each sprite a bit further to the right, so they're nicely placed in a row. The first time you execute the body, you draw the sprite at x-position 0 because index is 0. The next iteration, you draw the sprite at x-position livesSpr.size.width, the iteration after that at 2 * livesSpr.size.width, and so on. In this case, you use the counter not only to determine how often you execute instructions, but also to *change what the instructions do*. This is a very powerful feature of an iteration instruction such as while. Because of the looping behavior, a while instruction is also called a while *loop*. Figure 9-2 shows the Painter game where the number of lives is indicated at the upper left on the screen.

*Figure 9-2. The Painter game showing the player the remaining number of lives*

# A Shorter Notation for Incrementing Counters

Many while instructions, especially those that use a counter, have a body that contains an instruction for incrementing a variable. This can be done with the following instruction:

```
i = i + 1
```

As a side note, especially because of these kinds of instructions, it's unwise to express the assignment as "is." The value of i can, of course, never be the same as i + 1, but the value of i *becomes* the old value of i, plus 1. These kinds of instructions are very common in programs, so a special, shorter notation exists that does exactly the same thing:

```
i++
```

The ++ can be expressed as "is incremented." Because this operator is placed after the variable it operates on, the ++ operator is called a *postfix operator*. To increment a variable by more than 1, there is another notation,

```
i += 2
```

and it means the same as

```
i = i + 2
```

There is a similar notation for other basic arithmetic operations:

```
i -= 12        // this is the same as i = i - 12
i *= 0.99      // this is the same as i = i * 0.99
i /= 5         // this is the same as i = i / 5
i--            // this is the same as i = i - 1
```

This notation is very useful because it allows you to write shorter code. For example,

```
lives = lives - penalty
```

becomes

```
lives -= penalty
```

When you look at the example code belonging to this chapter and the ones following it, you will see that this shorter notation is used in many different classes to make the code more compact.

# A More Compact Looping Syntax

Many while instructions use a counting variable and therefore have the following structure:

```
var i = begin value
while i < end value {
    // do something useful using i
    i++
}
```

Because this kind of instruction is quite common, a more compact notation is available for it:

```
for var i = begin value ; i < end value ; i++ {
    // do something useful using i
}
```

The meaning of this instruction is exactly the same as the earlier while instruction. The advantage of using the for instruction in this case is that everything that has something to do with the counter is nicely grouped together in the header of the instruction. This reduces the chance of you forgetting the instruction to increment the counter (resulting in an endless loop). In the cases where "do something useful using i" consists of only a single instruction, you can leave out the braces, which makes the notation even more compact. Also, you can move the declaration of the variable i in the header of the for instruction. For example, look at the following code fragment:

```
for var index = 0; index < lives; index++ {
    let livesSpr = SKSpriteNode(imageNamed: "spr_lives")
    livesSpr.position = CGPoint(x: index * Int(livesSpr.size.width), y: 0)
    livesNode.addChild(livesSpr)
}
```

This is a very compact instruction that increments the counter and add the sprites at different positions. This instruction is equivalent to the while instruction shown earlier in this chapter.

Here's another example:

```
for var index = 0; index < livesNode.children.count; index++ {
    var livesSpr = livesNode.children[index] as SKNode
    livesSpr.hidden = lives <= index
}
```

Without actually understanding what the body does, can you (as an exercise) rewrite this for instruction into its equivalent while instruction?

If you look more closely at what this for instruction does, you see that it increments a counter index from zero to livesNode.children.count. The latter expression indicates the number of children that the node livesNode has. Inside the for loop, you see two instructions. The first instruction retrieves a particular child object from the node. This instruction works with a concept called an *array*. In Chapter 12, you'll learn more about arrays. Without going into too much detail, you can assume that this instruction retrieves a child node from the node livesNode using the value of the counter index. The result is that the for loop retrieves all the child nodes from livesNode one by one. The second instruction in the body sets the hidden status of the node that was retrieved. In other words, this for loop replaces the following instructions in the update method of GameWorld:

```
livesSpr5.hidden = lives <= 4
livesSpr4.hidden = lives <= 3
livesSpr3.hidden = lives <= 2
livesSpr2.hidden = lives <= 1
livesSpr1.hidden = lives <= 0
```

A very nice property of the new solution that uses `for` loops is that it's now really easy to change the maximum number of lives in the program. You only have to change the value of the `lives` variable in the `GameWorld` class and you're done! The rest of the code works independently of the initial value chosen for `lives`. It's a good idea to design your code in such a way that it's easy to change. This is just a simple example of how you can do that. The advantage is that not only is your code easier to change, it's also much more robust. There is a single place where the initial number of lives is set instead of multiple places. As a result, the chance that you will introduce a bug when you change the number of lives is much smaller.

The condition in a `while` or `for` loop doesn't necessarily have to be related to a counter. For example,

```
for var nr = 8; !isPrimeNumber(nr); nr++ {
    print(nr)
}
```

This `for` loop prints all the number 8 or higher, until the next prime number (which is 11). Therefore, the output of this piece of code is

```
8
9
10
```

Since in many cases you do need a counter, Swift also provides a shorter syntax for dealing with counters. Look at the following example:

```
for index in 0...9 {
    // do something
}
```

This `for` loop is equivalent to

```
for var index = 0; index <= 9; index++ {
    // do something
}
```

You can also define a range that excludes the last value, as follows:

```
for index in 0..<5 {
    // index will have values 0, 1, 2, 3, 4 respectively
}
```

This is equivalent to

```
for var index = 0; index < 5; index++ {
    // do something
}
```

The nice thing about the range notation for incrementing a counter is that it works very well with operations such as performing some task on objects in a list. You can also use variable names instead of constants to determine the range:

```
for index in 0..<lives {
    let livesSpr = SKSpriteNode(imageNamed: "spr_lives")
    livesSpr.position = CGPoint(x: index * Int(livesSpr.size.width), y: 0)
    livesNode.addChild(livesSpr)
}
```

If you simply want to execute a block of code a number of times and you don't need a counter, then you can omit the variable name and replace it by an underscore. For example, the following code prints "Hello!" ten times on the screen:

```
for _ in 1...10 {
    print("Hello!")
}
```

The use of a range in a for loop has one limitation: the starting value of the range should be smaller than the end value. In other words, this is not allowed:

```
for index in 3...1 {
    // do something
}
```

When you write down such an instruction in your code, the Xcode compiler will not generate a compiler error. Instead, when you run the program, a *runtime error* will be generated, immediately stopping the program. The reason that the compiler doesn't detect this is because ranges can also be defined by variable expressions. Therefore, there is no way in the syntax to define this constraint. Figure 9-3 contains the syntax diagram of the for instruction. As you can see, it contains the syntax for both the range notation and the full notation.

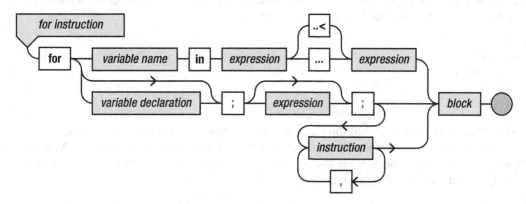

**Figure 9-3.** *Syntax diagram of the* for *instruction*

# A Few Special Cases

There are a few special cases that you need to know about when dealing with while and for loops. The following subsections discuss these cases.

## No Repeat at All

Sometimes the condition in the header of a while instruction is already false at the beginning. Look at the following code fragment:

```
var x = 1
var y = 0
while x < y {
    x++
}
```

In this case, the body of the while instruction isn't executed—not even once! Therefore, in this example, the variable x retains the value 1.

## Infinite Repeat

One of the dangers of using while instructions (and, to a lesser extent, for instructions) is that they might never end, if you're not careful. You can easily write such an instruction:

```
while 1 + 1 == 2 {
    x = x + 1
}
```

In this case, the value of x is incremented without end. This is because the condition 1 + 1 == 2 always yields true, no matter what is done in the body of the instruction. This example is quite easy to avoid, but often a while instruction ends in an infinite loop because of a programming error. Consider the following example:

```
var x = 1
var n = 0
while n < 10 {
    x = x * 2
}
```

The intention of this code is that the value of x is doubled ten times. But unfortunately, the programmer forgot to increment the counter in the body of the while instruction. As a result, the value of n will never be greater than or equal to ten, and the body of the while loop is infinitely repeated. What the programmer actually meant was

```
var x = 1
var n = 0
while n < 10 {
    x = x * 2
    n++
}
```

It would be a pity if you had to throw away your computer or mobile device after it was put into a coma because you forgot to increment the counter in the body of your while instruction. Fortunately, the operating system of most devices (including Macs, iPads, and iPhones) can stop the execution of a program by force, even if it hasn't finished. Once that's done, you can start to look for the cause of the program hanging. Although such hang-ups occur occasionally in programs, it's your job as a game programmer to make sure that once the game is publicly available, these kinds of programming errors have been removed from the game code. This is why proper testing is so important.

In general, if the program you wrote doesn't seem to do anything on startup, or if it hangs indefinitely, check out what is happening in the while instructions. A very common mistake is to forget to increment the counter variable, so the condition of the while instruction never becomes false and the while loop continues indefinitely. Many other programming errors may lead to an infinite loop. In fact, infinite loops are so common that a street in Cupertino, California has been named after them—and located on that street is Apple headquarters!

## Nested Repeats

The body of a while instruction or a for instruction is a block of instructions delimited by braces. Inside the block you can write any kind of instruction: an assignment, a method call, or another while or for loop. For example,

```
for y in 0...5 {
    for x in 0...y {
        let livesSpr = SKSpriteNode(imageNamed: "spr_lives")
        livesSpr.position = CGPoint(x: x * Int(livesSpr.size.width),
            y: y * -Int(livesSpr.size.height))
        livesNode.addChild(livesSpr)
    }
}
```

In this fragment, the variable y counts from 0 to 5. For each of these values of y, the body is executed, which consists of a for instruction. This second for instruction uses the counter x, which has as an upper limit the value of y. Therefore, in each progression of the outer for instruction, the inner for instruction goes on longer. The instruction that is repeated places a yellow balloon sprite at the position calculated by using the values of the x and y counters. The result of this loop is a number of balloons placed in the shape of a triangle (see Figure 9-4).

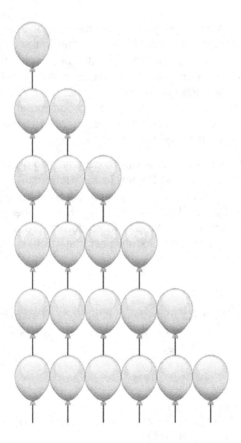

*Figure 9-4. Balloons in a triangle shape*

# Restarting the Game

When the player has lost all their lives, the game is over. How do you deal with this? In the Painter game, you want to show a Game Over screen. The player can tap on the screen, which will then restart the game. In order to add this to the game, you load an extra sprite when the game is started that represents the Game Over screen. You store this sprite as a property in the GameWorld class:

```
var gameover = SKSpriteNode(imageNamed: "spr_gameover")
```

In the initializer of GameWorld, you add this sprite to the main node representing the game world. Secondly, you assign a higher z-position to the sprite, so that it will be drawn on top of everything else. Finally, you set the hidden flag of the sprite, so it won't be shown yet to the player:

```
node.addChild(gameover)
gameover.zPosition = 2
gameover.hidden = true
```

Now you can use an if instruction in each of the game-loop methods to determine what you should do. If the game is over, you don't want the cannon and the ball to handle input anymore; you simply want to check if the player taps on the screen. If that happens, you reset the game. So, the handleInput method in the GameWorld class now contains the following instructions:

```
if (lives > 0) {
    cannon.handleInput(inputHelper)
    ball.handleInput(inputHelper)
} else if (inputHelper.hasTapped) {
    reset()
}
```

You add a reset method to the GameWorld class so you can reset the game to its initial state. This means resetting all the game objects. You also need to reset the number of lives to five. Here is the full reset method in GameWorld:

```
func reset() {
    lives = 5
    cannon.reset()
    ball.reset()
    can1.reset()
    can2.reset()
    can3.reset()
}
```

For the updateDelta method, you only need to update the game objects if the game isn't over. Therefore, you first check with an if instruction whether you need to update the game objects. If not (in other words, the number of lives has reached zero), you return from the method, like so:

```
if (lives <= 0) {
    return
}
// since you know that the player is still alive, you can update the game objects here
```

> **Note**   Check if the number of lives is smaller than or equal to zero. Are there cases in which the number of lives is less than zero? It is probably very unlikely, but it is possible that in one interation of the game loop two paint cans fall out of the screen simultaneously and the number of lives is decremented twice. If the number of lives was 1, then the new number of lives is -1.

The Game Over overlay should only be displayed if the player is no longer alive, so as the first instruction in the updateDelta method, you set the hidden status of the game over sprite accordingly:

```
gameover.hidden = lives > 0
```

In other words, the sprite remains hidden as long as the number of lives of the player is larger than zero. Figure 9-5 shows the Game Over overlay drawn on top of the game world.

*Figure 9-5. Game over!*

In Figure 9-5, notice that the Game Over overlay doesn't completely hide the other objects and the background. The reason is that the Game Over sprite has some *transparent* pixels. Often, sprites have transparent parts so the sprites seem to be integrated parts of the game world. The balloon, the ball, the paint cans, and the cannon barrel all are partly transparent, which is why they seamlessly integrate into the game world. When designing sprites, you need to make sure the image has these transparency values set correctly. Although doing this right can be a lot of work, modern image-editing tools such as Adobe Photoshop give you many means to define transparency in images. Just be sure you save the image in a format that supports transparency, such as PNG.

**Note**   You can use the (lack of) transparency of overlays to control what the player is seeing. In some cases, you might want things obscured (such as a "pause" screen in a time-sensitive game) or able to be seen (such as the Game Over screen in Painter).

# What You Have Learned

In this chapter, you have learned the following:

- How to store and display the current number of lives for a player
- How to repeat a group of instructions using the `while` or `for` instruction
- How to restart the game when the player has no lives remaining

# Chapter 10

# Organizing Game Objects

You saw in the previous chapters how to use classes to group variables that belong together. This chapter looks at the similarities between the different types of game objects and how you can express these similarities in Swift.

## Similarities Between Game Objects

If you look at the different game objects in the Painter game, you can see that they have a lot of things in common. For example, the ball, the cannon, and the paint cans all use three sprites that represent each of the three different colors. Also, most objects in the game have a velocity. Furthermore, some of the game objects have a method for handling input, some have an updateDelta method, and some have a reset method. Now, it isn't really a problem that these classes have similarities. The compiler or the players of the game won't complain about that. However, it's a pity that you have to copy code all the time. To give an example, the Cannon, Ball, and PaintCan classes all have the following computed property called color:

```swift
var color: UIColor {
    get {
        if (!red.hidden) {
            return UIColor.redColor()
        } else if (!green.hidden) {
            return UIColor.greenColor()
        } else {
            return UIColor.blueColor()
        }
    }
    set(col) {
        if col != UIColor.redColor() && col != UIColor.greenColor()
            && col != UIColor.blueColor() {
                return
        }
```

```
        red.hidden = col != UIColor.redColor()
        green.hidden = col != UIColor.greenColor()
        blue.hidden = col != UIColor.blueColor()
    }
}
```

The code is exactly the same, but you have to copy it for all three classes. And every time you want to add a different kind of colored game object, you probably need to copy this property again. If you only have to do that for one property, it's not that much of a problem. But there are more similarities between classes in Painter. For example, most game object classes in the Painter game have the same stored properties: velocity, red, green, and blue.

In general, it's better to avoid copying a lot of code. Why is that? Because if at some point you realize there is a mistake in that part of the code, you have to correct it everywhere you copied it to. In a small game like Painter, this isn't a big issue. But when you develop a commercial game with hundreds of different game-object classes, this becomes a serious maintenance problem. Furthermore, you don't always know how far a small game will go. If you aren't careful, you can end up copying a lot of code (and the bugs associated with it). As a game matures, it's a good idea to keep an eye out for where to optimize code, even if this means some extra work to find these duplications and consolidate them. For this particular situation, you need to think about how the different kinds of game objects are similar and whether you can group these similarities together, just as you grouped the properties in the previous chapters.

Conceptually speaking, it's easy to say what is similar between balls, paint cans, and cannons: they're all *game objects*. Basically, they are all located at a certain position; they all have a velocity (even the cannon, but its velocity is zero); and they all have a color that is red, green, or blue. Furthermore, most of them handle input of some kind and are updated.

# Inheritance

In Swift, you can group these similarities together in a generic class and then define other classes that are a *special version* of this generic class. In object-oriented jargon, this is called *inheritance*, and it's a very powerful language feature. Consider the following example:

```
class Vehicle {
    var numberOfWheels = 4
    var brand = ""

    func what() -> String {
        return "nrOfWheels = \(numberOfWheels), brand = \(brand)"
    }
}
```

Here you have a very simple example of a class for representing vehicles (you can imagine that this could be useful for a traffic-simulation game). To keep things simple, a vehicle is defined by a number of wheels and a brand. The Vehicle class also has a method called what that returns a description of the vehicle as a String value (text). This method could be useful if you wanted to create an app that presented a list of vehicles in a table. Note that I used a special mechanism in Swift to combine text and variables:

```
return "nrOfWheels = \(numberOfWheels), brand = \(brand)"
```

In Swift, this process of creating a String value by mixing constants or variables with text is called *string interpolation*. If you want to insert the value of a variable inside a text string, you simply write the name of the variable between \( and ). Here is an example that creates a variable of type Vehicle and that prints the vehicle data to the console:

```
var v = Vehicle()
v.brand = "volkswagen"
print(v.what()) // outputs "nrOfWheels = 4, brand = volkswagen"
```

Let's add an initializer to the class that accepts the brand name as a parameter:

```
init(_ b: String) {
    brand = b
}
```

Now you can create a vehicle and immediately assign it a brand name:

```
var v = Vehicle("volkswagen")
print(v.what())
```

There are different types of vehicles, such as cars, bikes, motorbikes, and so on. For some of these types, you would like to store additional information. For example, for a car, it could be useful to store whether it's a convertible; for the motorbike, how many cylinders it has; and so on. You can use the inheritance mechanism in Swift to do that. Here is an example of a class called Car:

```
class Car: Vehicle {
    var convertible = false
}
```

As you can see, behind the name of the class, there is a colon and then the word Vehicle. This means that the Car class *inherits from* Vehicle. In essence, this means that Car copies the functionality from Vehicle, including the what method:

```
var c = Car("mercedes")
print(c.what()) // outputs "nrOfWheels = 4, brand = mercedes"
```

The nice thing about inheritance is that you can replace or extend functionality. For example, suppose that you want the what method to return a string that also contains whether or not the car is a convertible. In order to achieve this, you can *override* the original what method and replace it by another one. Here is the new version of the Car class that overrides the what method:

```
class Car : Vehicle {
    var convertible = false

    override func what() -> String {
        return "nrOfWheels = \(numberOfWheels), brand = \(brand),
            convertible = \(convertible)"
    }
}
```

And later on, if you use the Car class:

```
var c = Car("mercedes")
print(c.what()) // outputs "nrOfWheels = 4, brand = mercedes, convertible = false"
```

Because the Car class inherits from Vehicle, this means that an object of type Car *is also an object of type* Vehicle. So, there are two important aspects of inheritance:

- There is a relationship between objects (a Car object is also a Vehicle).

- A class that inherits from another class copies its functionality (Car objects have the same (stored and computed) properties, and methods as Vehicle objects).

Because Car inherits from Vehicle, you also say that Car is a *subclass* or *derived class* of Vehicle, or that Vehicle is the *superclass*, or *parent class*, or *base class*, of Car. The inheritance relationship between classes is widely used; and in a good class design, it can be interpreted as "is a kind of." In this example, the relationship is clear: a car is a kind of vehicle. The other way around isn't always true. A vehicle isn't always a car. There could be other subclasses of Vehicle, such as the following:

```
class MotorBike: Vehicle {
    var cylinders = 4
    override init(_ b: String) {
        super.init(b)
        numberOfWheels = 2
    }
}
```

A motorbike is also a kind of vehicle. The Motorbike class inherits from Vehicle and adds its own custom property to indicate the number of cylinders. As you can see, the MotorBike class overrides the *initializer* of the Vehicle class. This is necessary because a motorbike doesn't have four wheels. So, when a MotorBike instance is created, you want to make sure that the number of wheels is set correctly. Although overriding a method or overriding an initializer is very similar, there is a crucial difference. When you override the initializer, Swift obligates you to call a designated initializer from the superclass. Furthermore, you have to call that initializer before you access any properties from the superclass. This is done to ensure that objects are properly initialized before you access their data. The Vehicle class contains a single (designated) initializer. This line of code calls that initializer:

```
super.init(b)
```

This is the first instruction in the Car initializer body, and it makes sure that the Vehicle part of the Car object is initialized. The keyword super is used to indicate that you call an initializer belonging to the superclass. super refers to an object, just like self. The main difference between self and super is that self refers to the object a method (or initializer) is currently manipulating, whereas super refers to that same object, but only *the part of the object belonging to the superclass*. In this example, it means that the type of self is Car, and the type of super is Vehicle.

Figure 10-1 illustrates the hierarchy of classes used in vehicle/car example. For a more expanded version of this hierarchy, see Figure 10-4.

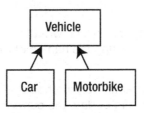

*Figure 10-1. Inheritance diagram of Vehicle and its subclasses*

# Game Objects and Inheritance

The "is a kind of" relationship also holds for the game objects in the Painter game. A ball is a kind of game object, and so are the paint cans and the cannon. You can make this inheritance relationship explicit in the program by defining a generic class called ThreeColorGameObject and having your actual game-object classes inherit from that generic class. You can then put everything that defines what a three-color game object is in that class, and the ball, the cannon, and the paint can will be special versions of that class. The Painter8 example belonging to this chapter shows how to do this.

Let's look at this ThreeColorGameObject class in more detail. You put into this class the properties that are commonly used by the different types of game objects in the game. You can define a basic skeleton of this class as follows:

```
class ThreeColorGameObject {
    var node = SKNode()
    var red = SKSpriteNode()
    var green = SKSpriteNode()
    var blue = SKSpriteNode()
    var velocity = CGPoint.zeroPoint
    ...
}
```

Each class that inherits from ThreeColorGameObject will have a node, three sprites, and a velocity. This is nice because now you only define these properties in one place, and they can be used in any class that inherits from ThreeColorGameObject.

One thing that you need to do is provide a way to initialize a three-color game object with three different sprites. When you define the ThreeColorGameObject class, you don't know yet which sprites to use because they will depend on the final type of the game object (cannons use sprites other than balls or paint cans). In order to solve this, let's add the following initializer:

```
init(_ spriteRed: String, _ spriteGreen: String, _ spriteBlue: String) {
    red = SKSpriteNode(imageNamed: spriteRed)
    green = SKSpriteNode(imageNamed: spriteGreen)
    blue = SKSpriteNode(imageNamed: spriteBlue)
    node.addChild(red)
    node.addChild(green)
    node.addChild(blue)
}
```

Whenever you inherit from this class, you define what the values of the sprite properties red, green, and blue should be, by passing the names of the images as a parameter to the ThreeColorGameObject initializer.

Next, you need to define the basic game-loop methods. The updateDelta method of the class only contains the instructions that update the current position of the game object based on its velocity:

```
func updateDelta(delta: NSTimeInterval) {
    node.position.x += velocity.x * CGFloat(delta)
    node.position.y += velocity.y * CGFloat(delta)
}
```

For completeness, let's also add methods for handling input and for resetting the game object, which can be overridden later on:

```
func handleInput() {
}

func reset() {
}
```

If you look at the ThreeColorGameObject class in the Painter8 example, you'll see also a few computed properties added. The first one is color, which reads and writes the color of the game object. The second property is called box, and it calculates the bounding box of the game object. This is a useful (read-only) property for determining whether two game objects collide. Here is the property definition:

```
var box: CGRect {
    get {
        return node.calculateAccumulatedFrame()
    }
}
```

The nice thing about adding methods and properties to `ThreeColorGameObject` is that any class that inherits from it now also has those methods and properties. This saves you a lot of code copying! For the complete `ThreeColorGameObject` class, see the Painter8 example belonging to this chapter.

# Cannon as a Subclass of ThreeColorGameObject

Now that you've created a very basic class for colored game objects, you can reuse this basic behavior for the actual game objects in your game by *inheriting* from this class. Let's first look at the Cannon class. Because you've defined the basic `ThreeColorGameObject` class, you can create the Cannon class as a subclass of that class. Here is a part of the definition of the Cannon class:

```
class Cannon: ThreeColorGameObject {
    var barrel = SKSpriteNode(imageNamed:"spr_cannon_barrel")

    init() {
        super.init("spr_cannon_red", "spr_cannon_green", "spr_cannon_blue")
        red.zPosition = 1
        green.zPosition = 1
        blue.zPosition = 1
        barrel.anchorPoint = CGPoint(x:0.233, y:0.5)
        node.position = CGPoint(x:-430, y:-280)
        node.zPosition = 1
        green.hidden = true
        blue.hidden = true
        node.addChild(barrel)
    }
    ...
}
```

The Cannon class introduces an extra property, called `barrel`. Also, the class has its own initializer. The first instruction in the Cannon initializer calls the designated initializer from the superclass. Between the parentheses, you see the three sprite parameters that this initializer expects. Then, the rest of the Cannon object is initialized.

Now that the new version of the Cannon class has been defined, you can start adding properties and methods to the class, just as you did before. For example, here is the handleInput method:

```
override func handleInput(inputHelper: InputHelper) {
    if !inputHelper.isTouching {
        return
    }
    let localTouch: CGPoint = GameScene.world.node.convertPoint(inputHelper.touchLocation,
    toNode: red)
    if !red.frame.contains(localTouch) {
        let opposite = inputHelper.touchLocation.y - node.position.y
        let adjacent = inputHelper.touchLocation.x - node.position.x
        barrel.zRotation = atan2(opposite, adjacent)
```

```
    } else if inputHelper.hasTapped {
        let tmp = blue.hidden
        blue.hidden = green.hidden
        green.hidden = red.hidden
        red.hidden = tmp
    }
}
```

As you can see, you can access properties such as node and red without any problem. Because Cannon inherits from ThreeColorGameObject, it contains the same (stored and computed) properties and methods. As you can also see, the word override indicates that this method replaces the original method (which had an empty body) from ThreeColorGameObject.

If you take a look at the Cannon class in the Painter8 example belonging to this chapter, you can see that the class definition is much smaller and easier to read than in the previous version because all the generic game-object properties and methods are placed in the ThreeColorGameObject class. Organizing your code in different classes and subclasses helps to reduce code copying and results in generally cleaner designs. There is a caveat, however: your class structure (which class inherits from which other class) must be correct. Remember that classes should only inherit from other classes if there is a "is a kind of" relationship between the classes. To illustrate this, suppose you want to add an indicator at the top of the screen that shows the current color of the ball. You could make a class for that and let it inherit from the Cannon class because it needs to handle input in a similar way:

```
class ColorIndicator : Cannon {
    ...
}
```

However, this is a very bad idea. A color indicator is certainly not a kind of cannon, and designing your classes this way makes it very unclear to other developers what the classes are used for. Furthermore, the color indicator would now also have a barrel, which doesn't make any sense. Class-inheritance diagrams should be logical and easy to understand. Every time you write a class that inherits from another class, ask yourself whether that class really "is a kind of" the class that you inherit from. If it isn't, then you have to rethink your design.

# The Ball Class

You define the new Ball class in a fashion very similar to the Cannon class. Just as in the Cannon class, you inherit from the ThreeColorGameObject class. The only difference is that you add an extra property that indicates whether the ball is ready to be shot:

```
class Ball : ThreeColorGameObject {
    var readyToShoot = false

    init() {
        super.init("spr_ball_red", "spr_ball_green", "spr_ball_blue")
        node.zPosition = 1
        node.hidden = true
    }
```

```
convenience init(position: CGPoint) {
    self.init()
    node.position = position
}
...
}
```

When a `Ball` instance is created, you need to call the designated `ThreeColorGameObject` initializer, just as you did with the `Cannon` class. In this case, you pass along the ball sprites as parameters.

The `Ball` class clearly illustrates what happens when you inherit from another class. Each `Ball` instance consists of a part that has been inherited from `ThreeColorGameObject` and a part that is defined in the `Ball` class. Figure 10-2 shows what the memory looks like for a `Ball` object without using inheritance. Figure 10-3 also shows a `Ball` instance, but using the inheritance mechanism introduced in this chapter.

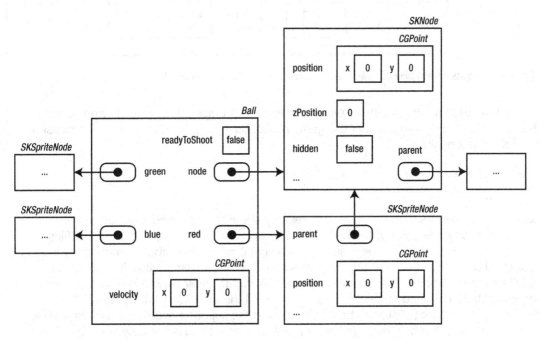

*Figure 10-2. Overview of the memory used by an instance of the Ball class (no inheritance)*

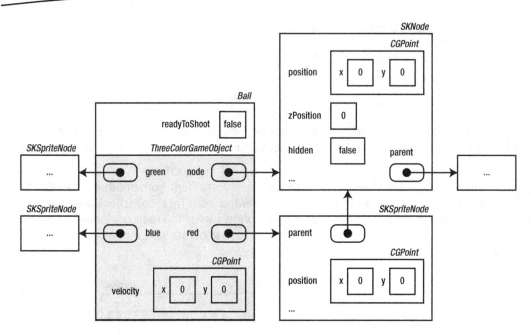

**Figure 10-3.** *An instance of the Ball class (which inherits from ThreeColorGameObject)*

The updateDelta method in the ThreeColorGameObject class contains only two instructions that calculate the new position of the game object based on its velocity, the time passed, and its current position:

```
node.position.x += velocity.x * CGFloat(delta)
node.position.y += velocity.y * CGFloat(delta)
```

Balls should do more than that. The ball velocity should be updated to incorporate drag and gravity; the color of the ball should be updated if needed; and if the ball flies outside the screen, it should be reset to its original position. You could simply copy the updateDelta method from the previous version of the Ball class so that it replaces the updateDelta method of ThreeColorGameObject. A slightly nicer way to do it is to define the updateDelta method in the Ball class but reuse the original updateDelta method from ThreeColorGameObject. This can be done by using the super keyword in a way very similar to how you used it to call the initializer of the superclass. Here is the new version of the updateDelta method in the Ball class:

```
override func updateDelta(delta: NSTimeInterval) {
    if !node.hidden {
        velocity.x *= 0.99
        velocity.y -= 15
        super.updateDelta(delta)
    } else {
        // calculate the ball position
        node.position = GameScene.world.cannon.ballPosition
```

```
        // copy the ball color
        self.color = GameScene.world.cannon.color
    }
    if GameScene.world.isOutsideWorld(node.position) {
        reset()
    }
}
```

In the body of the if instruction, you update the velocity and then call the updateDelta method of the superclass, which updates the position of the game object. The nice thing is that this approach allows you to separate different parts of (in this case) the updating process. Any game object with a position and velocity will need to update its position based on its velocity in each iteration of the game loop. You define this behavior in the updateDelta method of ThreeColorGameObject so you can reuse it for any class that inherits from ThreeColorGameObject!

# The PaintCan Class

The final class that inherits from ThreeColorGameObject is PaintCan. Have a look at the Painter8 example to see the complete class. PaintCan overrides the updateDelta method as well as the reset method. Just like before, it doesn't handle any input, so you don't have to override the handleInput method.

There is one interesting bit in the PaintCan class, and that is the part using the box computed property. Since any class inheriting from ThreeColorGameObject has that property, you can now use it to easily check whether two game objects collide. Take a look at the following lines of code:

```
var ball = GameScene.world.ball
if self.box.intersects(ball.box) {
    color = ball.color
    ball.reset()
}
```

These are just a few lines of code, but behind the scenes a lot is happening. Bounding boxes are computed as well as intersections between them, and the hidden statuses of colored sprites are changed. Because of the way the code is designed, you can do these tasks by writing only a couple of lines of code!

When looking at the game object classes, you can see that another interesting thing has happened. Because each game object class inherits from ThreeColorGameObject, the definitions in the ThreeColorGameObject class determine what methods and properties look like. In a sense, ThreeColorGameObject imposes constraints on any game object classes that inherit from it. For example, it enforces that the method for handling input is called handleInput (and not HandleInput, handleinput, or handle_input). This is another way in which inheritance helps to increase the quality of your code: it results in more consistent class definitions.

# Polymorphism

Because of the inheritance mechanism, you don't always have to know to what type of object a variable is pointing to. Consider the following declaration and initialization:

```
var someKindOfGameObject : Cannon = Cannon()
```

And somewhere else in the code, you do this:

```
someKindOfGameObject.updateDelta(delta)
```

Now suppose you change the declaration and initialization, as follows:

```
var someKindOfGameObject : ThreeColorGameObject = Cannon()
```

This is allowed, since Cannon is a subclass of ThreeColorGameObject. The other way (assigning a ThreeColorGameObject instance to a variable of type Cannon) is not allowed, since not every ThreeColorGameObject is a cannon (some of them are a ball or a paint can).

So, if someKindOfGameObject is of type ThreeColorGameObject, which version of the updateDelta method is called? It depends on the instance that the variable refers to. If that instance happens to be a Cannon instance, the updateDelta method of Cannon will be called. If it's a Ball instance, the updateDelta method of Ball will be called. When the program is executed, the right version of the updateDelta method is called automatically.

This effect is called *polymorphism*, and it comes in very handy sometimes. Polymorphism allows you to better separate code. Suppose a game company wants to release an extension of its game. For example, it might want to introduce a few new enemies, or skills that a player can learn. The company can provide these extensions as subclasses of generic Enemy and Skill classes. The actual game code will then use these objects without having to know which particular skill or enemy it's dealing with. It simply calls the methods that were defined in the generic classes.

# Inheriting from Existing Classes

Instead of creating a subclass of a class you wrote yourself, you can also inherit from classes written by other developers. In the Painter8 example, there are two hierarchies of game objects. One hierarchy is represented by the classes you created: the GameWorld instance contains references to the cannon, ball, and paint can objects. The second hierarchy is the one defined by the nodes in the scene graph. Generally, this is not an ideal solution. Because there are two hierarchies to maintain, inconsistencies can easily occur, leading to bugs and other undesired behavior.

A way to solve this problem is by merging these two hierarchies. The Painter9 example shows how this is done. The main difference between Painter8 and Painter9 is that in Painter9, the game object classes are all (indirectly) a subclass of SKNode, which is the main representation of a node in the scene graph in the SpriteKit framework. The ThreeColorGameObject class is now a subclass of SKNode. This means that the node property is no longer needed because any game object will already be a node itself.

If you take a look at the `ThreeColorGameObject` class in Painter9, you'll see that it is now a subclass of SKNode. Because of this, you need to do a few extra things. For one, you need to call the initializer of the superclass in your own initializers:

```
override init() {
    super.init()
    self.addChild(red)
    self.addChild(green)
    self.addChild(blue)
}

init(_ spriteRed: String, _ spriteGreen: String, _ spriteBlue: String) {
    super.init()
    red = SKSpriteNode(imageNamed: spriteRed)
    green = SKSpriteNode(imageNamed: spriteGreen)
    blue = SKSpriteNode(imageNamed: spriteBlue)
    self.addChild(red)
    self.addChild(green)
    self.addChild(blue)
}
```

The first initializer overrides the initializer of the superclass and makes sure that the three sprite nodes are added to this game object to ensure consistency, no matter what initializer is called. The second initializer is the same as before, except that it calls the initializer of the superclass, and sprites are now added to the game object itself instead of a separate node.

Finally, you see the following initializer:

```
required init?(coder aDecoder: NSCoder) {
    fatalError("init(coder:) has not been implemented")
}
```

When you inherit from SKNode, you are *required* to add this initializer (also indicated in the code itself by the `required` keyword). The reason this initializer is needed is because the SKNode class supports something called serialization. Serialization means that it's possible to initialize objects from data (for example, stored in a file). This is a useful feature for many games because it forms the basis of the save game mechanism. In Painter, there is no such mechanism, however, so the initializer contains a single instruction that stops the program with an error.

Because `ThreeColorGameObject` is a subclass of SKNode, any class inheriting from `ThreeColorGameObject` also is a subclass of SKNode, including the Cannon, the Ball and the PaintCan classes. As you can see in Painter9, the GameWorld class is set up in a very similar way as `ThreeColorGameObject`: it inherits from SKNode, so a separate node property is no longer needed.

# Hierarchies of Classes

You've seen several examples in this chapter of classes inheriting from a base game-object class. A class should inherit from another class only if the relationship between these two classes can be described as "is a kind of." For example: a Ball is a kind of ThreeColorGameObject, which in turn is a kind of SKNode. You can extend that hierarchy even further. For instance, you can write a class that inherits from the Ball class, such as BouncingBall, a special version of a standard ball that bounces off paint cans instead of only colliding with them. And you could make another class called BouncingElasticBall, which inherits from BouncingBall, but is a ball that deforms according to its elastic properties when it bounces against a paint can. Every time you inherit from a class, you get the data (encoded in properties) and the behavior (encoded in methods) from the base class for free.

Commercial games have a class hierarchy of different game objects with many different levels. Going back to the traffic-simulation example at the beginning of this chapter, you can imagine a very complicated hierarchy of all kinds of different vehicles. Figure 10-4 shows an example of such a hierarchy. The figure uses arrows to indicate an inheritance relation between classes.

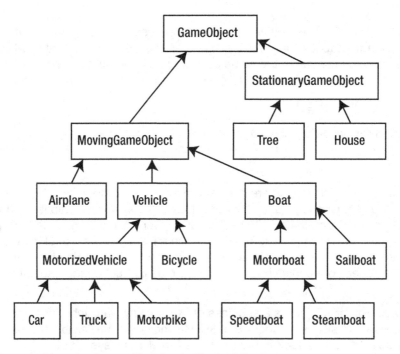

*Figure 10-4. A complex hierarchy of game objects in a traffic-simulation game*

At the very base of the inheritance tree is a GameObject class. This class contains only very basic information such as the position or the velocity of the game object. For each subclass, new properties and methods can be added, which are relevant for the particular class and its subclasses. For example, the property numberOfWheels typically belongs in the Vehicle class and not in MovingGameObject (because boats don't have wheels). The property flightAltitude belongs in the Airplane class, and the property bellIsWorking belongs in the Bicycle class.

When you determine the way your classes are structured, you have to make many decisions. There isn't a single best hierarchy; and, depending on the application, one hierarchy might be more useful than another. For instance, this example first divides the `MovingGameObject` class according to the medium the object uses to displace itself: land, air, or water. After that, the classes are divided in different subclasses: motorized or not motorized. You could choose to do this the other way around. For some classes, it isn't entirely clear where in the hierarchy they belong: do you say that a motorbike is a special type of bike (one with a motor)? Or is it a special kind of motorized vehicle (one with only two wheels)?

What is important is that the relationship between the classes themselves is clear. A sailboat is a boat, but a boat isn't always a sailboat. A bicycle is a vehicle, but not every vehicle is a bicycle.

# What You Have Learned

In this chapter, you have learned the following:

- How to use inheritance to structure related classes in a hierarchy
- How to override methods in a subclass to provide specific behavior for that class
- How to call a method or an initializer from the superclass, using the super keyword

# Chapter 11

# Finishing the Painter Game

In this chapter, you will finish the Painter game by adding a few extra features such as motion effects, sounds, and music, and maintaining and displaying a score. Finally, you will learn about characters and strings in a bit more detail.

## Adding Motion Effects

In order to make the game more visually appealing, you can make the paint cans swing back and forth slightly to simulate the effect of wind and friction on the falling motion. The PainterFinal program that belongs to this chapter is the final version of the game with this motion effect added to the cans. Adding such an effect isn't complicated. Thanks to the work you did in the previous chapter, only a single line needs to be added to the `updateDelta` method of the `PaintCan` class. Because `PaintCan` is a subclass of `ThreeColorGameObject`, which in turn is a subclass of `SKNode`, it has a `zRotation` property that you can use to rotate the paint can.

In order to achieve the motion effect, you use the `sin` function. By letting the value depend on the current position of the can, you get different values depending on that position. You then use this value to apply a rotation on the sprite. This is the line of code you add to the `updateDelta` method in the `PaintCan` class:

```
self.zRotation = sin(position.y / 50) * 0.04
```

This instruction uses the y-coordinate of the paint can position to get different rotation values. Furthermore, you divide it by 50 to get a nice slow movement, and you multiply the outcome by 0.04 to reduce the amplitude of the sine so the rotation looks more or less realistic. If you like, you can try out different values and see how they affect the behavior of the paint cans.

---

```
CREATING SPRITES
```

Even if you're not an artist, it helps to be able to make simple sprites yourself. It enables you to quickly make a prototype of the game—and maybe also find out there is an artist inside you. To create sprites, you first need good tools. Most artists use a painting program like Adobe Photoshop or a vector drawing program like Adobe Illustrator, but others work with such simple tools as Paintbrush or the more extensive and free GIMP. Every tool requires practice. Work your way through some tutorials, and make sure you get some insight into the many different features. Often, the things you want can be achieved in an easy way.

Preferably, create very large images of your game objects and then scale them down to the required size. The advantages are that you can change the required size in your game later and that you get rid of aliasing effects due to images being represented by pixels. When scaling images, anti-aliasing techniques blend the colors so the image remains smooth. If you keep the outside of the game object in the image transparent, then, when you scale, the border pixels will automatically become partially transparent. Only if you want to create the classic pixel style should you create the sprites in the actual size required.

Finally, look around on the Web. There are lots of sprites that you can use for free. Make sure to check the license terms so the pack of sprites you're using are legal for what you're building. You can then use them as a basis for your own sprites. But in the end, realize that the quality of your game increases significantly when you work with an experienced artist.

---

# Adding Sounds and Music

Another way to make the game more enjoyable is to add some sound. This game uses both background music and sound effects. In order to make dealing with sounds a bit easier in Swift, you add a Sound class that allows you to play back and loop sounds. Here is a part of that class (for the complete class, see the PainterFinal example):

```swift
class Sound {

    var audioPlayer = AVAudioPlayer()

    init(_ fileName: String) {
        let soundURL = NSBundle.mainBundle().URLForResource(fileName, withExtension: "mp3")
        audioPlayer = try! AVAudioPlayer(contentsOfURL: soundURL!)
    }
    ...

}
```

The class contains a stored property called audioPlayer that is responsible for playing the sound. In the initializer, you create a new audio player object based on the file name passed as a parameter. The syntax of creating the AVAudioPlayer object may look a bit unfamiliar to you. Creating an AVAudioPlayer object may result in an error (for example, if the sound file cannot be found). Swift forces you to choose whether to handle or ignore such errors. Since this kind of error handling is out of the scope of this book, I use try! to ignore any errors that may occur.

Now let's add some functionality to the Sound class to make playing a variety of sounds easier. One thing that many games need is the option to loop a sound. In general, background music should be looped; sound effects (such as firing a paint ball) shouldn't.

The Sound class contains a (computed) property called looping that indicates whether the sound should be looped or not. You can loop a sound by setting the property numberOfLoops in the audioPlayer object to an appropriate value. If you choose a value of 0, the sound will not loop (which is want you want for sound effects). A positive value indicates how often a sound should be looped. A value of -1 loops the sound indefinitely until the program is ended (which is a good option for background music). Here is the complete property:

```
var looping: Bool {
    get {
        return audioPlayer.numberOfLoops < 0
    }
    set {
        if newValue {
            audioPlayer.numberOfLoops = -1
        } else {
            audioPlayer.numberOfLoops = 0
        }
    }
}
```

Let's also add a property to change the volume of a sound that is playing. This is particularly useful because generally you want sound effects to be louder than background music. In some games, these volumes can be changed by the player (later in this book you will see how to do that). Whenever you introduce sound in your game, make sure to always provide volume or at least mute controls. Games without the ability to mute sounds will suffer the wrath of annoyed users via reviews! Here is the volume property, which is straightforward:

```
var volume: Float {
    get {
        return audioPlayer.volume
    }
    set {
        audioPlayer.volume = newValue
    }
}
```

Finally, you add a method called play, which does two things. First, it sets the location where to start playing the sound at the beginning (so, at time 0). Then, it calls the play method on the audioPlayer object:

```
func play() {
    audioPlayer.currentTime = 0
    audioPlayer.play()
}
```

Now you can use the Sound class to easily load and play a variety of sounds in your game. In the Painter game, there is background music as well as sound effects. For each specific sound you want to play, you add a property to the class that uses the sound. For example, for background music, the following property was added to GameWorld:

```
var backgroundMusic = Sound("snd_music")
```

In the initializer, you begin playing the background music in a loop at a low volume, as follows:

```
backgroundMusic.looping = true
backgroundMusic.volume = 0.5
backgroundMusic.play()
```

You also want to play sound effects. For example, when the player shoots a ball, they want to hear it! So, you play this sound effect when they start shooting the ball. In the Ball class, you add a property to represent the sound effect:

```
var shootPaintSound = Sound("snd_shoot_paint")
```

Then, you play the sound when the ball is shot, which is dealt with in the handleInput method of the Ball class:

```
if (!inputHelper.isTouching && readyToShoot && self.hidden) {
    self.hidden = false
    readyToShoot = false
    velocity.x = (inputHelper.touchLocation.x -
        GameScene.world.cannon.position.x) * 1.4
    velocity.y = (inputHelper.touchLocation.y -
        GameScene.world.cannon.position.y) * 1.4
    shootPaintSound.play()
}
```

Similarly, you also play a sound when a paint can of the correct color falls out of the screen (see the PaintCan class in the PainterFinal example for the actual code).

# Maintaining a Score

Scores are often a very effective way to motivate players to continue playing. *High scores* work especially well in that regard because they introduce a competitive factor into the game: you want to be better than AAA or XYZ (many early arcade games allowed only three characters for each name in the high-score list, leading to very imaginative names). High scores are so motivating that third-party systems exist to incorporate them into games. These systems let users compare themselves against thousands of other players around the world. In the Painter game, you keep it simple and add the property score to the GameWorld class in which to store the current score:

```
var score = 0
```

The player starts with a score of zero. Each time a paint can falls outside the screen, the score is updated. If a can of the correct color falls out of the screen, 10 points are added to the score. If a can isn't the right color, the player loses a life.

The score is a part of what is called the *economy* of a game. The game's economy basically describes the different costs and merits in the game and how they interact. When you make your own game, it's always useful to think about its economy. What do things cost, and what are the gains of executing different actions as a player? And are these two things in balance with each other?

You update the score in the `PaintCan` class, where you can check whether the can falls outside the screen. If so, you check whether it has the right color, and update the score and the number of player lives accordingly. Then you hide the `PaintCan` object so that it can fall again, like so:

```
let top = CGPoint(x: self.position.x, y: self.position.y + red.size.height/2)
if GameScene.world.isOutsideWorld(top) {
    if color != targetColor {
        GameScene.world.lives -= 1
    } else {
        GameScene.world.score += 10
        collectPointsSound.play()
    }
    self.hidden = true
}
```

In this code, you can also see that whenever a can of the right color falls off the screen, you play a sound effect stored in the `collectPointsSound` property.

# Characters and Strings

Since the game now maintains a score, it will also have to display this score on the screen somehow. This means you have to draw a number on the screen. In order to make clear to the player that this is a score and not some random number, you're also going to draw the text "Score: " in front of the number. Swift has a type for representing text called `String`. Just like numbers or Booleans, strings are a struct in Swift. Here is an example of declaring a string variable:

```
var name = "Patrick"
```

In Swift, strings are delimited by double quote characters. When using string values and combining them with other variables, you have to be careful when using quotes. If you forget the quotes, you're not writing text or characters anymore, but a piece of a Swift program! There is a big difference between the following:

- The string `"hello"` and the variable name `hello`
- The string `"123"` and the value `123`
- The string value `"+"` and the operator `+`

You use the + operator to combine (or *concatenate*) multiple strings:

```
var string1 = "hello "
var string2 = "world"
var string3 = string1 + string2 // string3 now contains "hello world"
```

Watch out: concatenation only makes sense when you're dealing with text. For example, it isn't possible to "concatenate" two numbers: the expression 1 + 2 results in 3, not 12. Of course, you can concatenate numbers *represented as text*: "1" + "2" results in "12". Making the distinction between text and numbers is done by using double quotes. If you want to combine strings and numbers (or variables of another type such as Boolean) into a single string, you can use the special \( ) notation, like so:

```
var age = 24
var info = "Peter is \(age) years old"
print(info) // prints the string "Peter is 24 years old"
```

This particular feature is called *string interpolation* and it's very useful in the Painter example for displaying the score. First, you add a label node to the game world:

```
var scoreLabel = SKLabelNode(fontNamed: "Chalkduster")
```

Then using string interpolation, you assign the current score to the label in the updateDelta method of GameWorld:

```
scoreLabel.text = "Score: \(score)"
```

Since the label is updated in every iteration of the game loop, the current score will now always be shown on the screen.

# Special Characters

Next to the \( ) notation, there are a few other special characters in strings that also use the backslash symbol, such as the following:

- \n for the line feed symbol
- \r for the carriage return symbol (note that for a new line in an iOS string, you can just use \n)
- \t for the tab symbol

This introduces a new problem: how to indicate the backslash character itself. The backslash character is indicated using the *double backslash*. In a similar way, the backslash symbol is used to represent the character for the double quotes:

- \\ for the backslash symbol
- \" for the double quote character

For example,

```
print("\"You are crazy,\" she said.") // output: "You are crazy," she said.
```

# Adding App Icons

The final thing to add to the Painter game is an app icon. App icons are needed in a variety of sizes, each with a different purpose. And some icons are needed in several resolutions (1x, 2x, or 3x). Figure 11-1 shows a screenshot of Xcode showing the icons that were added for the Painter game.

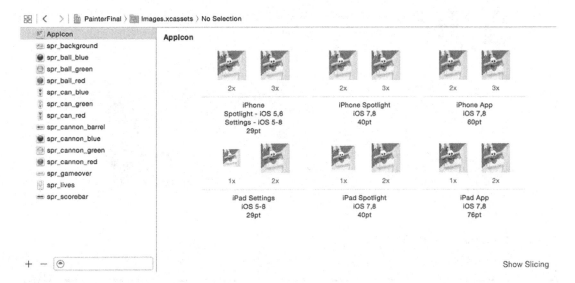

*Figure 11-1. Icons in the Painter game*

Designing a high quality icon for your app is really important. The icon is what most people will first see when they see your game is installed on a friend's device or when they look for nice games to play in the App Store. If your icon doesn't stand out, people will not buy your game. As a general tip, try to keep your icon simple, so that people can easily recognize it. Also, avoid putting text on an icon, since users will probably not be able to see the text on smaller screens. Finally, design your app icon in a way that's consistent with the game you create. If your game is very cartoon-like, then your app icon should be as well. If your game is very dark and moody, make sure your icon reflects this as well. And as with regular artwork, design your app at a high resolution, and then export it to scaled-down image files. There are tools available online to help you design and automatically export app icons in the right format, such as `http://appicontemplate.com` or `http://makeappicon.com`.

# A Few Final Remarks

Congratulations—you've completed your first game! Figure 11-2 shows the final game. While developing this game, you learned many important concepts. In the next game, you'll expand on the work you've already done. In the meantime, don't forget to play the game! You'll notice that it becomes really difficult after a few minutes because the paint cans come down faster and faster.

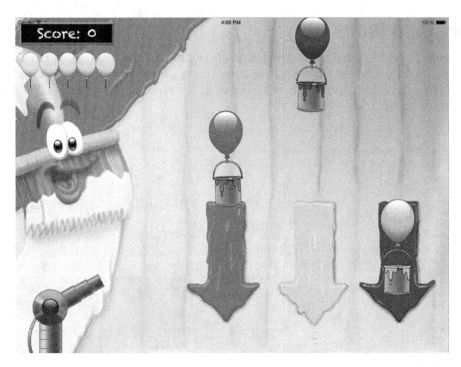

*Figure 11-2. The final version of Painter*

## WHO PLAYS GAMES?

You might think that games are primarily played by young males, but that isn't true at all. A huge percentage of people play games. In 2014 in the United States there were 188 million active gamers, which is more than half the total population (including babies). They play games on many different devices. 53% of the gamers play games on their smart phone and 41% play games on their wireless device (source: the Entertainment Software Association (ESA), 2014).

If you develop a game, you'd better first think about the audience you want for it. Games for young kids are different from games for middle-aged women. The games should have different kinds of gameplay, different visual styles, and different goals.

Although console games tend to take place in large 3D worlds, casual games on mobile devices are often 2D and are limited in size. Also, console games are designed such that they can (and need to be) played for hours and hours, whereas casual games are often designed to be playable in sessions of just a few minutes. There are also many types of *serious games*, which are games that are used to train of professionals such as firefighters, mayors, and doctors. Realize that the games you like aren't necessarily the games your target audience likes.

# What You Have Learned

In this chapter, you have learned the following:

- How to add music and sound effects to your game
- How to maintain and display a score
- How to use strings to represent and work with text

# Part III

# Tut's Tomb

*Tut's Tomb* is a game where the player has to collect treasures of the Pharaoh Tut (see Figure III-1 for a screenshot). All kinds of treasures fall down in the tomb, and by dragging treasures that are the same towards each other, you collect them and get points. Watch out, though: if a treasure stays in the tomb too long, it turns into a useless rock that takes up space. The treasures keep falling down faster and faster. If you don't remove enough treasures from the tomb, the tomb will be completely filled and the game is over. In the following chapters, you will develop this game. If you want to play the complete version to get a feel for how the game works, run the example belonging to Chapter 16!

*Figure III-1. A screenshot of Tut's Tomb*

# Advanced Input Handling

In this chapter, you will create a more advanced input handling mechanism. At the same time, a few important programming concepts, such as arrays and dictionaries, will be introduced. In the Painter game, input handling was rather basic. You only kept track of the last position that the player touched. For Painter, that was sufficient since the player plays the game using a single finger. In more complex games, this basic method of input handling is not enough. In particular, in Tut's Tomb, the player may use multiple fingers to drag objects over the screen. In this chapter, you are going to extend the InputHelper class and make it suitable for handling multitouch input.

## Creating a Touch Object

The main issue that you need to address is that the InputHelper class currently only keeps track of the information of a single touch. It stores the last recorded touch position, and whether or not the player has tapped (in other words, whether the player just started touching the screen with a finger). Here are the two properties that store this information:

```
var touchLocation = CGPoint(x: 0, y: 0)
var hasTapped: Bool = false
```

In order to deal with multitouch input, you need to store and track this information for multiple positions at the same time. Next to this, you also need a way to distinguish touches from each other, so that the player can, for example, use one finger to move one object and another to push a button. This means that each touch position needs a unique *identifier*. In order to facilitate this, let's create a type for representing a touch. Until now, you've used classes to create your own types. Another way to create a type is by using a *struct*. As explained earlier, structs, as opposed to classes, are copied by value and not by reference. This means that every time you copy a variable that has a struct as its type, the value is copied in memory. As a result, structs are generally preferred for smaller data structures. A touch is a good example of a smaller data structure. Here is an example of defining a struct to represent a touch:

```
struct Touch {
    var id = 0
    var location = CGPoint()
    var tapped = true
}
```

As you can see, defining a struct is the same as defining a class, except that you use the `struct` keyword instead of the `class` keyword. This struct has three properties: an identifier, a location, and a Boolean variable indicating whether or not the touch is a tap. You can now create a Touch object in a very simple way:

```
var myTouch = Touch()
```

By default, this Touch object will have the `id` 0, but what you want for each Touch object to have a unique identifier. There is a relatively simple way to achieve this. If you remember, class properties are properties that belong to a class, not to an object. The `world` property is a good example: it belongs to the GameScene class. No matter how many GameScene instances there are, there will always be a single `world` property, and you access it as follows:

```
GameScene.world
```

Similarly, structs know something called a *static property*. If a property is static, then it belongs to the struct and not to an instance of the struct. Take a look at the following struct definition:

```
struct Touch {
    var id = 0
    var location = CGPoint()
    var tapped = true

    static var idgen: Int = 0
}
```

This struct has a static property of `idgen`, which is initialized to 0. Since this property belongs to the struct and not to any particular instance, you can use it to generate unique identifiers. You do this by assigning the current value of the `idgen` property to the `id` property when the instance is created, and then incrementing the `idgen` property by 1 to generate the id for the new Touch instance. This job can be done in an initializer:

```
init() {
    id = Touch.idgen
    Touch.idgen++
}
```

There is an even shorter way to do this, by using the ++ *postfix* operator more smartly. When you increment a variable, the old value (before incrementing the variable) is returned by the ++ postfix operator. You can store this result in another variable, like so:

```
var a = 12
var b = a++ // after this instruction, a = 13 and b = 12
```

After the second instruction in this example has been executed, the variable b contains the old value of a (before incrementing), and a contains the incremented value. You can also write the ++ operator in front of a variable. This ++ *prefix* operator returns the *new* value (after incrementing), like so:

```
var c = 10
var d = ++c // after this instruction, c = 11, d = 11
```

In this case, after the second instruction both c and d contain the value after incrementing (11). If you apply this idea to the Touch struct, then you don't need an initializer anymore; you simply increment the idgen property and assign its old value to the id property:

```
struct Touch {
    var id = idgen++
    var location = CGPoint()
    var tapped = true

    static var idgen: Int = 0
}
```

The result is that you can now create Touch instances and each instance will automatically get a unique identifier:

```
var aTouch = Touch()            // aTouch has id 0
var anotherTouch = Touch()      // anotherTouch has id 1
var yetAnotherTouch = Touch() // yetAnotherTouch has id 2
```

# Arrays

Now that you have an easy way to generate touch locations carrying a unique identifier, you need to extend the InputHelper class so that it supports storing multiple instances of these touches. In Swift, a very convenient way to do this is by using *arrays*. An array is basically a numbered list. Have a look at the following examples:

```
var emptyArray: [Int] = []
var intArray = [4, 8, 15, 16, 23, 42]
```

Here you see two declarations and initializations of array variables. The first declaration is an empty array (no elements) that can contain Int values. The second variable, intArray, refers to an array of length 6. You can access the elements in the array by their index, where the first element in the array has index 0:

```
var v = intArray[0]  // contains the value 4
var v2 = intArray[4] // contains the value 23
```

You use square brackets to access elements in the array. You can also modify the values in the array using the same square brackets:

```
intArray[1] = 13 // intArray now is [4, 13, 15, 16, 23, 42]
```

It's also possible to add an element to the array:

```
intArray.append(-3) // intArray now is [4, 13, 15, 16, 23, 42, -3]
```

Finally, each array has a count variable that you can access to retrieve the length:

```
var l = intArray.count // contains the value 7
```

You can use arrays in combination with for loops to do interesting things. Here's an example:

```
for var i = 0; i < intArray.count; i++ {
    intArray[i] += 10
}
```

This walks through all the elements in the array and adds 10 to each. So, after this code is executed, intArray refers to [14, 23, 25, 26, 33, 52, 7]. Or you can use a for loop with a range to achieve the same thing:

```
for i in 0..<intArray.count {
    intArray[i] += 10
}
```

In addition to initializing an array in the way you just saw, there is another, more class-like way to create an array:

```
var myArray = Array<Int>(count: 3, repeatedValue: 10)
```

This example creates an array of size 3, each element being the value 10. So, the above instruction is the same as the following one:

```
var myArray = [10, 10, 10]
```

You can even create multidimensional arrays in Swift, like so:

```
var anotherArray: [[Int]] = [[1, 2, 3], [4, 5, 6]]
```

The anotherArray variable is an array of an array of integer values. So, as you can see, elements of arrays can also be arrays. Arrays of arrays are particularly useful to represent grid structures. Quite a few games use some kind of grid structure to represent the game world. For example, you can use a two-dimensional array to represent the playing field of a Tic Tac Toe game:

```
var tictactoe : [[String]] = [["x", "o", " "], [" ", "x", "o"], [" ", "o", "x"]]
```

The following is a simple way to represent a two-dimensional grid using a one-dimensional array:

```
var rows = 10, cols = 15
var myGrid = Array<Int>(count: rows * cols, repeatedValue: 0)
```

Accessing the element at row i and column j can now be done as follows:

```
var elem = myGrid[i * cols + j]
```

Figure 12-1 shows a part of the expression syntax diagram, with the syntax for specifying an array.

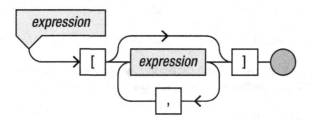

*Figure 12-1. Partial syntax diagram of expressions*

# Dictionaries

In addition to the array, Swift has a collection type called a *dictionary*. A dictionary is very similar to an array, except that it doesn't represent a numbered list, but rather a *mapping* from one type to another. A dictionary is a series of key/value pairs, where distinct keys are used to access the associated values. The keys and values can be of any type. This is in contract with an array, in which the "keys" are always the array indices. The following example should clarify this:

```
var translator = [String:String]()
translator["house"] = "maison"
translator["tree"] = "arbre"
translator["dog"] = "chien"
```

As you can see, the dictionary allows you to store a mapping. In this case, the mapping is from a string (the key) to another string (the value), which is useful if you want to implement a translation table. The types used don't have to be the same, though:

```
var ages = [String:Int]()
ages["mary"] = 45
ages["john"] = 12
```

# Optionals

Before continuing with the code example, let's take a closer look at one of the more innovative features of the Swift language: *optionals*. An optional is a mechanism that allows you to have a variable of a type that *optionally* refers to an actual object. This may not sound very useful, but consider again the translator example:

```
var translator = [String:String]()
translator["house"] = "maison"
translator["tree"] = "arbre"
translator["dog"] = "chien"
```

Now suppose you type the following instruction:

```
var houseTranslated = translator["house"]
```

Since you stored the "house" key in the dictionary, you can store the result of looking up the value in a variable. But now suppose that you type the following:

```
var carTranslated = translator["car"]
```

The translator dictionary doesn't contain an entry for a car. So what should happen in this case? You could imagine that the compiler generates an error when it compiles the program. But the compiler cannot know in all cases the contents of the translator dictionary. Suppose that the contents of this dictionary are retrieved from a server when the program starts? Or that they are entered by the user when the program is running? The compiler simply can't always know what is in the dictionary, so it cannot detect these kinds of errors. But if the compiler cannot detect it, what value is stored in the carTranslated variable if the entry doesn't exist? In Swift, this is the value nil. The value returned by the expression translator["car"] can be nil *in some cases*. This is why the type of that expression is called an *optional type*. You can recognize an optional type by the question mark after its name. The type of carTranslated is String?. You can also write that when you declare the variable:

```
var carTranslated: String? = translator["car"]
```

Because the carTranslated variable is an optional, you can assign it the value nil:

```
carTranslated = nil
```

You can also test whether it is `nil` in an `if` instruction:

```
if carTranslated == nil {
    print("Translation unavailable.")
}
```

Now suppose that you want to turn the result of the translation into capital letters. The String type has a property `capitalizedString` that does this. However, the following instruction will give a compiler error:

```
var strWithCapitals = carTranslated.capitalizedString
```

The reason that the compiler gives an error is that `carTranslated` may refer to nil instead of a string value. If that is the case, then the `capitalizedString` property cannot be used. In order to solve this, you can use something called *optional chaining*, as follows:

```
var strWithCapitals = carTranslated?.capitalizedString
```

Optional chaining checks if `carTranslated` is `nil`. If that is not the case, the result of the property is stored in `strWithCapitals`. If `carTranslated` is `nil`, the value `nil` is stored in `strWithCapitals`. This means that the `strWithCapitals` variable is itself also an optional type, `String?`.

If you are really certain that `carTranslated` will never contain a `nil` value, you can also *unwrap* it to an actual String type. This is done with an exclamation mark:

```
var strWithCapitals = carTranslated!.capitalizedString
```

Since the assumption is that `carTranslated` is never `nil`, the type of `strWithCapitals` is now String instead of String?. Be careful when using this, however. If your program has a bug leading to `carTranslated` unexpectedly being `nil`, the program execution will stop with an error.

Swift provides a nice extension of the `if` instruction to only execute a block of code if a value unwrap was successful:

```
if let carTranslated = translator["car"] {
    // do something
}
```

The body of this `if` instruction is executed only if the expression `carTranslated` is not nil. If that is the case, `carTranslated` is of type String and contains the unwrapped value of `translator["car"]`. As such, the `if` instruction above does the same thing as the following code:

```
let carTranslatedOptional = translator["car"]
if carTranslatedOptional != nil {
    let carTranslated = carTranslatedOptional!
    // do something
}
```

As you can see, the combined if instruction with value unwrapping is a useful extension, leading to shorter code that is easier to read.

---

**Note**    Optionals and the unwrapping mechanism are features that are currently only available in the Swift language. Other programming languages, such as C# or Java, do not have these features. By dealing explicitly with optional values in the programming language itself, Swift forces programmers to think about whether a value is guaranteed or whether it sometimes doesn't exist. So remember to think beforehand about how to deal with each situation when you write your code. This is a good thing because it leads to more robust programs. However, if you don't carefully design your classes and methods, you may end up with code riddled with question marks and exclamation marks, making your code very hard to understand.

---

# Storing Multiple Touches

Now you'll learn how to use arrays, dictionaries, and optional types to deal with multiple touches by creating a new InputHelper class. This class now contains a property called touches, which is an array of Touch objects:

```
var touches: [Touch] = []
```

There are three kinds of touch events that you need to deal with:

- The player starts touching the screen with one of his fingers.
- The player moves a finger already touching the screen.
- The player removes a finger from the screen.

For each of these cases, let's add a method to InputHelper that handles it. Later in this chapter, you'll deal with connecting these methods to actual touch events. The first case is when the player starts touching the screen. In that case, a Touch instance needs to be created, its location needs to be set to the recorded touch location, and finally the Touch instance should be added to the array. Here is the complete method:

```
func touchBegan(loc: CGPoint) -> Int {
    var touch = Touch()
    touch.location = loc
    touches.append(touch)
    return touch.id
}
```

As you can see, this method expects a CGPoint object representing the touch location as a parameter. The method returns the identifier of the Touch instance that was created. This is useful because then the caller of the method knows how to refer to that particular touch when using the InputHelper instance later.

When the player moves her finger, another method in InputHelper called touchMoved should be called:

```
func touchMoved(id: Int, loc: CGPoint) {
    if let index = findIndex(id) {
        touches[index].location = loc
    }
}
```

This method expects a touch identifier, and the new touch location as a parameter. It relies on a method called findIndex, which searches for the index in the touches array corresponding to the identifier and returns an optional Int value. In this method, you walk through all the elements in the touches array using a for loop. When you find the touch that matches the identifier of the touch data you're looking for, you return that data. If the touch data can't be found, you return nil. Here is the header and body of findIndex:

```
func findIndex(id: Int) -> Int? {
    for index in 0..<touches.count  {
        if touches[index].id == id {
            return index
        }
    }
    return nil
}
```

Once the index has been found, you set the location property of the Touch instance in the array to the new location, which is what the second instruction in the touchMoved method does.

Finally, when the player has removed a finger from the screen, the touchEnded method should be called, which removes the Touch instance from the array:

```
func touchEnded(id: Int) {
    if let index = findIndex(id) {
        touches.removeAtIndex(index)
    }
}
```

As you can see, removing an element from an array is done with the removeAtIndex method. This method takes an index as a parameter: the index indicates where the element should be removed. Here is an example:

```
var fib = [1, 1, 2, 3, 5, 8, 13]
fib.removeAtIndex(3) // fib now is [1, 1, 2, 5, 8, 13]
```

# Making Dealing with Touch Input Easier

You can add a few more methods to the `InputHelper` class to make it easier to use in games. The first is a simple method for retrieving the position of a touch with a given id:

```swift
func getTouch(id: Int) -> CGPoint {
    if let index = findIndex(id) {
        return touches[index].location
    } else {
        return CGPoint.zeroPoint
    }
}
```

It would also be useful to check whether the player is touching a certain area of the screen. For example, if you want to add a button to your game, you want to check whether the player has tapped in the area represented by the button sprite. The following method can be used in this case:

```swift
func containsTouch(rect: CGRect) -> Bool {
    for touch in touches {
        if rect.contains(touch.location) {
            return true
        }
    }
    return false
}
```

In the method body is a `for` loop that checks for each touch in the array, whether its position falls inside the rectangle. Depending on the outcome, the method returns either `true` or `false`. In order to find the id of the touch inside the rectangle, the following method can be called:

```swift
func getIDInRect(rect: CGRect) -> Int? {
    for touch in touches {
        if rect.contains(touch.location) {
            return touch.id
        }
    }
    return nil
}
```

This method is useful for checking whether a touch id is still valid:

```swift
func isTouching(id: Int) -> Bool {
    return findIndex(id) != nil
}
```

And finally, this method indicates whether the player has tapped (just started touching) inside a box or not:

```
func containsTap(rect: CGRect) -> Bool {
    for touch in touches {
        if rect.contains(touch.location) && touch.tapped {
            return true
        }
    }
    return false
}
```

There are more methods in the InputHelper class that will be useful later in the games you will develop in this book. For an overview, see the InputHelper class in the TutsTomb1 example belonging to this chapter.

# Linking Touch Events to the Input Helper Class

The InputHelper class is ready, but you still need to make sure that the touchBegan, touchMoved, and touchEnded methods are called when necessary. In the Painter game, you did this by adding touch event handling methods to the GameScene class. For example, this was the method that handled the start of a touch:

```
override func touchesBegan(touches: Set<UITouch>, withEvent event: UIEvent?) {
    let touch = touches.first!
    inputHelper.touchLocation = touch.locationInNode(self)
    inputHelper.nrTouches += touches.count
    inputHelper.hasTapped = true
}
```

The first parameter of this method is of type Set<UITouch>. Note that Set<UITouch> is also a *collection type*, similar to Array. The difference between arrays and sets is that an array has ordered information, whereas a set doesn't. Also, a set doesn't have duplicate elements, whereas this is allowed for arrays. Depending on what you need in your game, you can choose different data structures. A set, for example, may be useful for representing a player inventory, especially if the player can only have one of each item in his/her inventory.

It makes sense that the touches are also stored in a set, since you only allow for a particular touch to be stored once, and the order of the touches is not important. In the InputHelper class, you could have also used a set to store the touches instead of an array. Behind the Set word, you see the type UITouch between angled brackets. Recall that in Swift, and in many other programming languages that support so-called *generic types*, this means that the set contains objects of type UITouch. The type Set itself is a generic type because it can only be used if you indicate what kind of objects the set specifically contains. For example, you could also declare a set of strings:

```
var stringSet = Set<String>()
```

Inside the touchesBegan method, you want to handle the possibility of multiple touches. This means you need to deal with all the touches in the set. There is a special for loop syntax to do something for each element in a collection. Take a look at the following example:

```
var intArray = [2, 3, 4, 6]
for value: Int in intArray {
    print(value)
}
```

This example uses a for loop to perform a task for each element in the array. In many cases, you can leave out the type because it can be inferred from the collection that you are traversing:

```
var intArray = [2, 3, 4, 6]
for value in intArray {
    print(value)
}
```

Similarly, you can also perform a task for each element in a set:

```
for touch in touches {
    // handle the touch
}
```

Inside the body of the for loop, you use the touch variable (which is of type UITouch) to calculate the location of the touch and store it in a constant, like so:

```
let location = touch.locationInNode(self)
```

Then, you call the touchBegan method in InputHelper to add the touch to the array. This method returns an id that you store in a variable:

```
let id = inputHelper.touchBegan(location)
```

You can also use a dictionary to store the mapping between UITouch objects and the ids generated for the InputHelper class:

```
var touchmap = [UITouch:Int]()
```

You store the generated id in this map in the last instruction of the touchesBegan event handler method:

```
touchmap[touch] = inputHelper.touchBegan(location)
```

In the touchesMoved method, you need this id in order to update the touch location in the input helper. Just like in touchesBegan, you use a for loop to perform this task for each moved touch location. Here is the complete method:

```
override func touchesMoved(touches: Set<UITouch>, withEvent event: UIEvent) {
    for touch in touches {
        let touchid = touchmap[touch]!
        inputHelper.touchMoved(touchid, loc: touch.locationInNode(self))
    }
}
```

You first look up the id corresponding to that object in the dictionary. Then, the touchMoved method from the InputHelper class is called to update the touch location information.

```
let touchid = touchmap[touch]!
```

Note the exclamation mark at the end of the following instruction. This is needed because you need to unwrap the optional Int value returned by the dictionary lookup.

When the player stops touching the screen, the touch-to-id correspondence should be removed from the dictionary. This is achieved by assigning the nil value to the element in the dictionary, as follows:

```
let touchid = touchmap[touch]!
touchmap[touch] = nil
```

Finally, the touchEnded method is called to update the input helper:

```
inputHelper.touchEnded(touchid)
```

For the complete code to handle multitouch input, see the InputHelper and GameScene classes in the TutsTomb1 example belonging to this chapter.

# Dragging Sprites

As an example, let's use the new InputHelper class to drag sprites around on the screen. Take a look again at the TutsTomb1 program. Inside, you will find the updated InputHelper class, as well as a simple example that loads a few sprites, draws them on the screen, and allows you to move the sprites over the screen by dragging them. The program also contains a basic class called Treasure that is used for representing treasures in the Tut's Tomb game.

In the TutsTomb1 example, not much of that game has been implemented yet. There are just two Treasure objects drawn on the screen, which the player can drag around with their finger. Object dragging is implemented in the handleInput method of this class. This method consists of two parts. In the first part, you check whether the player has just started dragging the object. If that is the case, you need to store the id of that touch, so that later you can use the id to keep track of where the player is moving their finger. In the Treasure class, there is a property called touchid (of type Int?) that stores the id of the touch currently dragging the object. If the object is not being dragged, the id is set to nil. Once the player starts dragging, you store the id of the touch in the property:

```
if inputHelper.containsTap(self.box) {
    touchid = inputHelper.getIDInRect(self.box)
}
```

The next step in the handleInput method is to update the position of the treasure to follow the finger of the user as long as the user is touching the screen with that finger. As soon as the player stops touching the screen with that finger, you reset the touchid property to nil. This is all covered in the following instructions:

```
if let touchUnwrap = touchid {
    if inputHelper.isTouching(touchUnwrap) {
        self.position = inputHelper.getTouch(touchUnwrap)
    } else {
        touchid = nil
    }
}
```

And that's it! As you can see, dragging functionality is not that hard to implement, but it really helps if you have a few useful methods for dealing with (multi)touch input. In this case, the containsTap method makes it very simple to know when a player starts dragging an object around.

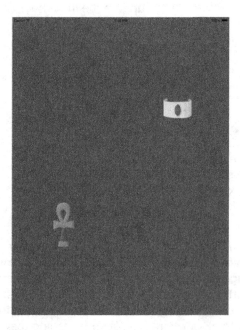

*Figure 12-2. The TutsTomb1 example*

# What You Have Learned

In this chapter, you have learned the following:

- How to deal with multitouch input for games
- What arrays and dictionaries are and how to use them
- What optionals are and how you should use them

# Game Physics

In the Painter game, you created a very basic mechanism for objects moving around in the game world and colliding with each other. In Tut's Tomb, this is no longer sufficient. Objects need to fall according to gravity, they need to bounce off walls, and they need to handle collisions differently. In this chapter, you are going to adapt your game structure so that it is more suitable for these advanced interactions. You will see that it's quite simple to add physically correct behavior to your game objects in SpriteKit.

## A Basic Class for Game Objects

Most games have a complicated structure of game objects. First, there might be a background consisting of various layers of moving objects (mountains, air, trees, and so on). Then there are interactive objects moving around. These objects may be enemies of the player, so they need some level of intelligence; they can also be more static, such as power-ups, trees, doors, or ladders. A game object that represents a house might consist of many other game objects, such as a door, stairs, windows, and a kitchen (which may, in turn, consist of different game objects).

Given these different types of game objects and the relations between them, you can say that game objects generally form part of a *hierarchy*, which represents the game world. Most games use some kind of hierarchy of game objects. Especially in 3D games, such a hierarchy is very important because of the complexity of three-dimensional environments. Objects in 3D games are normally represented not by sprites, but by one or more 3D models. The advantage of a hierarchy is that these objects can be grouped together, so that if you pick up a vase that contains a scroll with magic writing on it, the scroll moves along with the vase.

In the Painter game, the basic type of game object was represented by the ThreeColorGameObject class. Until now, this is how you've represented game objects, simply because it was sufficient for the basic examples you were working on. If you want to develop bigger, more complicated games, you have to let go of the basic premise that a game object is a three-colored sprite.

In SpriteKit, the most basic game object is an object of type SKNode. The only thing that SKNode assumes is that a game object is supposed to be a part of some kind of hierarchy (representing the game world). The games you create in this book rely on a design that defines how game objects are a part of the game loop in the game object classes themselves. For example, in Painter, the Cannon class handles input related to the cannon, and the Ball class handles input related to the ball. Also, the ball position and any game object interaction are handled in an update method part of the Ball class. Finally, whenever the game is restarted, each game object is reset to its original state. This means that it's probably useful if game objects have a handleInput method, an update method, and a reset method.

In the TutsTomb2 example, you can find a class called GameObjectNode, which is a subclass of SKNode. The GameObjectNode class adds exactly the three game loop methods mentioned in the previous paragraph. Since any object of type GameObjectNode is also an SKNode object, it may have children. If, for example, the handleInput method is called on a GameObjectNode instance, you need to make sure that any children of type GameObjectNode also handle input. So, inside the body of the handleInput method, you use a for loop to traverse the children, cast them to a GameObjectNode instance, and if the casting succeeds, call the handleInput method on the child object, like so:

```
func handleInput(inputHelper: InputHelper) {
    for obj in children {
        if let node = obj as? GameObjectNode {
            node.handleInput(inputHelper)
        }
    }
}
```

Note the special notation used for assigning an optional value to a variable in an if instruction. The as? operator attempts to cast an object to a given type (in this case, GameObjectNode). If the cast is not possible, the operator returns nil. So, if node contains an actual GameObjectNode instance, the handleInput method is called on it. If you take a look at the GameObjectNode class, you'll see that something very similar is done for the updateDelta and reset methods.

# Game Object Subclasses

Since the Tut's Tomb game deals with treasures that are falling down, the TutsTomb2 example contains a Treasure class, which is now a subclass of GameObjectNode. The Treasure class overrides the handleInput method to implement dragging.

Another class that is a subclass of GameObjectNode is GameWorld. The game world is filled with game objects in the setup method, which is called in the GameScene class, when the scene is initialized. Here is the part of the setup method that adds a few Treasure instances to the game world:

```
for i in 0...4 {
    var treasure = Treasure()
    treasure.position = CGPoint(x: -250 + i * 120, y: 200)
    treasures.addChild(treasure)
}
```

As you can see, this code creates five Treasure instances, positions them according to the loop counter i, and adds them to the treasures node, which is part of the game world.

The nice thing about GameWorld being a subclass of GameObjectNode is that now the game loop methods are automatically called on its children as well, due to the way GameObjectNode is designed. This means that if you add Treasure instances as children of another game object, then handleInput method calls are now automatically propagated to the treasures. The handleInput method of GameWorld is called in GameScene, which in turn calls the handleInput method on all the children (and children's children) of game objects part of the game world, including the treasures. This results in a nice, clean design that will make creating more complex game object interactions later much easier. As you can see in the TutsTomb2 example, the handleInput method of Treasure calls the handleInput method of its superclass (GameObjectNode). This way, you make sure that the chain of handleInput method calls is not broken, even if in the future you decide to add child nodes to a Treasure instance.

# Adding Physics to Game Objects

Until now, you have made game objects move by changing their position in the game loop. In Painter, some objects, such as the ball, had a velocity property, which you manipulated in order to make the ball move. In the physical world, things are slightly more complicated. Objects move because forces are exerted on them. For example, any object in the world is subject to a gravity force. If you push an object in some direction, you are applying a force to that object. And when objects collide with each other, they need to respond naturally to these collisions.

If you want the game world to behave in a more physically correct manner, you need to have a model that simulates the physical world as a part of the game. The nice thing about the SpriteKit framework is that it already has a physics engine integrated in it that you can use to add physically plausible behavior to your game objects. In the Painter game, you coded the physics yourself. For example, you did this in the Ball class:

```
velocity.x *= 0.99
velocity.y -= 15
```

The first line is a simple model for air friction. The second line is an approximation of what gravity does to the velocity of the object. In Tut's Tomb, you are going to use the physics engine of SpriteKit to simulate physics, instead of writing the code yourself. As you'll see, adding physics to your game world is really easy. Any instance of (a subclass of) SKNode has a property called physicsBody that allows you to control the way the object is a part of the physics system. If you want to add physical behavior to an object, the physicsBody property should refer to a SKPhysicsBody instance. This instance is an often simplified representation of the game object in the physical world. For example, in the Treasure class, you could add the following line to the initializer:

```
self.physicsBody = SKPhysicsBody(circleOfRadius: 100)
```

This creates a physical representation for the treasures. In this case, the physical representation is a circle with a given radius. You can also use another shape, such as a rectangle:

```
self.physicsBody = SKPhysicsBody(rectangleOfSize: CGSize(width: 100, height: 100))
```

You can also use the shape of a sprite (texture) to create the shape of the physics body:

```
self.physicsBody = SKPhysicsBody(texture: sprite.texture!, size: sprite.size)
```

If you want your game to run smoothly on many different devices, then it is a good idea to make sure the physics calculations do not become too complicated. For 2D games, this is generally not really a big issue anymore, but if you have many game objects with physical behavior moving around and colliding with each other, you may choose to use simplified shapes to deal with the physics more efficiently. And if a shape already looks a lot like a rectangle or a circle, it will probably still look good if you do the physics calculations with the simplified shape.

In Tut's Tomb, you are going to use the actual sprite shapes for the physics calculation. Now that Treasure instances have a physicsBody, they instantly exhibit physical behavior. In the TutsTomb2 example, a few Treasure instances have been added to the game world, just for testing purposes.

If you were to run the game without adding any extra objects, you would see the five objects you added fall out of the screen immediately. This is because those objects are subject to a gravity force by default. In order to contain the game objects in the world, you need to create the ground and walls. So let's add a floor to the game world. This floor also needs a physics body so that it can interact with the other game objects:

```
let floor = SKNode()
floor.position.y = -400
var square = CGSize(width: GameScene.world.size.width, height: 200)
floor.physicsBody = SKPhysicsBody(rectangleOfSize: square)
```

As you can see, the floor is an SKNode object with a physics body attached to it, so there is no actual floor sprite. You simply want the objects to not fall down any further. In order to represent the floor in the physical world, you use a simplified shape–a rectangle in this case. But wait, since the floor is a physical object as well, won't it simply fall down just like the other game objects? Yes, it will, so you explicitly tell the physics system that the floor is at a fixed location in the game world, and it doesn't respond to dynamics (including forces). Here is how you do that:

```
floor.physicsBody?.dynamic = false
```

Finally, you add the floor object to the game world:

```
addChild(floor)
```

In a similar way, you also add a ceiling, a left wall, and a right wall to the game world. See the TutsTomb2 example for the complete code.

Now that the game world has a floor, a ceiling and sidewalls, the game objects fall down and collide with the enclosing walls and each other. You get all this behavior for free when you use the physics engine provided by SpriteKit. Sometimes it's useful for debugging to show the actual physics bodies on the screen. You can do this by setting the showPhysics property in the SKView object. The following line in the GameViewController class does this:

```
skView.showsPhysics = true
```

# Interaction

Since you defined a physics body for each game object, you can now manipulate the object by applying forces to it. For example, you could give a physics body a velocity, as follows:

```
physicsBody?.velocity = CGVector(dx: 10, dy: 10)
```

As you can see, the physicsBody property is optional, which makes sense because if the object is not part of the physics system, the property is nil. The velocity property of physicsBody is of type CGVector, which represents a two-dimensional vector. Once you assign a velocity to an object, it automatically calculates its own position according to that velocity as the game progresses. In the Treasure class, you use this to allow for dragging of a physics-based object:

```
var moveVector = inputHelper.getTouch(touchid)
moveVector.x -= position.x
moveVector.y -= position.y
physicsBody?.velocity = CGVector(dx: moveVector.x * 10, dy: moveVector.y * 10)
```

First, you calculate the vector that represents the direction in which the physics body should move. You do this by retrieving the touch position, and subtracting the current object position from it. In order for the object to move towards the touch position fast enough, the x and y factors of the velocity vector are multiplied by a constant value (10). Once you assign that vector to the velocity property of the physics body, the object position is automatically updated.

Another type of interaction you want to handle is collisions between objects. In games, often some kind of action needs to be taken when objects collide with each other. If the player collides with a power-up, player health should be increased. If the player collides with an enemy, the player is damaged. If the player collides with a star, the player should be awarded points.

In SpriteKit, you can indicate which object is responsible for handling collisions (or *contacts*). If this object then has a specific method, that method will be called whenever there is a contact between physical bodies. SpriteKit uses a Swift feature called a *protocol* to enforce this. A protocol is simply a definition of a collection of method (or property) headers to help developers write more coherent code. Here is an example of a protocol called SKPhysicsContactDelegate:

```
protocol SKPhysicsContactDelegate : NSObjectProtocol {
    optional func didBeginContact(contact: SKPhysicsContact)
    optional func didEndContact(contact: SKPhysicsContact)
}
```

As you can see, this protocol contains two method headers, didBeginContact and didEndContact. Let's change the GameWorld class so that it adheres to the SKPhysicsContactDelegate protocol. This is done in a way very similar to inheritance:

```
class GameWorld : GameObjectNode, SKPhysicsContactDelegate {
    // To do: class body
}
```

If a class adheres to a protocol, you can also say that a class *implements* the protocol. In this case, GameWorld now implements the protocol SKPhysicsContactDelegate. The protocol describes that any class that implements it, and optionally defines the methods didBeginContact and didEndContact. There are also protocols that oblige a class that implements it to define methods or properties, or even initializers. Take a look at the following protocol:

```
protocol NSCoding {
    func encodeWithCoder(aCoder: NSCoder)
    init(coder aDecoder: NSCoder)
}
```

If a class implements this protocol, it has to have the method as well as the initializer defined in the protocol. This protocol is implemented by SKNode, and it is one of the reasons why any subclass of SKNode, including GameObjectNode, needs to define a particular initializer:

```
required init?(coder aDecoder: NSCoder) {
    fatalError("init(coder:) has not been implemented")
}
```

In the GameWorld class, you add the following method defined in the SKPhysicsContactDelegate protocol:

```
func didBeginContact(contact: SKPhysicsContact) {
    let firstBody = contact.bodyA.node as? Treasure
    let secondBody = contact.bodyB.node as? Treasure
    print("Contact at position \(contact.contactPoint)")
}
```

As you can see in the body of the method, the contact parameter contains information about what bodies are in contact, and where the contact is in the game world. Just for testing purposes, the contact location is printed to the screen whenever a contact between two physics bodies has started. You can also implement the didEndContact method, and then you can take an action whenever two objects stop being in contact. For example, when the player removes a diamond from a table, you could set off an alarm. In the next chapters, you're going to define more complex behavior when there is contact between game objects.

You need to do one more thing to make sure that didBeginContact is called whenever there is contact between two physical bodies: you need to tell the scene that the object responsible for contact handling is the GameWorld instance. You do this by adding the following line of code to the didMoveToView method of GameScene:

```
physicsWorld.contactDelegate = GameScene.world
```

This completes the TutsTomb2 example. Figure 13-1 shows a screenshot of the game so far. Run the example yourself, and see how it works. Play around with the settings of the physics engine. For example, can you change the gravity? Also, try to change the shapes that are used for the game object physical bodies and see how the gameplay changes.

*Figure 13-1. A screenshot of the TutsTomb2 example program*

**Note**   One of the interesting things you can do with physics in games is play around with the parameters of the physics engine. Most physics engines (including the one provided with SpriteKit) allow you to change things such as the gravity force, or which objects are affected by gravity. This is useful for games that take place on alien worlds with different gravities. Also, it's more important that a game is playable than that it has correct physics. In strategy games, airplanes fly as fast as soldiers can walk on the ground. This is completely unrealistic, but it makes the game playable. Don't hesitate to change the settings of the physics engine to improve the gameplay. Have a look at the properties and methods of the SKPhysicsBody class to get an idea of the possibilities.

# What You Have Learned

In this chapter, you have learned the following:

- How to organize game objects in a scene graph by using a basic game object class

- How to add physical behavior to your game

- How to interact with objects in a physical world by dragging them

- How to take an action when two objects collide with each other

# Chapter 14

# Gameplay Programming

This chapter looks into the gameplay programming of the Tut's Tomb game. You will learn how to use actions as an easy way to add behavior to the game world. Also, you'll deal with interactions between game objects (for example, when two treasures of the same type collide).

## Game Object Behavior

Previously, the way in which you added behavior to the games was by defining handleInput and update methods as a part of each game object class, and then making sure that those methods were called in each instance during the game loop. The nice thing about this approach is that each game object is responsible for its own behavior. The behavior of the ball in Painter is defined in the Ball class; the behavior of a treasure in Tut's Tomb is defined in the Treasure class.

Defining behavior in methods that are a part of the class is nice: when you look at the class definition, you immediately see what the behavior of an instance of that class entails. This approach also has its limitations. Most importantly, there is no way to copy behavior between different classes. The paint cans in Painter display the behavior of falling down again and again, with random time intervals. In Tut's Tomb, treasures also fall down, but there is no simple way to copy the behavior from the paint cans to the treasures, apart from copying and pasting the code between the classes.

Generally speaking, game objects often have a lot in common in terms of their behavior. Most platform games will have some kind of patrolling enemy moving from left to right and back again. Objects, such as bonus lives for the player, appear in the scene randomly or at fixed time intervals. Game objects may have simple special effects such as rotation or scaling (for example, for a bomb about to explode). Wouldn't it be nice if you could somehow separate this behavior from the game objects itself, so that it can be copied more easily between classes?

# Actions

The SpriteKit framework offers a very nice solution for defining game object behavior in a more general manner: by using so-called *actions*. In SpriteKit, you can attach these actions to instances of SKNode and determine how often and in which order they are executed. You can think of actions as simple blocks of predefined behaviors that can be combined in any way you desire. You can even define your own custom actions and add them to your game objects. Let's look at a few examples.

When you want a game object to have predefined behavior in the form of an action, you need to do two things. First, you need to define the action, and then you need to tell the game object to run the action. Defining actions is done by using the SKAction class. Take a look at the following action definition:

```
let rotate = SKAction.rotateByAngle(CGFloat(2 * M_PI), duration: 3)
```

The SKAction class has a number of class methods that you can call. Each creates an action of some kind. In this example, a rotate action is defined that rotates an object around its origin by $2\pi$ radians (360 degrees) over a timespan of three seconds. You can, for example, define this action in the initializer of your game object class. Then, you can tell the game object to run this action, as follows:

```
self.runAction(rotate)
```

Now, when you create the game object, it will rotate once around its origin. Here is another example of an action:

```
let fadein = SKAction.fadeInWithDuration(5)
self.runAction(fadein)
```

This action fades in a game object (from completely transparent to fully opaque) during 5 seconds. Here is another example:

```
let playSound = SKAction.playSoundFileNamed("snd_music.mp3", waitForCompletion: false)
```

This action plays a sound effect. Playing a sound effect using actions is easier than the method explained earlier in this book. However, with actions such as this one, there is no means to control the volume of the sound, so although using actions to play sounds can be very convenient, you may need more control over sounds in your game.

Instead of running only a single action, you can also create a sequence of actions, and run the sequence, like so:

```
let seq = SKAction.sequence([fadein, rotate])
```

The sequence method expects an array of SKAction objects and it creates a new action that is now the sequence of the actions in the array. You can run the sequence just like you run any other action:

```
self.runAction(seq)
```

And instead of running an action only once, you can also create actions that repeat, like so:

```
let repeat = SKAction.repeatActionForever(seq)
self.runAction(repeat)
```

You can even create an action that simply executes a block of code. Here is an example:

```
let customAction = SKAction.runBlock({
    // write your own code here
})
```

As you can see, actions in SpriteKit are a very powerful tool to define behavior for game objects. In the next section, you're going to use actions to define some behavior in the Tut's Tomb game.

# Using Actions to Drop Treasures

In Tut's Tomb, treasures need to drop down every few seconds. Actions are very useful here to define this behavior in a simple manner. The action of dropping a treasure needs to be repeated indefinitely, and the game needs to wait a bit between dropping treasures in order to not overwhelm the players with treasures immediately. In this section, you are going to define this action in the GameWorld class.

In order to make the game more interesting over time, new types of treasure will appear once in a while. Every time a treasure drops, you'll increment a counter. The value of the counter determines the variety in treasure types. Let's change the Treasure class to support this behavior. The first thing that is needed is an initializer that takes a treasure type as a parameter:

```
init(type: UInt32) {
    super.init()
    self.type = type
    sprite = SKSpriteNode(imageNamed: "spr_treasure_\(self.type)")
    sprite.zPosition = 1
    self.position.y = 500
    self.addChild(sprite)
    self.physicsBody = SKPhysicsBody(texture: sprite.texture!, size: sprite.size)
    self.physicsBody?.contactTestBitMask = 1
}
```

This initializer creates a sprite node depending on the treasure type. The treasure type is expressed as an integer value. The UInt32 type stands for a 32-bit, unsigned integer value. The word "unsigned" means that the integer has no sign. In other words, the type doesn't make a distinction between positive and negative numbers. This is good because the various treasure types are expressed as positive numbers. You can now add a *convenience* initializer that randomly creates a treasure within a range of types:

```
convenience init(range: UInt32) {
    let finalRange = min(range, 20)
    let tp = arc4random_uniform(finalRange)
    self.init(type: tp)
}
```

This convenience initializer does three things. First, it makes sure that the range is never higher than the maximum number of sprites that are available (20, in the case of Tut's Tomb). The second line generates a random integer number within the range, and finally, you call the designated initializer.

Now that you have extended the Treasure class in this way, you can easily define an action that drops treasures. First, let's declare a counter property in the GameWorld class:

```
var counter = 0
```

In the GameWorld initializer, you are going to define the actions needed to drop treasures. You drop a treasure by creating a Treasure instance and adding it to the game world. The Treasure initializer already places the object at the right position (see the initializer code in this section). Depending on the current value of the counter, you can calculate a desired range. For example, you could start with a range of 5 and increase it by 1 every 10 treasures:

```
let r: UInt32 = 5 + self.counter/10
```

Creating a Treasure instance according to this range, and adding it to the game world can now be done in a single line of code:

```
self.treasures.addChild(Treasure(range: r))
```

The only other thing that needs to be done in the action for dropping a treasure is incrementing the counter. As a result, this is the action that drops a treasure:

```
let dropTreasureAction = SKAction.runBlock({
    let r: UInt32 = 5 + self.counter/10
    self.treasures.addChild(Treasure(range: r))
    self.counter++
})
```

As you can see, this action is defined as a block of instructions that needs to be executed. In order to wait between dropping treasures, you can use the waitForDuration method that creates a waiting action. Here is a sequence of the two actions, where the game waits for two seconds after dropping a treasure:

```
let seq = SKAction.sequence([dropTreasureAction, SKAction.waitForDuration(2)])
```

The total action then infinitely repeats this sequence:

```
let totalAction = SKAction.repeatActionForever(seq)
self.runAction(totalAction)
```

As a result of this action, a treasure will drop down every two seconds. In order to make it look like the treasure falls out of a chimney, let's add a chimney sprite to the game world that is drawn over the position where the treasures appear before they fall down. The chimney is drawn at a higher z position, so that the treasures are drawn behind it:

```
let chimney = SKSpriteNode(imageNamed:"spr_chimney")
chimney.zPosition = 10
chimney.position.y = 510
addChild(chimney)
```

The TutsTomb3 example belonging to this chapter contains the code explained in this section. When you run it, you'll see that treasures fall down at a regular interval of two seconds. (see Figure 14-1). Play around with the example code and see if you can modify what the actions do. Can you make treasures appear more often?

*Figure 14-1. Treasures falling down in the TutsTomb3 example*

# Special Types of Treasure

In order to make the game a bit more interesting, there are a few special types of treasure. The first type is a rock. If a treasure stays in the scene for too long, it turns into a useless rock that doesn't get removed from the scene (even if it collides with another rock). The second special treasure type is a magical crystal that removes anything it collides with from the screen (even a useless rock). In the code, you need a way to distinguish between the various types of treasure. One way to do this is by defining constant values that represent special types of treasure. For example, you could define the following constants in the Treasure class:

```
static let RockType: UInt32 = 99
static let MagicType: UInt32 = 100
```

Note that I used static properties here, so that they can be referred to without needing a Treasure instance. The constants are of type UInt32, just like the regular treasure types.

Another option is to use a separate class or struct that defines the special types. Take a look at this code:

```
struct TreasureType {
    static let Rock : UInt32 = 99
    static let Magic : UInt32 = 100
}
```

Here, a separate struct is used to define the various types of treasure. This is the approach used in the TutsTomb3 (and subsequent) examples. Because the constants in the struct are static, you don't need an instance of the struct to access these properties. For example,

```
if type == TreasureType.Rock {
    sprite = SKSpriteNode(imageNamed: "spr_rock")
}
```

In this code (taken from the Treasure initializer), you check whether the type passed as a parameter is a rock. If so, you load the rock sprite.

In some cases, you want to create a magic crystal instead of a regular treasure. This is done by the following (part of an) if instruction:

```
if arc4random_uniform(6) == 0 {
    sprite = SKSpriteNode(imageNamed: "spr_magic")
    self.type = TreasureType.Magic
}
```

Here you see that I used a random number generator to sometimes create a magic crystal instead of a regular treasure.

Sometimes, you will need a type to represent different categories of things, similar to the different types of treasure. Swift has a special feature for that, called *enumerations*. Enumerations are quite handy for representing a variable that has a category value or that represents a particular state. For example, you might want to store the type of character that a player represents by using an enumeration. You can decide yourself what kind of different states are in your type. So, before you can use an enumeration, you first have to define it:

```
enum CharacterClan {
    case Warrior
    case Wizard
    case Elf
    case Spy
}
```

The enum keyword indicates that you are going to define an enumeration. After that, you write the name of the enumeration and, between braces, the different cases. Each case is preceded by the case keyword.

The type definition can be placed inside a method, but you may also define it at the class body level, so that all the methods in the class can use the type. You may even define it at the global scope (outside of the class body). Here is an example of using the CharacterClan enumeration:

```
let myClan = CharacterClan.Warrior
```

In this case, you have created a variable of type CharacterClan, which may contain one of four values: CharacterClan.Warrior, CharacterClan.Wizard, CharacterClan.Elf, or CharacterClan.Spy. If the type of a variable is defined, you don't need to write the full name of the enumerated type. For example,

```
let myClan: CharacterClan = .Warrior
```

Another example of using enumerations would be to define a type for indicating the days in the week or the months in a year:

```
enum MonthType {
    case January, February, March, April, May, June, July, August, September, October, November,
        December
}

enum DayType {
    case Sunday, Monday, Tuesday, Wednesday, Thursday, Friday, Saturday
}

let currentMonth = MonthType.February
let today = DayType.Tuesday
```

As you can see in these examples, you don't have to write the case keyword in front of every case. This makes it easier to create enumerated types with many different cases.

Although enumerations are very useful in games, I didn't use them in the TutsTomb3 example to represent the various types of treasure. The reason is that you need a numerical value for the type since that determines which sprite to load. Enumerations are not numerical values. The struct defined in the TutsTomb3 example behaves very much like an enumeration in the code, but the cases are numerical values. Some programming languages, such as C#, allow for enumerations to be used as numerical values. This can be quite handy, but it doesn't fit that well in Swift's quite strict typing system.

# Turning Treasures Into Rocks

If a treasure stays too long in the scene, it will be replaced by a rock. This can be achieved quite easily using actions. The SKNode class has a version of runAction that takes two parameters instead of one. The first parameter is the action to run, and the second parameter is a block of code that should be executed once the action is finished. If you use a waiting action, then you can use this approach to execute a block of code after a certain amount of time has passed:

```
self.runAction(SKAction.waitForDuration(20), completion: {
    // this code will be executed after 20 seconds
})
```

Within the block are the instructions that replace this treasure by a rock. The first step is creating a rock, using the special rock type:

```
var rock = Treasure(type: TreasureType.Rock)
```

You assign the current treasure position to the rock, so it will be placed at the same spot as the treasure that is being replaced:

```
rock.position = self.position
```

Then, you add the rock to the scene, by adding it as a child to the parent of this treasure (which is the treasures node in the GameWorld class):

```
self.parent?.addChild(rock)
```

Finally, you remove the current treasure from its parent, so that it is no longer drawn:

```
self.removeFromParent()
```

Take a look at the Treasure class in the TutsTomb3 example belonging to this chapter to see the complete code of the action. Figure 14-2 shows that some of the treasures have turned into rocks!

*Figure 14-2. Treasures turning into useless rocks*

# Handling Physics Contacts

Before concluding this chapter, let's take a look at the final part of the gameplay: handling contact between treasures. In the previous chapter, you saw how to add physical behavior to game objects. You also saw that contacts can be handled if you define a particular method inside the GameWorld class, which implements the SKPhysicsContactDelegate protocol:

```
func didBeginContact(contact: SKPhysicsContact) {
    let firstBody = contact.bodyA.node as? Treasure
    let secondBody = contact.bodyB.node as? Treasure

    // handle contact between the two bodies here
}
```

You handle the contact between the two bodies by looking at a few different cases. The first case is that the casting of the body nodes to Treasure instances was not successful. This happens if one of the bodies actually is not a treasure at all (instead, for example, a wall).

In that case, you simply return from the method because you don't have to do anything in particular when a treasure collides with a wall:

```
if firstBody == nil || secondBody == nil {
    return
}
```

If two objects collide and they are of the same type (or one of them is a magic crystal), both objects will be removed from the scene. In order to avoid removing objects from the scene multiple times (which can happen when separate parts of the objects are in contact at the same time), you need to check whether you already handled a contact between these two objects. If either of the objects has no parent (in other words, it has already been removed from the scene), the contact was already handled, and the code is as follows:

```
if firstBody?.parent == nil || secondBody?.parent == nil {
    return
}
```

Yet another case is where two rocks collide. In that case, you also return from the method because when two rocks collide, nothing happens–they simply stay in the scene, like so:

```
if firstBody?.type == TreasureType.Rock &&
    secondBody?.type == TreasureType.Rock {
    return
}
```

The final case is the one where objects need to be removed from the scene. This happens if the type of the two treasures matches, or either one of the treasures is a magic crystal. Both objects are removed from the scene in that case, by using the removeFromParent method:

```
if firstBody?.type == secondBody?.type || firstBody?.type == TreasureType.Magic
    || secondBody?.type == TreasureType.Magic {
    firstBody?.removeFromParent()
    secondBody?.removeFromParent()
}
```

Take a look at the GameWorld class in the TutsTomb3 example for the complete code of the method. Note that the order in which the if instructions are written inside the method body is important. For example, dealing with rocks works correctly because of the order. If the if instruction comparing the rock types was placed at the end of the method body, then two rocks would also be removed from the scene when they collide, which is undesirable. It's important that you think carefully about which cases to handle when you write code like this. Bugs are easily introduced if you don't watch out!

# What You Have Learned

In this chapter, you have learned the following:

- How to program gameplay aspects and interaction between game objects

- How to use actions to define game object behavior

- How to handle physical contact in the Tut's Tomb game

# Game States

In the previous chapter, you programmed the main gameplay elements of the Tut's Tomb game. However, the game as it stands is far from complete. For example, nothing happens when the tomb is completely filled with treasures. Also, when you start the program, the game immediately begins without any warning. What is still needed is a way to incorporate menus and overlays in the game so the player can get help or start playing the game. When the player is, for example, in a menu screen, the type of interaction with the game is very different from when the player is solving a level or trying to survive as long as possible. When programming a game, you have to think about how to incorporate these different *game states* and switch between them.

Modern games have many different game states, such as menus, maps, inventories, splash screens, intro movies, and much more. This chapter shows how to add different game states to the Tut's Tomb game. Because this game isn't yet very complicated, you can get away with using a few simple extensions to your current classes. However, game-state management needs to be handled properly if you want to build a commercial game. Chapter 18 covers a software design using classes that can handle game states in a very nice and generic way.

## Better Layer Handling

An important thing when dealing with different game states is that things are drawn at different layers. You use the zPosition property of the SKNode class for that. Using fixed numbers to represent layers may not always be very easy to remember. You have to keep track of which layer represents the scene, which one represents an overlay, and which one represents a background. In the TutsTomb4 example, I used a struct to represent the different layers, very similar to how I defined the various treasure types (see the GameScene.swift file):

```
struct Layer {
    static let Background: CGFloat = 0
    static let Scene: CGFloat = 1
    static let Scene1: CGFloat = 2
```

```
        static let Scene2: CGFloat = 3
        static let Overlay: CGFloat = 10
        static let Overlay1: CGFloat = 11
        static let Overlay2: CGFloat = 12
}
```

As you can see, I define a few useful layers for the background, the scene, and the overlays. Now you can very easily define the layer by using these constants:

```
background.zPosition = Layer.Background
```

Take a look at the code in the TutsTomb4 example to see how these layers are used to structure the order in which objects in the game world are drawn.

# Adding a Title Screen

One of the first things you can do to make a game look more complete is add a title screen. The title screen allows the player to get ready to play the game instead of being immediately launched into it. You can extend the GameWorld class so that it loads and displays a title screen consisting of a single image. You create a SKSpriteNode instance for that and add it to the game world, like so:

```
var titleScreen = SKSpriteNode(imageNamed:"spr_title")
...
titleScreen.zPosition = Layer.Overlay2
addChild(titleScreen)
```

You assign it the layer Layer.Overlays2 so you can be sure the title is drawn on top of everything. But you have to do a little extra work to properly handle input and update the game world because you want the game to start only when the title screen is no longer visible. You can do that by adding a few instructions to the handleInput method to distinguish between two states, the state in which you show the title screen and the state in which you're playing the game:

```
if !titleScreen.hidden {
    if inputHelper.hasTapped {
        titleScreen.hidden = true
        self.runAction(totalAction)
    }
} ... else {
    super.handleInput(inputHelper)
    ...
}
```

Looking at the if instructions, you can see that if the title screen is visible, the game reacts only when the player taps on the screen. In that case, you set the title screen's hidden flag to true so it isn't drawn anymore. Also, you start the action that drops a treasure every few seconds. As a result, whenever the title screen is visible, the only thing the game reacts to is the player touching the screen. If the title screen isn't visible, you call the `handleInput` method of the super class; in other words, the game reacts to the player as it should when the player is playing the game.

You follow very much the same procedure for the `updateDelta` method, where you update the game world only if the title isn't visible:

```
if titleScreen.hidden {
    super.updateDelta(delta)
}
```

When a player starts the game, they now see a title screen before the game starts (see Figure 15-1). You aren't done yet. In the next section, you add a simple button GUI element that shows a help frame.

*Figure 15-1. The Tut's Tomb title screen*

# Adding a Button to Show a Help Frame

This section explains how to add a button to a game, which you use to display a help frame. To do that, you add another class, `Button`, to the program. You inherit from the `GameObjectNode` class and add some simple behavior that checks whether the player pressed a button. In the Button class, you declare a Boolean property that indicates whether the button was tapped. Then you override the handleInput method to check whether the player has tapped on the button on the screen. If the touching position is within the boundaries of the button sprite at that time, you know the player has tapped on the button, and you set the value of the property to true. How can you check whether the touch position is within the boundaries of the sprite? By using the box property of the GameObjectNode class and use the containsTap method in the InputHelper class. Here is the complete handleInput method of Button:

```
override func handleInput(inputHelper: InputHelper) {
    super.handleInput(inputHelper)
    tapped = inputHelper.containsTap(self.box)
}
```

For the complete Button class, see the TutsTomb4 example. Now let's add a Help button to the game world. In the GameWorld class, you add a property to represent the Help button:

```
var helpbutton = Button(imageNamed: "spr_button_help")
```

The next step is to position the Help button on the screen and add it to the game world. In Tut's Tomb, the Help button should always be shown in the top right of the screen, regardless of the device that is used. To write the code that achieves this, you add a method called topRight to the GameWorld class that calculates the position corresponding to the top right of the screen:

```
func topRight() -> CGPoint {
    return CGPoint(x: size.width/2, y: size.height/2)
}
```

Using this method, you can now calculate the desired position of the Help button:

```
var helppos = topRight()
helppos.x -= helpbutton.sprite.size.width/2 + 10
helppos.y -= helpbutton.sprite.size.height/2 + 10
```

Because the origin of a sprite is its center by default, you need to subtract half of the help button sprite width and height of the top right position. You subtract another 10 pixels so that there is a slight margin between the button and the edges of the screen.

Because you want to display a help frame when the player presses the Help button, you also add a help frame to the game world. You set its hidden flag to true so it isn't yet visible:

```
var helpframe = SKSpriteNode(imageNamed: "spr_help")
helpframe.zPosition = Layer.Overlay2
helpframe.hidden = true
```

Now you have to make sure that when the player taps the help button, the help frame is shown. You can do this using the following if instruction in the handleInput method of the GameWorld class:

```
if helpbutton.tapped  {
    helpframe.hidden = false
    self.removeAllActions()
}
```

You have to make sure the game isn't updated when the help frame is displayed. This is partly done by calling the removeAllActions method, which disables the action that drops treasures. You also need to make sure that game objects are only updated if the help frame isn't visible. Therefore, you change the updateDelta method of the GameWorld class as follows:

```
if titleScreen.hidden && helpframe.hidden {
    super.updateDelta(delta)
}
```

Figure 15-2 shows the game when the help frame is displayed.

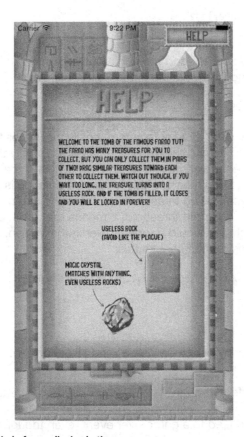

*Figure 15-2. Screenshot of the help frame display in the game*

# Overlays

A very common way of presenting information to the player is to use *overlays*. Overlays are basically images that can be displayed on top of the game world to present information or to provide a user interface such as a menu, a mini map, status information, and more. The help frame introduced in the previous section is another example of an overlay.

Overlays can present an entirely new game state (such as a Game Over overlay), or they can supplement the game world by providing information to the player. For example, many strategy games provide information about the number of units selected, available resources, ongoing building processes, items gathered, and so on. These kinds of overlays are generally always on the screen, and together they're called the *heads-up display* (HUD). Tut's Tomb has a very basic HUD: it consists of a frame that displays the current score (which you'll add in the next chapter), and a Help button the user can tap to view a frame with help information.

Next to the HUD, you want to show a Game Over overlay when the tomb is filled entirely with treasures. You add this overlay to the game world, and set its hidden status to true:

```
var gameover = SKSpriteNode(imageNamed: "spr_gameover")
self.addChild(gameover)
gameover.zPosition = Layer.Overlay2
gameover.hidden = true
```

The origin of the sprite is its center, and the origin of the game scene is also in the center. The latter is achieved by the following line in the GameScene class:

```
anchorPoint = CGPoint(x: 0.5, y: 0.5)
```

The result is that the Game Over overlay is automatically nicely positioned in the middle of the screen. You only have to extend the GameWorld class to display the overlay when needed. You first need to check when the game is actually over, which is the case if the tomb is completely filled. So how do you measure this? A simple solution is to extend the method dealing with physics contacts. If two treasure objects are in contact and the y-position of either one of them is above a certain threshold, it means that probably the tomb is quite full, since otherwise the collision would happen lower in the screen. In the didBeginContact method, the following if instruction checks this:

```
if firstBody?.position.y > 400 || secondBody?.position.y > 400 {
    gameover.hidden = false
    self.removeAllActions()
}
```

If the game is over, the overlay becomes visible, and all actions are removed so that treasures no longer fall down.

This solution is not yet perfect, though. The player could drag a treasure and hold it below the chimney. The treasure falling down would then collide with the treasure that the player was dragging, which would lead to a game over event, even though the tomb might be completely empty. A simple way to solve this is by not letting the player drag a treasure as soon as it reaches a threshold slightly lower than the game over threshold. This is done by extending the handleInput method of the Treasure class, as follows:

```
if position.y >= 200 {
    touchid = nil
    if physicsBody?.velocity.dy >= 0 {
        physicsBody?.velocity = CGVector.zeroVector
    }
    return
}
```

If the y position is larger than the threshold of 200, you stop dragging the treasure by setting the touch id to nil. Another thing you need to deal with is the player dragging the treasure up at a high velocity. In order to avoid this, you set the velocity of the physics body to zero if the treasure is moving upward. You measure this by checking the dy property of the physics body velocity.

In the handleInput method of GameWorld, you check whether the game over overlay is visible. If that is the case, the player can tap on the screen to restart the game:

```
if !gameover.hidden {
    if inputHelper.hasTapped {
        gameover.hidden = true
        self.reset()
        self.runAction(totalAction)
    }
}
```

You override the reset method because you need to do a little extra work when the game restarts. Notably, you have to clear the treasures node so that the tomb is empty again, and you reset the counter to 0, so that the game starts with a limited range of treasures. Furthermore, you call the reset method from the superclass so that all game objects in the game world are reset as well:

```
override func reset() {
    super.reset()
    self.treasures.removeAllChildren()
    self.counter = 0
}
```

The final thing you need to do is make sure that the game world is no longer updated when the game is over. This means yet another change in the updateDelta method of GameWorld, as follows:

```
if titleScreen.hidden && helpframe.hidden && gameover.hidden {
    super.updateDelta(delta)
}
```

Figure 15-3 shows the Game Over state.

*Figure 15-3. Too bad . . .*

## DESIGNING GAMES

On game-development teams, the programmer normally isn't responsible for the design of the game, but it's still very useful to have a basic understanding of this process. The programmer must turn the game design into code and must be able to advise the designer about what will work and what will be difficult to achieve. For this collaboration to be successful, everyone has to speak the same language.

Designing a game primarily consists of defining the game mechanics, the setting of the game, and choosing the game levels. Game mechanics involve such things as the rules of the game, the way players control the game, the goals and challenges, and the reward structure. Psychology and educational science play an important role here. They help you understand how players get in the flow (the mood in which they're fully committed to playing the game); how goals, challenges, and rewards can support each other; and how to vary and adapt the game's difficulty.

The game's setting deals with the story, the characters, and the virtual world in which the game takes place. A good story can be a strong motivator for players, and discovering the story while playing can be a very satisfying task. Characters need to evoke empathy from the player to give meaning to the tasks that must be performed. And the game world enhances these aspects and adapts the game to certain demographics.

Level design is sometimes done by special level designers, but in smaller teams it's often the responsibility of the game designer. Careful level design leads to a good learning curve. It keeps the player challenged and motivated, and it should result in pleasant surprises.

Many books have been written about game design, and you're strongly encouraged to read some of them. You can also find lots of information on all aspects of game development on sites like www.gamasutra.com.

# What You Have Learned

In this chapter, you have learned the following:

- How to add a HUD and overlays to the game
- How to define a simple button that shows a frame
- How to deal with a few different game states such as a title screen and a Game Over state

# Chapter 16

# Finishing the Tut's Tomb Game

In this chapter, you will finish the Tut's Tomb game. As a first step, you will add a score indicator to the game, using a custom game font. Second, you will add a nice visual effect by showing glitter on the treasures in the game. Finally, you will add sound and music. Take a look at the TutsTombFinal game example. This contains all the code explained in this chapter.

## Adding a Score

In Tut's Tomb, every time two treasures of the same type collide, they disappear from the screen and the player gets points. You need to display those points somewhere on the screen. In this game, the score is shown in the top left part of the screen. In the GameWorld class, you add a scoreObj property that will represent the node for maintaining and displaying the current score. The type of this property is Score, which is a class that will be discussed in this chapter. When the game world is set up, the Score instance is positioned in the top left of the screen (with a top and side margin), and is added to the GameWorld node like so:

```
var scorepos = GameScene.world.topLeft()
scorepos.x += scoreObj.sprite.size.width/2 + 10
scorepos.y -= scoreObj.sprite.size.height/2 + 10
scoreObj.position = scorepos
self.addChild(scoreObj)
```

The Score class is a subclass of GameObjectNode. It contains a sprite, a label to display the score, and an integer property to keep track of the current score. In the class initializer, the sprite and label properties are positioned and added to the node:

```
sprite.zPosition = Layer.Overlay
self.addChild(sprite)

label.position = CGPoint(x: 100, y: 0)
label.zPosition = Layer.Overlay1
label.fontColor = UIColor.blackColor()
label.fontSize = 20
label.verticalAlignmentMode = .Center
label.horizontalAlignmentMode = .Right
label.text = "0"
self.addChild(label)
```

The label is initialized with a font color and size, as well as an alignment. The alignment indicates how the text is displayed with respect to the label position, which is (100, 0). The vertical alignment mode is "center." This means that the text is displayed such that the vertical middle of the text is at y-position 0, local to the score node object to which the text belongs. The horizontal alignment mode is "right," which results in the text being right-aligned. In terms of positioning, this means that the local x-position (which is 100) indicates the right edge of the label text. There are a few other options for aligning text. For example, you can vertically align text at the top, center, bottom, or baseline (the latter means the virtual line on which the text is written, which is different from bottom alignment, since depending on the font used, some characters may stick out below the baseline, such as the g or the p character). Play around with the various alignment options and label positioning to see how it works. If you want to learn more about a certain property or method in Xcode, Control-Click it, and select Jump to Definition. Xcode will then show you the definition. You can also hold down Command and click a property or method to achieve the same thing.

The Score class uses a stored integer property called scoreValue to keep track of the current score. Accessing the score should be done through a computed property score:

```
var score: Int {
    get {
        return scoreValue
    }
    set {
        scoreValue = newValue
        label.text = String(self.scoreValue)
    }
}
```

The reason why a computed property is used is that it allows you to also change the label text when the score is changed. In the didBeginContact method of GameWorld, the score is incremented if there is a contact between two treasures of the same type (or if there is a magic crystal involved):

```
if firstBody?.type == secondBody?.type || firstBody?.type == TreasureType.Magic
    || secondBody?.type == TreasureType.Magic {
    self.scoreObj.score += 10
    ...
}
```

When the score is incremented, the set part of the score property is called, and the score label text is updated as well.

# Controlling Access

Suppose that the scoreValue property is declared as follows in the Score class:

```
var scoreValue: Int = 0
```

Although the property is supposed to be accessed only within the Score class, there is nothing that prevents a developer from writing this:

```
self.scoreObj.scoreValue += 10
```

If by accident the score is updated in this fashion, it will lead to a problem in the game because the label text will not be changed, even though the score has changed. Is there a way to enforce that a property can only be accessed within the class and not outside it? Yes, there is! Swift knows three keywords for controlling access to both properties and methods in a class: private, internal, and public, also called *access modifiers*.

If you use the *private* access modifier, you can only access the property or method within the source file where it is defined. So, code written in other source files will not be able to directly access such a property. For example, in the TutsTombFinal example, this is how the scoreValue property is declared:

```
private var scoreValue: Int = 0
```

If you were to now try to access the scoreValue property in the GameWorld class, which is defined in another source file, the compiler would give you an error. Sometimes, it's useful to make methods private as well. For example, you might add a low-level method to your class that you use internally to compute something, but you don't want it to be called from somewhere else. You'll see an example of such a method later in this chapter.

*Internal* access means that properties and methods are accessible from any file within the *target* where it's defined. A target is what Xcode builds when you click the Play button. So, in the context of this book, a target will mostly be an app, but it can also be a library of classes that belong together or an OS X application. By default, properties and methods have internal access. So, the declaration

```
var lives: Int = 0
```

is equivalent to

```
internal var lives: Int = 0
```

Finally, a *public* property or method can be accessed from any source file, and even outside of the target. The latter is especially useful when you develop a library of classes that you would like to use for multiple games.

# Using a Custom Font

If you want to set your game apart, you have to carefully think about the fonts that you are using in your game. You generally want to avoid using fonts such as Times New Roman or Arial, since everybody knows and uses those fonts already. There are lots of free fonts available that you can use in your game. If you decide to use a custom font, make sure that you are allowed to use it. Not all fonts can be used for commercial purposes.

Just like sprites and sounds, fonts are a type of game asset. If you use a particular font in your game, you should package this font with your app so that you are sure the game looks the same for all players. Packaging your font with the game is quite easy, but it involves a few steps.

First, you need to add the font file to your game project. In the TutsTombFinal example, you can see that there is a folder called Fonts, which contains a TrueType font file.

The next step is ensuring that Xcode copies the font so that it is a part of the target. In Xcode, click the project name on the left side of the window, and select the TutsTombFinal target. Then go to the Build Phases tab. If you open the Copy Bundle Resources list, it needs to show the font. If it is not there, drag it from the project file list to the Copy Bundle Resources list (see Figure 16-1).

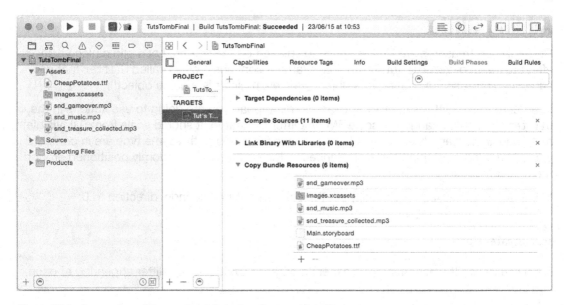

**Figure 16-1.** *An overview of the assets copied when the target is built*

Now that the font is added to the project and copied when the target is built, you need to indicate in the project settings that your target will use that particular font. Click the Info.plist file in the Supporting Files folder, and you'll see a list of items. There is a key called "Fonts provided by application" and you'll see that it contains a single item: the custom font used in the Tut's Tomb game. If you start a new project for your own game and you want to add a custom font, you need to add the "Fonts provided by application" key yourself to this list by clicking the plus sign that appears when you hover over the Information Property List dictionary. You can then add a new key and add your custom fonts to that key.

The final step is creating a label node using your font. Note that a font name used in a Swift program is not necessarily the same as the name of the font *file*. There is no real convenient way to find the font name belonging to a font file. If you insert the following code snippet in your program somewhere, the program will list all the fonts that it knows:

```
let fontFamilies = UIFont.familyNames()
for familyName in fontFamilies {
    let fontNames = UIFont.fontNamesForFamilyName(familyName)
    print("\(familyName): \(fontNames)")
}
```

You can then find the name of the font you want to use in the list that is printed to the console. Figure 16-2 shows the score label in TutsTombFinal using a custom font for displaying the score value.

# Adding Glitter

Currently, the treasures are simple sprites displayed on the screen. Let's add a nice visual effect to them: glitter. The TutsTombFinal example contains a class called `Glitter` that you can use to represent a glitter game object (yes, even glitter is a game object!).

In order to make glitter smoothly appear and disappear, you are going to use actions in the `Glitter` class that change the scale. When glitter is created, it should scale from 0 (invisible) to 1 (regular size) and back again. Whenever two treasures of the same type are in contact, you add a number of this `Glitter` instances to the game world, randomly positioned around the contact location.

In the `Glitter` initializer, you initially set the scale in both the x and y direction to 0:

```
self.xScale = 0
self.yScale = 0
```

Then you define the actions for the glitter. In order to avoid a lot of glitter appearing at once, you start with a waiting action:

```
let waitAction = SKAction.waitForDuration(0.1, withRange: 0.2)
```

This waiting action chooses a random waiting time around 0.1 seconds, within a range of 0.2 seconds. As a result, each added glitter shows up at a slightly different time. Then, you define a scale up and a scale down action:

```
let scaleUpAction = SKAction.scaleTo(1, duration: 0.3)
let scaleDownAction = SKAction.scaleTo(0, duration: 0.3)
```

Finally, you create a sequence of these actions, and run them:

```
let totalAction = SKAction.sequence([waitAction, scaleUpAction, scaleDownAction])
self.runAction(totalAction, completion: {
    self.removeFromParent()
})
```

Once the action is completed, a block of instructions is executed. In this case, the block contains a single instruction that removes the glitter from the game world.

The only thing left to do is add glitter to the scene. In order to help do that, let's add a method to the `GameWorld` class that adds a number of glitter around a given position. Because this method should only be used in the `GameWorld` class, this is a good example of a method with *private* access. Here is the header of the method:

```
private func addGlittersAroundPosition(pos: CGPoint, number: Int)
```

As you can see, the method expects a position and a number. Inside the method body, you use a `for` loop to create and add a `Glitter` object a number of times. In order to randomly position the object, you can use polar coordinates. In other words, instead of representing a position by an x and y coordinate, you represent it by a radius and an angle. If you randomly choose a radius in a range, and a random angle between 0 and $2\pi$, the glitter will appear in a circle around the given position. You can go from the polar coordinates back to regular (Cartesian) coordinates by using the sine and cosine mathematical functions. Here is the complete body of the addGlittersAroundPosition method:

```
for _ in 1...number {
    var glitter = Glitter()
    glitter.position = pos
    var radius = randomDouble() * 100
    var angle = randomDouble() * 2 * M_PI
    glitter.position.x += CGFloat(cos(angle) * radius)
    glitter.position.y += CGFloat(sin(angle) * radius)
    self.addChild(glitter)
}
```

Note the use of the underscore in the for loop since there is no need for an actual counter variable. In the didBeginContact method, you can then call this method to add glitter around the contact location. Take a look at the code in the TutsTombFinal example to see how that is done. Figure 16-2 shows the game with glitter!

*Figure 16-2.* The TutsTombFinal game with glitter

# Adding More Glitter

Because glitter doesn't care where it's positioned, you can add glitter anywhere in the game at any time you want. For example, to make the magic crystal more magical, you can define an action that continuously adds glitter around it. The Treasure class contains an addGlitter method that adds glitter randomly around the position of the treasure sprite. You can then simply define an action that repeatedly adds glitter to a magic crystal object. This action consists of calling the addGlitter method, and waiting for a bit. Here is the code that defines the action:

```
let addGlitterAction = SKAction.runBlock({
    self.addGlitter()
})
let waitAction = SKAction.waitForDuration(0.1)
let totalAction = SKAction.repeatActionForever(
    SKAction.sequence([addGlitterAction, waitAction]))
self.runAction(totalAction)
```

Figure 16-3 shows a magic crystal with glitter.

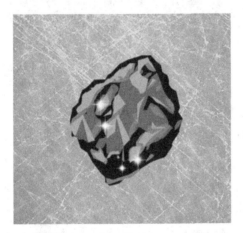

*Figure 16-3. Shiny!*

# Adding Music and Sound Effects

Just like in the Painter game, you want to add music and sound effects to the game to make it more attractive. As you've seen, playing music and sounds is very easy in Swift. You can use the Sound class that you created earlier for Painter. This is another good example of reusing code: you created the Sound class once, and you're using it for all the games in this book!

Quite a few of the classes designed for Tut's Tomb will be useful for the other games in this book. When you start building your own games, you'll probably end up with a collection of similar classes that you will use often. When building games, it's a good idea to think ahead. What classes can you reuse for other projects? What is the best way to design a class so you might be able to use it again later? As you develop more and more classes, it may be useful to keep a list; you can then quickly scan the list as you develop new items and implement things you might not have thought of before.

When the game starts, you begin playing the background music, as follows (see the GameWorld class):

```
backgroundMusic.looping = true
backgroundMusic.volume = 0.5
backgroundMusic.play()
```

And when two treasures of the same type collide, you also play a sound effect (also in the GameWorld class):

```
if firstBody?.type == secondBody?.type || firstBody?.type == TreasureType.Magic
    || secondBody?.type == TreasureType.Magic {
    self.scoreObj.score += 10
    ...
    treasureCollectSound.play()
}
```

Finally, you play a sound when the game is over (again in the GameWorld class):

```
if firstBody?.position.y > 400 || secondBody?.position.y > 400 {
    gameover.hidden = false
    self.removeAllActions()
    gameoverSound.play()
}
```

This completes the Tut's Tomb game. You can play the game by running the TutsTombFinal example belonging to this chapter. As an exercise, see if you're able to extend the game yourself with new features. For example, you could add extra animation effects when treasures collide. Or how about adding a leaderboard/high-score list? In any case, happy treasure hunting!

---

| LEADERBOARDS |
| --- |

Why do games contain leaderboards and high-score lists? Early games didn't have them because there was no semi-permanent storage available in the game consoles. So, nothing could be remembered between playing sessions. Also, there was no Save Game option, which had an important effect on game mechanics: a player always had to start from the beginning, even if they were experienced.

Once storage became available, designers started to introduce leaderboards. Being better than somebody else always gives a feeling of satisfaction, and it adds an important goal for the player. But this only makes sense if multiple people are playing the game on the same device. If you're the sole player, the only thing you can do is try to beat yourself. Fortunately, nowadays computers and game consoles are connected to the Internet. As a result, you can store leaderboards online and compete with the whole world.

But this adds an additional problem: a goal is only interesting when it's reachable. Being the best player among a couple of millions is unreachable for most people. So, worldwide leaderboards can actually reduce player satisfaction. To remedy this, games often introduce sub-leaderboards. For example, you can have a leaderboard that is restricted to your own country or to scores reached this week. You can also see how you rank among your friends. Carefully designing your game's scoring system and the way such scores are shown on leaderboards can make a crucial difference in the satisfaction it gives to your players.

# What You Have Learned

In this chapter, you have learned the following:

- How to use custom fonts in your game
- How to restrict access to properties and methods
- How to create glitter and attach it to game objects

# Part IV

# Penguin Pairs

In this part of the book, you will develop the game *Penguin Pairs* (see Figure IV-1). I will introduce a few new techniques for programming games, such as game objects in a grid layout, file I/O, better game-state management, storing game data between playing sessions, and more.

Penguin Pairs is a puzzle game, the goal of which is to make pairs of penguins of the same color. The player can move the penguins by clicking or tapping them and selecting the direction in which the penguin should move. A penguin moves until it's stopped by another character in the game (this can be a penguin, a seal, a shark, or an iceberg) or it drops from the playing field, in which case it falls into the water and is eaten by hungry sharks. The different levels of the game introduce new gameplay elements to keep the game exciting. For example, there is a special penguin that can match any other penguin, penguins can get stuck in a hole (meaning they can't move), and penguin-eating sharks can be placed on the board. You can run the final version of this game by trying the example program belonging to Chapter 21.

*Figure IV-1.* *The Penguin Pairs game*

# Chapter 17

# Menus and Grids

Penguin Pairs is a puzzle game, and often, board games and puzzle games are based on placing objects in some kind of grid. There are many examples of such games: Chess, Tetris, Tic-Tac-Toe, Sudoku, Candy Crush, and many more. Often the goal in these games is to modify the configuration of the grid in some way to achieve points. In Tetris, completely filled rows have to be constructed; and in Sudoku, numerical properties must hold for rows, columns, and subgrids.

Structures such as grids often impose a set of rules that binds the playing pieces to certain positions or configurations on the playing board. For example, in a chess game, the pieces can only be placed (meaningfully) on the white and black squares on the playing board. You aren't allowed to place your queen halfway between two squares. In computer games, these kinds of restrictions are easier to enforce: you just have to make sure the position where you place your game object is a valid one.

Grids are also useful in other parts of the game. For example, you may want to show a grid of buttons to let the player choose between levels. This is why grids are also often used for organizing GUI elements on the screen. In addition to grid layouts, this chapter also introduces a few new GUI elements such as a slider and an on-off button that are needed for the Penguin Pairs game. You will notice that this chapter is a bit math-heavy, due to having to deal with grid locations, slider positions, and what not. It's worthwhile to understand these things well, though. Once you've done the hard work of creating the classes and methods, you can use them over and over again for any games you develop in the future.

## Game Objects in a Grid Layout

Before writing the code, let's first think about what a grid is, and what kinds of parameters help define a grid. Figure 17-1 shows an overview of all the important parameters of a grid. A grid generally consists of a number of cells. The grids I use in this book have cells with a fixed width and height. Furthermore, the grid will have a number of rows and columns. Since in the SpriteKit framework the positive y axis points upward, let's also define the grid in this way. So, the lowest row in the grid is row 0, the row above that row 1, and so on. The leftmost column is column 0 and the column index increases in the direction of the positive x axis (see also Figure 17-1). Finally, there may be space between the cells in a grid (for example, if you want to show a grid of buttons). This space, also called *padding*, is defined for both the x and y direction.

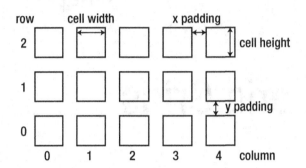

*Figure 17-1. Overview of a grid structure with three rows and five columns*

The way I approach laying out objects in a grid is by creating a GridLayout class of which an instance is attached to a node in the scene. The GridLayout instance will be responsible for laying out the child nodes of the node to which it is attached. The order of the children in the children array belonging to SKNode determines where each child is located on the grid. In the grid in Figure 17-1, the bottom five cells (row 0) are filled with the first five elements in the array, the next five children in the array fill row 1, and so on. Instead of adding each child node directly to the SKNode instance, you call an add method in the GridLayout class to add the child node and calculate its position on the grid.

In the PenguinPairs1 example, you'll find the complete code of the GridLayout class. The class has several properties in order to maintain information about the grid size (following Figure 17-1):

```
var cellWidth: Int = 0, cellHeight: Int = 0, rows: Int = 0, columns: Int = 0
var xPadding: Int = 0, yPadding: Int = 0
var target: SKNode? = nil
```

The target property is the SKNode object whose children will be laid out in a grid. In the GameWorld class, you create a node to contain a number of buttons:

```
var levelButtons = GameObjectNode()
```

In the GameWorld setup method, you create a layout object, and assign the levelButtons node as its target:

```
var layout = GridLayout(rows: nrRows, columns: nrCols, cellWidth: 150, cellHeight: 150)
layout.xPadding = 5
layout.yPadding = 5
layout.target = levelButtons
```

Now let's create a few useful methods and properties in the GridLayout class. First, it is useful to be able to calculate the total width and height of the grid, given its cell width and height and the padding. As you can see in Figure 17-1, the total width of the grid is the number of cells times the cell width, and added to that is the number of cells minus 1 times the x padding. The height is calculated in a similar way. Here are the two properties in GridLayout that calculate the total grid width and height:

```
var width : CGFloat {
    get { return CGFloat(columns * cellWidth + (columns - 1) * xPadding) }
}

var height : CGFloat {
    get { return CGFloat(rows * cellHeight + (rows - 1) * yPadding) }
}
```

Let's also add a method that can convert a row and column index on the grid to a local position in the node. Let's assume that the grid's origin is its center (just like with sprites). The bottom left point of the grid is then (-width/2, -height/2). For the x-position, you then add the column index times the sum of the cell width and x padding. For the y-position, you do the same with the row index and the sum of the cell height and y padding. This gives you the bottom left point of the desired cell. Finally, you add half the cell width and height in order to position the child nicely in the center of the grid cell. Here is the method that performs this computation:

```
func toPosition(col: Int, row: Int) -> CGPoint {
    let xpos = -width/2 + CGFloat(col * (cellWidth + xPadding) + cellWidth / 2)
    let ypos = -height/2 + CGFloat(row * (cellHeight + yPadding) + cellHeight / 2)
    return CGPoint(x: xpos, y: ypos)
}
```

Similarly, you defined a method called toGridLocation that converts a position to a column and row index. Check out the code yourself in the PenguinPairs1 example. You can now define a method called add that adds a node to the target and automatically positions it correctly. Here is the complete method:

```
func add(obj: SKNode) {
    if let target_unwrapped = target {
        let r = target_unwrapped.children.count / columns
        let c = target_unwrapped.children.count % columns
        target_unwrapped.addChild(obj)
        obj.position = toPosition(c, row: r)
    }
}
```

Because target is an optional variable, you first unwrap it and then work with the unwrapped target. First, you calculate the row and column index belonging to the node that will be added, using the number of children in the children array. Then, you add the object to the target, and call the toPosition method to calculate its actual position.

Finally, you define a method called at that allows you to retrieve an object at a particular location in the grid. This method returns an optional SKNode object. It's optional because in some cases there may not be an SKNode object, for example if the supplied column or row index is out of range of the grid dimensions. Here is the complete method:

```
func at(col: Int, row: Int) -> SKNode? {
    if col < 0 || col >= columns || row < 0 || row >= rows {
        return nil
    }
    if let target_unwrapped = target {
        var index = row * columns + col
        return target_unwrapped.children[index] as? SKNode
    }
    return nil
}
```

Now you can use the GridLayout class to organize child objects into a grid structure. In the remaining chapters of this book, you will use this class whenever you need game objects in a grid layout.

The PenguinPairs1 example uses the GridLayout class to show a grid of level buttons on the screen. In the GameWorld class, the level buttons are created and added to the grid. The first step is to determine the number of rows and columns needed in the grid. The levels will be read from a text file, just like with Penguin Pairs. Therefore, the code is structured so that based on the number of levels, you can decide how many columns the grid needs, and then the code calculates the number of rows required:

```
let nrCols = 6, nrLevels = 12
var nrRows = nrLevels / nrCols
if nrLevels % nrCols != 0 {
    nrRows++
}
```

Now you can define the layout to which the level buttons should conform, and define x and y padding values to allow for some space between the buttons. You also set a node as the target of this layout:

```
var layout = GridLayout(rows: nrRows, columns: nrCols, cellWidth: 150, cellHeight: 150)
layout.xPadding = 5
layout.yPadding = 5
layout.target = levelButtons
```

You use a nested for loop to fill the grid with level buttons, defined as simple SKSpriteNode instances for now:

```
for var i = nrRows - 1; i >= 0; i-- {
    for var j = 0; j < nrCols; j++ {
        if i*nrCols + j < nrLevels {
            var level = SKSpriteNode(imageNamed: "spr_level_unsolved")
            level.zPosition = Layer.Scene
```

```
        layout.add(level)
    } else {
        layout.add(SKNode())
    }
    }
}
```

The if instruction inside the nested for loop is needed because the bottom row may be only partly filled with buttons. At the other locations in the grid, an empty SKNode instance is added. You can see the result by running the PenguinPairs1 example belonging to this chapter. Figure 17-2 shows a screenshot.

*Figure 17-2. A grid of level buttons in the PenguinPairs1 example program*

# Class Extensions

Before continuing to adding a menu to Penguin Pairs, let's go back to the class design used in the two previous games and reconsider what can be done to improve it. For the Tut's Tomb game, I defined a class called GameObjectNode, which was a subclass of SKNode, and added methods for basic game loop interaction. This brought along some inconvenience: in order for this to work correctly, every node in the scene should be a GameObjectNode instance, or an instance of a subclass of GameObjectNode. Wouldn't it be much easier if you could simply extend the functionality of the SKNode class itself? The good news is: you can! Swift has a mechanism called *class extensions*. It allows you to add functionality to an existing class and use that extended class definition in your project. If you open the SKNode_Extension.swift file belonging to the PenguinPairs2 example, you'll see something like this:

```
import SpriteKit

extension SKNode {
    ...

    func handleInput(inputHelper: InputHelper) {
        ...
    }
```

```
func updateDelta(delta: NSTimeInterval) {
    ...
}

func reset() {
    ...
}
}
```

This tells the compiler that within the PenguinPairs2 project, the SKNode class is extended by (among others) three methods. As a result, any SKNode instance you create from now on will have the methods and properties defined in the extension. This means you no longer need a separate GameObjectNode class. Moreover, subclasses of SKNode, such as SKSpriteNode, will now also automatically have the methods and properties defined in the extension. This is very useful. For example, you could rewrite the Button class to simply be a subclass of SKSpriteNode:

```
class Button: SKSpriteNode {

    var tapped = false

    init(imageNamed: String) {
        let texture = SKTexture(imageNamed: imageNamed)
        super.init(texture: texture, color: UIColor.whiteColor(), size: texture.size())
    }

    required init?(coder aDecoder: NSCoder) {
        fatalError("init(coder:) has not been implemented")
    }

    override func handleInput(inputHelper: InputHelper) {
        super.handleInput(inputHelper)
        tapped = inputHelper.containsTap(self.box) && !self.hidden
    }
}
```

Class extensions are very useful if you'd like to extend the functionality of an existing class in a framework. The SKNode extension is a good example of this. Because you directly extend the SKNode class, the extension is smoothly transferred to all classes in the SpriteKit framework that inherit from SKNode. As a result, it leads to less duplication of code. In the remaining chapters of this book, I'll use class extensions to add functionality to existing classes.

Class extensions are yet another tool in the toolkit of a developer to design a software architecture in a nice, generic way. However, as with any tool, you have to watch out how you use it. If you rely too much on class extensions, it may no longer be clear to you which part of a class was original and which part was added by you. When you start a new project, you may end up sifting through your previous projects to gather the bits and pieces you added to the existing classes and copy them to your new project. And if a new version of the SpriteKit framework is released, your extensions of SpriteKit classes may no longer make any sense (although this latter argument can be made for any piece of code that uses SpriteKit classes).

# Setting Up a Menu

Now that the SKNode class has been extended with game loop functionality, let's use it to create a menu for the Penguin Pairs game. When thinking about menus, you may think of a pull-down menu (like File or Edit) or buttons at the top of an application. Menus can be flexible, though, especially in games, where a menu is often designed in the style of the game and may in many cases cover part of the screen or even the entire screen. As an example, let's see how to define a basic *options* menu screen containing two controls: one for switching hints on or off, and one for controlling the volume of the music. First, you need to draw the elements surrounding these controls. You add a background to the menu and then add a text label to describe the Hints control. You use the SKLabelNode class for that. You define the text that should be drawn and place it at the appropriate position (the following code is taken from the GameWorld class in the PenguinPairs2 example belonging to this chapter):

```
let background = SKSpriteNode(imageNamed: "spr_background_options")
background.zPosition = Layer.Background
self.addChild(background)

let onOffLabel = SKLabelNode(fontNamed: "Helvetica")
onOffLabel.horizontalAlignmentMode = .Right
onOffLabel.verticalAlignmentMode = .Center
onOffLabel.position = CGPoint(x: -50, y: 50)
onOffLabel.fontColor = UIColor(red: 0, green: 0, blue: 0.4, alpha: 1)
onOffLabel.fontSize = 60
onOffLabel.text = "Hints"
self.addChild(onOffLabel)
```

Similarly, you add a text label for the music volume controller. For the complete code, see the PenguinPairs2 example belonging to this chapter.

# Adding an On/off Button

The next step is adding an on/off button that shows a hint (or doesn't) during game play. Later in the chapter, you will see how the value of this button is used. Just as you did for the Button class, you make a special class for on/off buttons, called (not surprisingly) OnOffButton. In the PenguinPairs2 example, this class is a subclass of SKSpriteNode, just like the new Button class. It has two (stored) properties of type SKTexture, each of which represents a texture (image):

```
var onTexture  = SKTexture(imageNamed: "spr_button_on")
var offTexture = SKTexture(imageNamed: "spr_button_off")
```

Depending on the state of the button, a different texture will be selected for the sprite node. The button has two states: *off* and *on* (see also Figure 17-3). The *on* state is chosen when the SKSpriteNode instance is initialized:

```
init() {
    super.init(texture: onTexture, color: UIColor.whiteColor(), size: onTexture.size())
}
```

*Figure 17-3. The two textures used for the on/off button*

An important aspect of the button is that you need to be able to read and set whether it's on or off. Because the button has two possible textures, you can define that the button is in the *off* state if the current texture points to the offTexture property, and that it's in the *on* state if the current texture points to the onTexture property. You can then add a Boolean computed property that gets and sets this value. Here is the definition of that property:

```
var on: Bool {
    get {
        return self.texture == onTexture
    }
    set {
        if newValue {
            self.texture = onTexture
        } else {
            self.texture = offTexture
        }
    }
}
```

Finally, you need to handle taps on the button to toggle its on and off states. Similar to what you did in the Button class, you check in the handleInput method whether the player tapped within the bounding box of the button. Here is the complete handleInput method:

```
override func handleInput(inputHelper: InputHelper) {
    super.handleInput(inputHelper)
    if inputHelper.containsTap(self.box) && !self.hidden {
        self.on = !self.on
    }
}
```

Note that you only toggle the button state if it is visible. In the GameWorld class, you add an OnOffButton instance to the game world, at the desired position:

```
var onOffButton = OnOffButton()
...
onOffButton.position = CGPoint(x: 200, y: 50)
self.addChild(onOffButton)
```

# Defining a Slider Button

Next, you add a second kind of GUI control: a slider. This slider will control the volume of the background music in the game. It consists of two sprites: a back sprite that represents the bar, and a front sprite that represents the actual slider. Therefore, the Slider class inherits from SKNode and contains (among others) two SKSpriteNode properties to represent each sprite. Because the back sprite has a border, you need to take this into account when you move or draw the slider. Therefore, you also define left and right margins that define the border width on the left and right side of the back sprite. The complete list of stored properties is given as follows:

```
var back = SKSpriteNode(imageNamed: "spr_slider_bar")
var front = SKSpriteNode(imageNamed: "spr_slider_button")
let leftMargin = CGFloat(4), rightMargin = CGFloat(7)
var dragging = false
var draggingIndex: Int?
```

As you can see, you also set a Boolean property dragging to false and you add a property draggingIndex that is an optional of type Int. You need these properties to keep track of when the player is dragging the slider and what the touch ID is so you update the slider position when needed, even when the touch location isn't within the boundaries of the back sprite.

# Calculating World Positions of Game Objects

Because you need to track whether the player is touching the slider, you need to calculate the bounding box of a node. If you look at the SKNode extension, you can see that it defines the box property, which was also a part of the original GameObjectNode class. In GameObjectNode, the get part of the box property contained a single line:

```
return self.calculateAccumulatedFrame()
```

This worked fine for the Tut's Tomb game because that game used a very simple hierarchy of nodes. If a hierarchy becomes more complex, a node's local position may be different from its actual position in the world. This is also the case for the slider. In the Slider initializer, the front part of the slider is positioned locally at the left side of the back sprite:

```
front.position = CGPoint(x: leftMargin - back.size.width/2 + front.size.width/2, y: 0)
```

However, the Slider node itself is also placed at a certain position in the scene:

```
musicSlider.position = CGPoint(x: 200, y: -100)
```

As a result, the local position of the slider bar is different from its actual position in the world. This is a problem if you want to check whether or not the player is touching the bar. Touch locations are calculated in the world space. The calculateAccumulatedFrame method returns the bounding box at the local node position. This means that an extra step is required to translate the local position into the world position. The new box property uses the convertPoint method to do this:

```
if parent != nil {
    boundingBox.origin = scene!.convertPoint(boundingBox.origin, fromNode: parent!)
}
```

Note that it only performs the calculation if the node has a parent, because if it hasn't, then its local position is the same as the world position. Since the bounding box is *positioned locally to its parent*, you need to convert the node position from the *parent* node to the *scene* node (which is the node at the root of the game world). For directly accessing the root of the game world, you use the scene property, which is a part of SKNode.

For convenience, let's also add a worldPosition property that calculates the position of the node in world coordinates. Here is the complete property (which also uses the convertPoint method):

```
var worldPosition: CGPoint {
    get {
        if parent != nil {
            return parent!.convertPoint(position, toNode: scene!)
        } else {
            return position
        }
    }
}
```

# Completing the Slider Class

The next step is adding a property value to the Slider class that allows you to retrieve and set the value of the slider. You want a value of 0 to indicate that the slider is fully moved to the left, and a value of 1 to indicate the fully right position of the slider. You can calculate the current value by looking at the position of the *front* sprite, and seeing how much it's moved to the right. Therefore, the following line of code calculates the slider value from the slider position:

```
return (front.position.x - front.size.width/2 - (back.position.x - back.size.width/2) -
    leftMargin) / (back.size.width - front.size.width - leftMargin - rightMargin)
```

In the upper part of the fraction, you calculate how far to the right the front sprite has been moved. You calculate this locally to the back left position plus the left margin. You then divide this by the total length that the slider can move. This `return` instruction forms the get part of the value property. For the `set` part of the property, you need to convert a value between zero and one to the front slider x-position. This amounts to rewriting the previous formula such that the front x-position is the unknown, which is then calculated as follows:

```
front.position.x = newValue * (back.size.width - front.size.width - leftMargin -
    rightMargin) + leftMargin - back.size.width/2 + front.size.width/2
```

Now that you have a way to set and get the slider value, you need to write the code to handle player input. The first step is checking whether the player is currently touching the screen. If that isn't the case, you simply reset the dragging status variables to their initial values, and you're done:

```
if !inputHelper.isTouching {
    dragging = false
    draggingIndex = nil
    return
}
```

If instructions are executed that are written after this `if` instruction, you know the player is touching the screen.

You need to check whether the player is actually touching the button. If that is the case, you assign a new value to the `draggingIndex` variable and set `dragging` to true:

```
if inputHelper.containsTouch(back.box) {
    draggingIndex = inputHelper.getIDInRect(back.box)
    dragging = true

}
```

Then, you check whether the player is currently dragging. If not, you are done and you return from the method:

```
if !dragging {
    return
}
```

The final step is updating the slider position since the player is currently dragging. The first step is unwrapping the dragging index. Then, you retrieve the position where the player is touching the screen:

```
if let draggingUnwrap = draggingIndex {
    let touchPos = inputHelper.getTouch(draggingUnwrap)
    ...
}
```

Next, you calculate what the x-position of the slider should be. Because the touch position is in world coordinates, you subtract the world position of the back sprite from it to get the local position of the slider. This yields the following expression:

```
touchPos.x - back.worldPosition.x
```

You need to do a little more work, though, because you have to make sure the slider can't move outside of its range. You therefore need to clamp the slider position within a certain range. In order to do this, let's add a function that can perform this clamping operation:

```
func clamp(number:CGFloat, min:CGFloat, max:CGFloat) -> CGFloat
{
    if number < min {
        return min
    }
    else if number > max {
        return max
    }
    return number
}
```

Now you use that function to calculate the clamped value of the slider, and you store it as the slider's new x-position:

```
front.position.x = clamp(touchPos.x - back.worldPosition.x,
    leftMargin - back.size.width/2 + front.size.width/2,
    back.size.width/2 - front.size.width/2 - rightMargin)
```

This completes the code to handle the player input. You can then use the value property in that class to change the volume of the music according to the value of the slider (see the updateDelta method of the GameWorld class):

```
backgroundMusic.volume = Float(musicSlider.value)
```

This completes the PenguinPairs2 example. Figure 17-4 shows what it looks like.

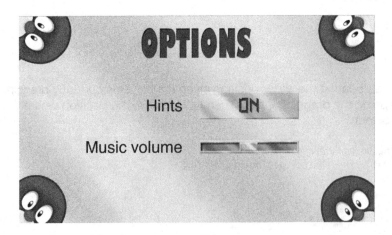

*Figure 17-4. The PenguinPairs2 example*

Most games contain some menu screens. With these screens, the player can set options, choose levels, watch achievements, and pause the game. Creating all these additional screens can be a lot of work that doesn't contribute to the actual game play, so developers tend to put less effort into them. But that is a very wrong decision.

An artist once said, "Your game is as good as its worst screen." If one of the menu screens has poor quality, the player will get the feeling that the game is unfinished and the developer didn't put enough effort into it. So make sure all your menu screens look beautiful, and are easy to use and navigate.

Think carefully about what you put in these screens. You might be tempted to create options for everything: the difficulty of the game, the music to play, the color of the background, and so on. But remember, you're the person who should create the game, not the player. You or your artist should determine what gives the most interesting game play and the most compelling visual style, not the user.

Try to avoid options as much as possible. For example, should a player really set the difficulty? Can't you adapt the difficulty automatically by monitoring the player's progress? And do you really need a level-selection screen? Can't you simply remember where the player was the last time, and immediately continue there? Keep your interface as simple as possible!

# What You Have Learned

In this chapter, you have learned the following:

- How to create a menu with a variety of buttons and sliders

- How to retrieve the values of buttons and sliders, and translate that information into changing game settings such as the background music volume

- How to use class extensions to add functionality to existing third-party classes

# Chapter 18

# Game State Management

Normally, you don't immediately start playing when a game application starts. For example, in the Tut's Tomb game, you see a title screen before playing. More complicated games may have a title screen, a menu for options, menus for selecting different levels, screens to display the high score after finishing a level, a menu to select different characters and attributes, and so on. In Tut's Tomb, adding a title screen wasn't that difficult because the title screen itself had very little interaction. However, when you look at the example in the previous chapter, you can see that building a screen with a few options and controls can result in quite a lot of code. You can imagine that when you add more menus and screens to the game, it's going to be a pain to manage which objects belong to which screen and when they should be drawn or updated.

Generally, these different menus and screens are called *game states*. In some programs, they're called *scenes*, and the object responsible for managing the scenes is the *director*. Sometimes a distinction is made between game *modes* and game *states*. In that case, things like menus, the main playing screen, and so on are game *modes*, whereas "level finished" and "game over" are game *states*.

This book follows a simplified paradigm and calls everything *game states*. To deal with these different game states, you need a *manager*. In this chapter, you develop the main classes needed for such a structure and learn how to use it to display different menus and switch between them while keeping the code cleanly separated.

## Basics of Managing Game States

When you want to deal properly with game states, you need to make sure of the following:

- Game states should be run completely independently. In other words, you don't want to have to deal with the options menu screen or the Game Over screen while you're in the game-playing state.

- There should be an easy way to define game states, find game states, and switch between them. That way, when the player presses the Options button in the title screen, you can easily switch to the options menu state.

In the examples you've seen until now, there was always some kind of game world class. Looking at it from the view of game states, each of these worlds represents a single (playing) game state. You need to define such a class for each different state. The nice thing is that you already have a lot of code in place that helps you do this. The SKNode class is particularly useful because it represents a node possibly containing a whole subtree of game objects, which is a sufficient basis for representing a game state. In the previous games, the classes that represented the game world inherited from the SKNode class. In the remaining examples in this book, the classes that represent a *game state* will also inherit from SKNode. So, if you have an options menu, a title screen, a level-selection screen, and a help menu, you make a separate class for each of these game states. The only thing you still need to provide is a way to manage the various game states in the game. You do this by creating a *game state manager*.

# The Game State Manager

In this section, you create a class called GameStateManager, which you will use to manage the various game states in the Penguin Pairs game. An important design criterion for the game state manager is that it should be easily accessible. Also, there should be only a single game state manager instance that is accessible everywhere. In the Painter and Tut's Tomb game, the game world was easily accessible because it was a class property of the GameScene class. For the game state manager, I'll do something slightly different.

As you gain more experience in writing software, you'll notice that you tend to use similar design solutions for problems. In software engineering, these similar solutions are called *design patterns*. Some of those design patterns are quite well-known and are commonly used in a lot of applications, including games. In this case, the "problem" that you want to solve is that you want a class to have a single instance, which is accessible everywhere. The design pattern that solves this is called the *singleton*. Here is a very simple example of a class using a singleton design pattern:

```
class MyClass {
    static let instance = MyClass()
    var aProperty = 12
}
```

As you can see, the class MyClass contains a class property called instance, which itself is an instance of MyClass. Accessing this single instance is easy, and you use that instance to access the aProperty property:

```
print(MyClass.instance.aProperty) // prints '12' to the console
```

The nice thing about this approach is that it avoids global variables, and the class design itself indicates that there should only ever be a single instance of the class. Let's follow this exact same procedure for the game state manager and define a singleton class called GameStateManager. In the PenguinPairs3 example belonging to this chapter, you can find an implementation of the game state manager as a singleton.

This class is set up in such a way that it allows you to store different game states (that is, different SKNode instances), so you can select what the current game state is, and the manager then adds that node to itself as a child so that the selected node becomes active and visible.

The various game states are stored as nodes in an array, which is a property of the GameStateManager class:

```
var states : [SKNode] = []
```

You also define an additional property to keep track of the currently active game state (which is an instance of SKNode):

```
var currentGameState: SKNode? = nil
```

When the GameStateManager instance is created, there are no game states yet, so there is no currently active game state either. As a result, the currentGameState property is an optional value.

# Assigning Names to Nodes

When you're dealing with different game states and game objects, it is useful if there is some way to identify these states/objects. In the SpriteKit framework, it's possible to assign a name to a node. You can use that name later to look up the node in the scene. For example, this is how you define a node with a name:

```
var someNode = SKNode()
someNode.name = "playingField"
```

The SKNode class has a method called childNodeWithName, which you can use to search for nodes. By default, this method searches the children of the node it is called on until it finds a matching child. It will then stop and return this node. When searching through the nodes, you can use regular expression syntax. Here are a few examples of searches:

```
var node = self.childNodeWithName("playingField") /* searches the children of
    this node for the first node called "playingField" */
node = self.childNodeWithName("playing*") /* searches the children of this node
    for the first node that has a name starting with "playing" */
node = self.childNodeWithName("/playingField") /* searches the children of the
    root node for the first node called "playingField" */
node = self.childNodeWithName("//playingField") /* searches through the entire
    node tree and returns the first node it finds called "playingField" */
```

Using the naming scheme of nodes, you can write a simple get method as a part of the
GameStateManager class that retrieves a game state (SKNode instance), given a name:

```
func get(name: String) -> SKNode? {
    for state in states {
        if state.name == name {
            return state
        }
    }
    return nil
}
```

Selecting the currently active game state is done by calling a method called switchTo. You
have to be careful when switching game states. Once you switch to another game state,
any objects in the current game state can no longer be found (since that game state is no
longer active) Because of this, it is safer to only switch to another game state at the end of
each update cycle. In order to achieve this, the GameStateManager class has a property called
plannedSwitch that optionally contains a game state title that should be switched to. In the
switchTo method, this property is assigned the title passed as a parameter:

```
func switchTo(name: String) {
    plannedSwitch = name
}
```

Now you need to override the updateDelta method in the GameStateManager class to actually
make the switch. The first step in this method is simply calling the updateDelta method of
the superclass to ensure all game objects are properly updated:

```
super.updateDelta(delta)
```

Then, you check whether a switch to another game state is needed. This is the case if the
plannedSwitch property contains a value, and if this value is a valid game state title. If either
of these conditions aren't true, you return from the method:

```
if plannedSwitch == nil || !has(plannedSwitch!) {
    return
}
```

Switching to another game state is then rather straightforward. First, you remove any
children (states) currently active:

```
self.removeAllChildren()
```

Then, you locate the new game state, and add it as a child to the node that the game state
manager represents:

```
currentGameState = get(plannedSwitch!)
self.addChild(currentGameState!)
```

As a last instruction in the updateDelta method, you set the value of the plannedSwitch property to nil again, since the game state switch has been made.

The only thing left to do is to make the game state manager an integral part of the game, so you call its game-loop methods in the update method of the GameScene class:

```
override func update(currentTime: NSTimeInterval) {
    GameStateManager.instance.handleInput(inputHelper)
    GameStateManager.instance.updateDelta(delta)
    inputHelper.reset()
}
```

# Adding States and Switching Between Them

Now that you have your game state manager, you can start adding different states to it. A very basic game state is the title menu state. In the PenguinPairs3 example, you add a class called TitleMenuState to the application that represents this state. The title menu state consists of four game objects: a background and three buttons. You can reuse the Button class that you developed earlier for the Tut's Tomb game. Here is the initializer of the TitleMenuState class:

```
override init() {
    super.init()
    self.name = "title"

    let layout = GridLayout(rows: 3, columns: 1, cellWidth: Int(playButton.size.width),
        cellHeight: Int(playButton.size.height))
    layout.yPadding = 5
    let buttons = SKNode()
    buttons.position.y = -200
    self.addChild(buttons)
    layout.target = buttons

    playButton.zPosition = Layer.Scene
    optionsButton.zPosition = Layer.Scene
    helpButton.zPosition = Layer.Scene
    layout.add(helpButton)
    layout.add(optionsButton)
    layout.add(playButton)

    let background = SKSpriteNode(imageNamed: "spr_background_title")
    background.zPosition = Layer.Background
    self.addChild(background)
}
```

As you can see, the GridLayout class is used here to very easily position the buttons. Because you need to do something when a button is pressed, you have to override the handleInput method. In that method, you check whether each of the buttons is pressed, and if so, you switch to another state. For instance, if the player taps the Play Game button, you need to switch to the level menu:

```
if playButton.tapped {
    GameStateManager.instance.switchTo("level")
}
```

You add similar alternatives for the other two buttons. Now the title menu state is basically done. In the GameScene class, the only thing you need to do is make an instance of TitleMenuState and add it to the game state manager. You do the same thing for all the other states in the game. After that you set the currently active state to be the title menu, so the player sees the title menu when the game starts:

```
GameStateManager.instance.addChild(TitleMenuState())
GameStateManager.instance.addChild(HelpState())
GameStateManager.instance.addChild(OptionsMenuState())
GameStateManager.instance.addChild(LevelMenuState(nrLevels: 12))

// the current game state is the title screen
GameStateManager.instance.switchTo("title")
```

The help and option menu states are set up in a fashion similar to TitleMenuState. In the class initializer, you add your game objects to the game world, and you override the handleInput method to switch between states. For example, both the help and option menu states contain a Back button that returns you to the title screen:

```
if backButton.tapped {
    GameStateManager.instance.switchTo("title")
}
```

Have a look at the HelpState and OptionsMenuState classes in the PenguinPairs3 example to get an idea of how the different states are set up and how you switch between states.

# The Level Menu State

A slightly more complicated game state is the level menu. You want the player to be able to select a level from a grid of level buttons. You want to be able to display three different states with these level buttons because a level can be locked, unlocked but not yet solved by the player, or solved. In order for this to work, you require some sort of persistent storage across game plays, which will be discussed in the next chapter.

Before you can create the LevelMenuState class, you add a class called LevelButton that inherits from Button. In the LevelButton class, you keep track of the level index that the button refers to and whether the level is solved, unsolved, or locked to the player.

Depending on the level status, the button should have a different appearance. Because the button has three different states, you load three textures, one for each state. In summary, here are the stored properties defined in LevelButton:

```
var levelIndex = 0
var locked = SKTexture(imageNamed: "spr_level_locked")
var unsolved = SKTexture(imageNamed: "spr_level_unsolved")
var solved = SKTexture(imageNamed: "spr_level_solved")
```

Later on, you will adapt the LevelButton class to display one of these textures depending on the status of the level. For now, you simply display the unsolved texture when the button is created. Also, you add a text label in the initializer, which is drawn on the belly of the penguin, so the player can see which level each button refers to, like so:

```
let textLabel = SKLabelNode(fontNamed: "Helvetica")
textLabel.position = CGPoint(x: 0, y: -25)
textLabel.fontColor = UIColor(red: 0, green: 0, blue: 0.4, alpha: 1)
textLabel.fontSize = 24
textLabel.text = String(levelIndex)
textLabel.horizontalAlignmentMode = .Center
textLabel.zPosition = Layer.Overlay
self.addChild(textLabel)
```

Finally, in the handleInput method, you check whether the button has been tapped. If the player has tapped the level button, and the level is not locked, the game should switch to the respective level. Let's assume that a level with index *x* has the name "levelx". Also, when the player switches to a level, you may want to reset that level so that the player can start immediately from the beginning. In summary, here is the complete handleInput method:

```
override func handleInput(inputHelper: InputHelper) {
    super.handleInput(inputHelper)
    if self.texture == locked {
        return
    }
    if tapped {
        GameStateManager.instance.switchTo("level\(levelIndex)")
        GameStateManager.instance.reset()
    }
}
```

Note that in the PenguinPairs3 example, this method is actually commented out, since there are no level states yet.

As you can see, adding different states to a game and switching between them isn't very hard, as long as you think about the design of the software beforehand. By thinking in advance about which classes are needed and how the functionality of your game should be split up between them, you can save yourself a lot of time later. In the next chapter, you further extend this example by creating the actual levels. Figure 18-1 shows a screenshot of the level menu state.

*Figure 18-1.* *The level menu screen in Penguin Pairs*

# What You Have Learned

In this chapter, you have learned the following:

- What design patterns are and what the singleton pattern offers
- How to define different game states using a game state manager
- How to switch between game states depending on the player's actions

# Chapter 19

# Storing and Recalling Game Data

Many games consist of different levels. Casual games such as puzzles and maze games may have several hundreds of levels. Until now, your games have relied on randomness to keep the gameplay interesting. Although randomness is a powerful tool to achieve replayability, in a lot of cases game designers want more control over how a game progresses. This control is generally achieved by designing *levels*. Each level is its own game world in which the player has to achieve some sort of objective.

With the tools you've used until now, for each level in a game you write a specific class in which you fill that specific level with game objects and add the behavior you want. This approach has a few disadvantages. The most important disadvantage is that you're mixing the *game logic* (gameplay, win condition, and so on) with the *game content*. This means every time you want to add another level to the game, you have to write a new class, which leads to a lot of extra time spent on development. Furthermore, if a game designer wants to add a level to a game that you built, the designer needs in-depth knowledge of how your code works. And any mistake the designer makes in writing the code will result in bugs or crashes in your game.

A much better approach is to store level information separately from the actual game code. While the game is loading, this level information is retrieved. Ideally, the information needs to be stored in a simple format that non-programmers can understand and work with. That way, levels can be designed by someone without that person having to know how the game converts the data into playable game levels. The most convenient way to store the level information is in a text format. You can use text very easily to describe a level. Have a look at the following example:

```
RHBQKBHR
PPPPPPPP
........
........
........
........
pppppppp
rhbqkbhr
```

This text data describes the starting position in the Chess game, where each character represents a chess piece (lowercase for white pieces and uppercase for black pieces). If you create a chess game that reads such a description from a file, you can very easily modify the file to allow for different starting points. For example, you could let a designer create a number of different classic chess situations taken from actual games between chess masters. You wouldn't have to make any changes to your game code. You could even decide to create a superchess game and make the board bigger, by adding columns and rows (assuming that the code loading the game data supports this). All this can be done without knowing how the Chess game actually works. Because it is simple text, the format is relatively easy to understand, even for someone with little or no programming experience. You can adopt this technique to create various levels for your game without any code modification. This is especially useful for bigger games, which generally will also have a bigger team of people involved. By separating out level design from code writing, you allow non-programmers who excel at tasks such as game design and graphics design to help you more effectively create awesome games.

You will deal with the different levels in Penguin Pairs in a similar fashion. In this chapter, you will see how to build such a level-loading scheme into your games. Another thing you will look at is storing and recalling the state of the different game over sessions. Games such as Painter and Tut's Tomb don't retain any information from previous times when the player played the game, which in those games doesn't really matter. In the case of Penguin Pairs, it does matter because you don't want the player to have to start all over every time the game is launched. If the player finishes a level, the app should remember it the next time the player launches the game, so the player can continue where they left off.

# Structure of a Level

Let's first look at what kind of things can be in a level in the Penguin Pairs game. First, there is some kind of background image. Let's assume that this background is fixed when you load the level, so there is no need to store any information about it in the text file.

In the level are a number of different animals, such as penguins, seals, and sharks. There are also icebergs, background blocks that penguins can move on, and a few more things. You want to store all this information in the level file. One possibility is to store every object's position and type, but that would make the variable complicated. Another possibility is to divide the level into small blocks, also called *tiles*. Every block has a certain type (this could be a penguin, a playing field tile, a transparent tile, a seal, and so on). A tile can be represented by a single character, and you can store the structure of the level in a text file just like in the Chess example:

```
#.......#
#...r...#
#.......#
#.      .#
#.      .#
#.      .#
#.......#
#...r...#
#.......#
```

In this level definition, a number of different blocks are defined. An iceberg (wall) tile is defined by the # sign, a penguin by an r character, a background tile by a . character, and an empty tile by a space character. Later on in this chapter, you will write a method that uses this information to create the various tiles and store them somewhere (probably in an SKNode instance).

In addition to the tiles, you need to store a few other things for each level:

- A level title
- A hint for the level
- The number of pairs to be made
- The width and height of the level (needed for file reading purposes)
- The location and direction of the hint arrow

So, you can define a complete level in a text file as follows:

```
Splash!
Don't let the penguins fall in the water!
1
9 9
3 7 1
#.......#
#...r...#
#.......#
#.     .#
#.     .#
#.     .#
#.......#
#...r...#
#.......#
```

For every level, you add similar lines of text to the text file. If you open the file levels.txt part of the PenguinPairs4 example, you'll see that it contains a number of different levels. The very first line in the text file indicates how many levels are defined in the text file (in the case of Penguin Pairs: 12).

# Reading Data From Files

Now that the Penguin Pairs levels have been defined in a text file, you need to write the code that actually reads this text file. Reading a text file in Swift is rather straightforward. It basically consists of two steps: first you need to define which file needs to be read, and then you can use the String type, which has an initializer that reads the contents of a file. For example, the following two lines read the levels.txt file:

```
let filePath = NSBundle.mainBundle().pathForResource("levels", ofType:"txt")
let data = try! String(contentsOfFile: filePath!, encoding: NSUTF8StringEncoding)
```

After reading the file in this way, you end up with a string containing the entire text file. It's useful to split this string into multiple strings, where each string is a single line in the text file. You can use the method componentsSeparatedByString for that, which divides a string into multiple substrings stored in an array (note the use of the newline character as a separator):

```
let multipleStrings = data.componentsSeparatedByString("\n")
```

Before continuing to use the file data to read in the Penguin Pairs levels, let's design a simple class to make file reading even easier. In the PenguinPairs4 example, you'll find the FileReader class, which reads a file and provides a means of simple access. In the initializer, a file passed as a parameter is read, and its data is stored in an array of strings. So now you can read a file simply by creating a FileReader instance. For example, in the GameScene class, this is how you read the level data:

```
let levels = FileReader(filename: "levels")
```

The next step is accessing the file data. You can do that directly by accessing the array of strings part of the FileReader instance. Another way to do this is by using an *iterator design*. Basically, this means that the FileReader instance keeps track of which part of the data you retrieved while it iterates through the file data. Note the addition of the property named it to the FileReader class to keep track of where in the string array you are reading:

```
var it = -1
```

Next, define a method called nextLine, which increments the it property and returns the next line. Here is the complete method:

```
func nextLine() -> String {
    if (it >= fileData.count - 1) {
        return ""
    } else {
        it++
        return fileData[it]
    }
}
```

So, every time you want to read the next line in the file, you simply call the nextLine method to retrieve it. Note that the interesting bit in the method is happening in these two lines:

```
it++
return fileData[it]
```

First, you increment the iterator, and then you return the element in the array that the iterator corresponds to. There is a neat trick you can apply to condense these two lines of code into a single one. It hinges on the fact that the ++ postfix operator returns a result. In other words, you could do something like this:

```
var result = it++
```

The result variable will now contain the *old* value of it. In other words, if it had the value 3, then after this instruction, result would contain the value 3 (it's old value) and it would contain the value 4. You can also do this:

```
var anotherResult = ++it
```

In this case, anotherResult will contain the *new* value of it (after it has been incremented) since you used the prefix ++ operator. So if it was 3, after this instruction both it and anotherResult will contain the value 4. To go back to the file reading example, this means that you can replace the two lines in the nextLine method with the following single line:

```
return fileData[++it]
```

Every time you need to read a line from the file, you can use the nextLine method. For example, right after loading the file in the GameScene class, you retrieve the first line of the file in order to obtain the number of levels:

```
let nrLevels = levels.nextLine().toInt()!
```

You then use a for loop to create a state for each level:

```
for i in 1...nrLevels {
    GameStateManager.instance.addChild(LevelState(fileReader: levels, levelNr: i))
}
```

As you can see, you pass along the FileReader instance to the LevelState initializer, so that each level state can retrieve its own level data (more about that later).

# The Tile Class

Before looking into creating the actual levels, let's first do a bit of preparation and write a basic Tile class. This class is a subclass of the SKSpriteNode class. For now, you don't consider more complicated items in the level such as penguins, seals, and sharks. You only look at background (transparent) tiles, normal tiles, and wall (iceberg) tiles. Let's introduce an enumerated type to represent these different varieties of tiles:

```
enum TileType {
    case Wall
    case Background
    case Normal
}
```

The Tile class is a basic subclass of SKSpriteNode. It simply adds a property that represents the type of tile:

```
private var tileTipe: TileType = .Background
```

To accommodate transparent tiles, you provide a convenience initializer that loads a wall sprite image, and sets the node to hidden:

```
convenience init() {
    self.init(imageNamed: "spr_wall", type: .Background)
    self.hidden = true
}
```

When you load the level, you create a tile for each character and store it in a grid structure using the GridLayout class.

# The Level State

In the previous chapter, you saw how to create multiple game states such as a title screen, a level-choice menu, and an options menu. In this section, you add several *level states*. Each level state is a subclass of SKNode and adds its own game objects to the world. The LevelState initializer expects a FileReader instance (in order to read level data), as well as the level number belonging to the level. Here is part of the LevelState initializer:

```
init(fileReader: FileReader, levelNr : Int) {
    super.init()
    self.levelNr = levelNr
    self.name = "level\(levelNr)"

    // to do: fill this level with game objects according to the level data
}
```

As you can see, each level gets assigned a unique name. Level 1 is called "level1", level 2 is called "level2", and so on. You also need to keep track of animals such as the penguins, seals, and sharks. You do this in a separate node stored as a property of LevelState so you can look animals up quickly later.

```
var animals = SKNode()
```

Now you can start creating game objects to fill the game world. First, you add a background image to the game world:

```
let background = SKSpriteNode(imageNamed: "spr_background_level")
background.zPosition = Layer.Background
self.addChild(background)
```

Next to this, you also add the various buttons (quit, retry, and hint) that are a part of the level. Check the LevelState.swift file part of the PenguinPairs4 example to see the code.

After adding a background and buttons, you can start reading the data stored in the text file. The first step is reading the level title, help information, the number of required pairs, the level size, and hint information, and then storing all these in local variables, to be used later on to construct the game world:

```
let title = fileReader.nextLine()
let help = fileReader.nextLine()
let nrPairs = fileReader.nextLine().toInt()!
let sizeArr = fileReader.nextLine().componentsSeparatedByString(" ")
let width = sizeArr[0].toInt()!, height = sizeArr[1].toInt()!
let hintArr = fileReader.nextLine().componentsSeparatedByString(" ")
```

The next step is actually creating the field of tiles. For this, define a class called `TileField`, which is a subclass of `SKNode` but it adds a grid layout. Furthermore, it also has a method `getTileType`, which returns the type of a tile at a certain location in the grid. Later, this method is going to be useful for checking if a penguin has fallen off the playing field, for example. Here is the complete class:

```
class TileField : SKNode {

    var layout: GridLayout

    init(rows: Int, columns: Int, cellWidth: Int, cellHeight: Int) {
        layout = GridLayout(rows: rows, columns: columns,
            cellWidth: cellWidth, cellHeight: cellHeight)
        super.init()
        layout.target = self
    }

    required init?(coder aDecoder: NSCoder) {
        fatalError("init(coder:) has not been implemented")
    }

    func getTileType(col: Int, row: Int) -> TileType {
        if let obj = layout.at(col, row: row) as? Tile {
            return obj.type
        }
        return .Background
    }
}
```

In the `LevelState` initializer, you create the `TileField` instance, with the appropriate height, width, and cell size:

```
let tileDimension = 75
var tileField = TileField(rows: height, columns: width,
    cellWidth: tileDimension, cellHeight: tileDimension)
tileField.name = "level\(levelNr)_tileField"
self.addChild(tileField)
```

Now you can start retrieving actual level data from the text file. The next step is reading all the remaining lines pertaining to this level and storing them in an array so you can iterate through the array later on:

```
var lines: [String] = []
for i in 0..<height {
    var newLine = fileReader.nextLine()
    while count(newLine) < width {
        newLine += " "
    }
    lines.append(newLine)
}
```

As you can see, there is an additional while loop that adds space characters to the line you just read. This is done to avoid problems due to level lines not being the same width. Consider the following level definition:

```
 .
r.r
 .
```

This is a very simple level with two penguins. The width of the level is three cells. However, in the first and last line of the level definition, the level only has two cells defined (first a space, and then a dot), due to the layout of the level. You could ask your level designer to add enough spaces to the text file to make sure all lines are of equal width, but that is risky. The level designer might forget to do it, and it's easily addressed in the code itself using the while loop. This is a good example of why you sometimes need to write extra code to make things more robust. By adding the while loop, you save the level designer a lot of headaches; it makes designing levels a much more stable experience.

Now that you have all the level data stored in an array of strings, you use another for loop to go through each of the lines and create all the tiles:

```
for i in 0..<height {
    var currLine = lines[height-1-i]
    var j = 0
    for c in currLine {
        j++
        // create the tile at row i and column j
    }
}
```

Note that you start with the last line in the array. This is because the grid is filled from bottom to top (following the direction of the y axis). Depending on the character you are currently handling, you need to create different kinds of game objects and add them to the tile field. You could use an if instruction for that:

```
if c == "." {
    // create an empty tile
} else if c == " " {
    // create a background tile
```

```
} else if c == "r" {
    // create a penguin tile
} else {
    // do something else
}
```

In principle, this code would work. But you have to write the condition again and again. There is another option that allows you to write this in a slightly cleaner way. Swift offers a special kind of instruction for handling cases: switch.

> **Note** When defining levels in a text-based format, you have to decide what kind of object each character represents. These decisions influence the work of both level designers, who have to enter the characters in the level data files, and developers, who have to write the code to interpret that level data. This shows how important documentation is, even during active development. A "cheat sheet" is nice to have so that when you write this code, you don't have to remember all the ideas you had for level design. A cheat sheet is also useful if you work with a designer, to make sure you're both on the same page.

## Using `switch` to Handle Alternatives

The switch instruction allows you to specify alternatives, and the instructions that should be executed for each alternative. For example, the previous if instruction with multiple alternatives can be rewritten as a switch instruction as follows:

```
switch c {
    case ".": // create an empty tile
    case " ": // create a background tile
    case "r": // create a penguin tile
    default: // do something else
}
```

The switch instruction has a few handy features that make it very useful for handling different alternatives. Have a look at the following code example:

```
if x == 1 {
    one()
} else if x == 2 {
    two()
    alsoTwo()
} else if x == 3 || x == 4 {
    threeOrFour()
} else {
    more()
}
```

You can rewrite this with a `switch` instruction as follows:

```
switch x {
    case 1:
        one()
    case 2:
        two()
        alsoTwo()
    case 3, 4:
        threeOrFour()
    default:
        more()
}
```

When a `switch` instruction is executed, the expression after the switch keyword is evaluated. Then the instructions after the word `case` and the particular value are executed. If there is no case that corresponds to the value, the instructions after the `default` keyword are executed. The values behind the different cases need to be constant values (numbers, strings between double quotes, or variables declared as constant). As you can see, a case can represent multiple values; in the example, 3 and 4 fall under the same case. For each case, multiple instructions may be executed (see for example, case 2).

An important detail is that a `switch` instruction must be *exhaustive*, in order words: all cases need to be handled. This is most easily solved by using a *default* case, as you can see in the example above. The default case is what happens when neither of the explicit cases in the `switch` instruction occur. Figure 19-1 shows a diagram of a `switch` instruction.

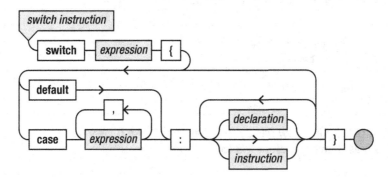

**Figure 19-1.** *Syntax diagram for the `switch` instruction*

# Loading Different Kinds of Tiles

You can use the `switch` instruction to load all the different tiles and game objects. For each character in the level data, you need to perform a different task. For example, when the character "." is read, you need to create a normal playing-field tile. The following instructions do that:

```
let tileSprite = "spr_field_\((i + j) % 2)"
var tile = Tile(imageNamed: tileSprite, type: .Normal)
tile.zPosition = Layer.Scene
tileField.layout.add(tile)
```

The sprite used for the tile is alternatively `spr_field_0.png` or `spr_field_1.png`. By switching the sprite using the formula $(i + j) \% 2$, you get an alternating checkerboard pattern, as you can see by running the PenguinPairs4 program belonging to this chapter. Another example is adding a transparent background tile:

```
var tile = Tile()
tile.zPosition = Layer.Scene
tileField.layout.add(tile)
```

When you have to place n animal, two things need to be done:

- Place a normal tile.
- Place the animal.

Because animals sometimes need to move around on the playing board and you need to interact with them, you create a class called `Animal` to represent an animal such as a penguin, a seal, or a shark. Later in this section, you see what this class looks like. In the `switch` instruction, you then create a normal tile and a penguin, as follows:

```
let tileSprite = "spr_field_\((i + j) % 2)"
var tile = Tile(imageNamed: tileSprite, type: .Normal)
tile.zPosition = Layer.Scene
tileField.layout.add(tile)
var p = Animal(type: String(c))
p.position = tile.position
p.initialPosition = tile.position
p.zPosition = Layer.Scene1
animals.addChild(p)
```

The first step is creating a regular tile and adding it to the tile field. Then you create the `Animal` instance. The `Animal` initializer gets the current character as a parameter, so that you can load the correct sprite in the `Animal` initializer. After creating the `Animal` object, you set its position to the position of the tile you created so it's placed correctly. You also set a property called `initialPosition` to that same value. You do this so that if the player gets stuck and presses the Retry button, you know the original position of each animal in the level.

In the `Animal` initializer, you pass the character along as a parameter. There are a few different kinds of animals. Depending on the kind of animal, you need to do different things in the initializer. One particular type of animal is the boxed animal. This represents an animal locked in a hole in the ice. Boxed animals cannot be moved by the player. In the level description, a boxed animal is represented by an uppercase character. You check whether the character is in uppercase, and store that information as a Boolean value in the property boxed, belonging to the Animal class:

```
boxed = type.uppercaseString == type
```

Then you write a few instructions to convert the type of animal into the sprite name:

```
var spriteName = "spr_animal_\(type)"
if boxed && type != "@" {
    spriteName = "spr_animal_boxed_\(type.lowercaseString)"
}
```

If the animal is in a box, or it is an empty box (represented by the "@" character), you use another sprite name. To complete the Animal class, you add a few convenient methods to check whether you're dealing with a special case such as a multicolored penguin, an empty box, a seal, or a shark. Multicolored penguins can pair with any other colored penguin, an empty boxed in a level can be used to move a penguin into, a seal can be moved around but never makes a pair, and a shark eats anything that comes into its path. For the complete Animal class, see the example PenguinPairs4 program belonging to this chapter.

Now that you've dealt with all these different cases in the switch instruction, you can load each level. Have a look at the LevelState class in the example to see the complete level-creation process. Figure 19-2 shows a screenshot of one of the levels after it's been loaded.

*Figure 19-2. One of the levels in the Penguin Pairs game*

# Maintaining the Player's Progress

To complete this chapter, this section shows you a nice way to keep track of the player's progress over different playing sessions. You want the game to remember where the player was when they last played the game. There are several ways to do this. One way is to let the player do this job and simply open all the levels to the player by default. This is a solution, but it doesn't really motivate the player to solve each level in sequence. Another way is to use a text file in which you store the player status. The third option is to use so-called *user defaults*. This is a feature that allows you to keep track of settings and preferences of players of your game with very little effort. You retrieve the current set of user defaults by writing a single line of code:

```
var defaults = NSUserDefaults.standardUserDefaults()
```

The defaults variable acts as a kind of dictionary, in which you can store key-value pairs that retain their value over different playing sessions. For example, you can store whether the player wants to see hints in Penguin Pairs by storing a Boolean value in the defaults variable:

```
defaults.setBool(true, forKey: "hints")
```

Similarly, reading data from the user defaults is also very straightforward:

```
let showHints = defaults.boolForKey("hints")
```

When a player starts the Penguin Pairs game for the first time, of course there is no default information present yet pertaining to the game. In that case, you need to fill the defaults variable with the "default defaults." In the case of Penguin Pairs, this means hints are on, background music is played at a volume of 0.5, and all levels are locked, except for the first level, which has the status "unsolved." This data can be stored again in a text file, and read the first time a player starts the Penguin Pairs app.

In order to do something slightly different, you are not going to read this data from a regular text file, but from a Property List file (plist). This is a very handy text-based file format. Behind the scenes, it uses XML to structure text, but the Xcode environment has a very useful tool that allows you to edit these files very easily. If you click the defaults.plist file in the PenguinPairs4 project, you will see an editor screen (see Figure 19-3). In this editor screen, you can change the content of the defaults file. You can add items to the list, or remove them.

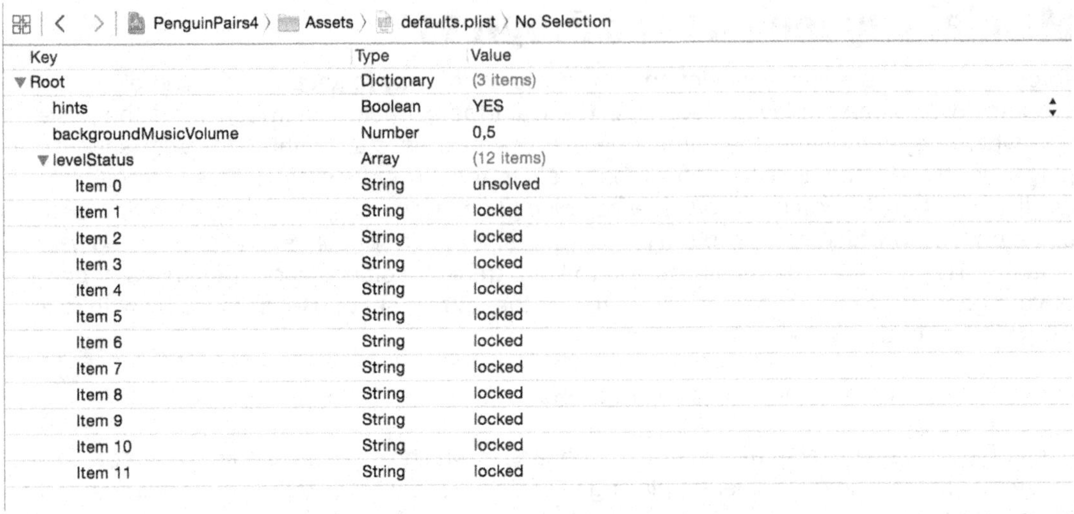

| Key | Type | Value |
| --- | --- | --- |
| ▼ Root | Dictionary | (3 items) |
| hints | Boolean | YES |
| backgroundMusicVolume | Number | 0,5 |
| ▼ levelStatus | Array | (12 items) |
| Item 0 | String | unsolved |
| Item 1 | String | locked |
| Item 2 | String | locked |
| Item 3 | String | locked |
| Item 4 | String | locked |
| Item 5 | String | locked |
| Item 6 | String | locked |
| Item 7 | String | locked |
| Item 8 | String | locked |
| Item 9 | String | locked |
| Item 10 | String | locked |
| Item 11 | String | locked |

*Figure 19-3. A screenshot of the property list editing environment in Xcode*

Reading data from a property list file is quite straightforward. You can read the file and store its content in a dictionary with only a few lines of code:

```
var filePath = NSBundle.mainBundle().pathForResource("defaults", ofType:"plist")
let defaultPreferences = NSDictionary(contentsOfFile: filePath!)!
```

Now you can go through all the items in the dictionary and add them to the user defaults, using a for loop as follows:

```
for (key, value) in defaultPreferences {
    defaults.setObject(value, forKey: key as! String)
}
```

In order to deal with the user defaults neatly, the PenguinPairs4 example has a class DefaultsManager. This class implements the singleton design pattern, just like the game state manager. It allows you to easily read and write the user preferences. For example, in the options menu state, the user preference for the background music volume is retrieved and the slider is set to the corresponding value:

```
musicSlider.value = CGFloat(DefaultsManager.instance.musicVolume)
```

Take a look at the PenguinPairs4 example yourself to see how it deals with default values and preferences.

| THE CURSE OF SAVED GAMES |
| --- |

Most games contain a mechanism that lets the player save their progress. This is normally used in one of three ways: to continue playing later, to return to a previous save point when the player fails later in the game, or to exploit alternative strategies or storylines. These possibilities all sound reasonable, but they also introduce problems; when you design a game, you must carefully consider when (and how) to allow the player to save and load the game state.

For example, in older first-person shooters, all enemies were at fixed locations in the game world. A common strategy among players became to save a game, run into a room to see where the enemies were (which led to instant death), load the saved game, and, armed with the information about the location of the enemies, carefully clean out the room. This made the game a lot easier to play, but it was definitely not the intention of the creators. This can be partially remedied by making it difficult to save a game or to load a saved game. Other games only allow saves at particular save points. Some even make reaching a save point part of the challenge. But this can lead to frustration because the player may have to replay sections of the game over and over if there is one very difficult spot. The most interesting games are the ones where you never have to return to save points because you never really fail, but this is extremely difficult to design.

So think carefully about your saving mechanism. When will you allow saves? How many different saves will you allow? How does saving work in the game? How does the player load a saved game? Does it cost the player something to save or load a game? All of these decisions will influence the gameplay and player satisfaction.

# What You Have Learned

In this chapter, you have learned the following:

- How to create a tile-based game world by reading data from a text file
- How to use the `switch` instruction to handle different cases
- How to retrieve and store level-status data with user defaults

# Chapter 20

# Interaction Between Game Objects

In this chapter, you are going to program the main gameplay for the Penguin Pairs game. You will learn how to move penguins around on the board and what to do when a penguin collides with another game object, such as a shark or another penguin.

## Defining Operators

Since you will be dealing with moving and colliding penguins, you will be doing quite a lot of calculations with two-dimensional points and vectors (represented by CGPoint instances). At the moment, computing things with these points is a bit of a hassle. For example, in the LevelState class, this is how you have to position the Quit button:

```
quitButton.position = GameScreen.instance.topRight
quitButton.position.x -= quitButton.center.x + 10
quitButton.position.y -= quitButton.center.y + 10
```

It would be much easier if you could do something like this:

```
quitButton.position = GameScreen.instance.topRight - quitButton.center -
    CGPoint(x: 10, y: 10)
```

Unfortunately, it's not defined in Swift what the minus operator does with two CGPoint instances. Fortunately, it is very easy to define what the minus operator should do because Swift simply lets you write a function to define that behavior:

```
func - (left: CGPoint, right: CGPoint) -> CGPoint {
    return CGPoint(x: left.x - right.x, y: left.y - right.y)
}
```

As you can see, the minus operator creates a new CGPoint instance and returns it. Now that this function is defined, you can subtract CGPoint instances. Easy, isn't it? You can also define other operators, such as the == operator, which compares two CGPoint instances and returns true if they are the same point:

```
func == (left: CGPoint, right: CGPoint) -> Bool {
    return (left.x == right.x) && (left.y == right.y)
}
```

Take a look at the Math.swift file to see a bunch of these operators defined in order to make computing things with CGPoint instances a lot easier.

# Selecting Penguins

Before you can move penguins around, you need to be able to *select* a penguin. When you tap an animal such as a penguin or a seal, four arrows should appear that allow you to control the direction in which the animal should move. To display these arrows and handle the input, you can add a class called AnimalSelector. The animal selector contains four arrows, and it inherits from the SKNode class. When you tap on a penguin, the animal selector appears, consisting of four arrows, each pointing in a different direction (see Figure 20-1).

*Figure 20-1. The animal selector arrows that appear around a penguin after tapping it*

Each of the four arrows is an instance of the Button class. The initializer of the AnimalSelector class expects a spacing parameter that controls how far away each arrow is placed from the location of the animal that is selected. If you choose a value of 75 for the spacing, then each arrow is placed nicely on the grid, since the grid cell width and height is 75 points.

Because the selector controls a particular animal, you also have to keep track of which one it controls. Therefore, you also add a property named selectedAnimal to the AnimalSelector class, which contains a reference to the target animal. In the initializer, you position the four arrows according to the value of spacing. Initially, you assume that no animal is selected yet, so the animal selector is hidden. The following is the complete AnimalSelector initializer:

```
init(spacing: Int) {
    super.init()
    arrowRight.position = CGPoint(x: spacing, y: 0)
    arrowUp.position = CGPoint(x: 0, y: spacing)
    arrowLeft.position = CGPoint(x: -spacing, y: 0)
    arrowDown.position = CGPoint(x: 0, y: -spacing)
    self.addChild(arrowRight)
    self.addChild(arrowUp)
    self.addChild(arrowLeft)
    self.addChild(arrowDown)
    self.hidden = true
}
```

In the handleInput method, you first check whether the selector is visible. If not, it doesn't need to handle input:

```
if hidden {
    return
}
```

You then check whether one of the arrows was tapped. If so, you calculate the desired animal velocity:

```
super.handleInput(inputHelper)
var animalVelocity = CGPoint.zeroPoint
if arrowRight.tapped {
    animalVelocity.x = 1
} else if arrowLeft.tapped {
    animalVelocity.x = -1
} else if arrowUp.tapped {
    animalVelocity.y = 1
} else if arrowDown.tapped {
    animalVelocity.y = -1
}
animalVelocity *= 500
```

Note the use of the custom operator and how it is defined for multiplying a point by a constant. Once you calculated the desired animal velocity, you assign it to the velocity property of the selected animal:

```
selectedAnimal?.velocity = animalVelocity
```

Finally, if the player has tapped anywhere but on the selected animal (for example, on another penguin or in another part of the screen), you hide the animal selector again and set the selectedAnimal property to nil:

```
if inputHelper.hasTapped && !inputHelper.containsTap(selectedAnimal!.box) {
    self.hidden = true
    selectedAnimal = nil
}
```

In the handleInput method in the Animal class, you have to handle tapping an animal. However, there are some situations when you don't have to handle this, such as the following:

- The animal isn't visible.
- The animal is in a hole in the ice.
- The animal is a shark.
- The animal is already moving.

In all these cases, you don't do anything, and you return from the method:

```
if hidden || boxed || isShark || velocity != CGPoint.zeroPoint {
    return
}
```

If the player didn't tap on the animal, you can also return from the method. Therefore, you add the following if instruction that verifies this:

```
if !inputHelper.containsTap(box) {
    return
}
```

Now that you know the player has tapped on the animal, you should assign the animal selector to it. The first step is finding the animal selector game object:

```
if let animalSelector = childNodeWithName("//animalSelector") as? AnimalSelector {
    // do something
}
```

The expression passed to the childNodeWithName method consists of the regular expression part (//) that tells the method to search in the entire tree, and the name of the animal selector objects. Once you've found the animal selector, you can make the selector visible, set its position, and assign the animal as the selector's target animal. However, you only do this if the player has not tapped on the animal selector or if it is hidden. If the player tapped on the selector, then you first want to handle that tap, so you don't move the selector to another animal. This leads to the following instructions:

```
if !inputHelper.containsTap(animalSelector.box) || animalSelector.hidden {
    animalSelector.position = self.position
    animalSelector.hidden = false
    animalSelector.selectedAnimal = self
}
```

As you can see, properly handling user input can be complicated sometimes. You need to take care of all possible actions that a player can take and handle the input appropriately. If you don't do this right, you risk introducing bugs in the game that can lead to a crash (which is bad) or to a possibility for the player to cheat (which is even worse, especially in online multiplayer games).

The instructions you just wrote allow the player to select animals at will and tell them to move in a particular direction. Now you need to handle the interaction between the animal, the playing field, and other game objects.

# Updating Animals

Interaction between animals and other game objects is done in the updateDelta method of the Animal class. The main reason for doing this in the Animal class is that then each animal handles its own interaction. If you add multiple animals to the game (as you're doing here), you don't have to change anything in the code that handles the interaction. By default, you call the updateDelta method of the superclass. Although technically not necessary, it is a good idea to still do this. If in the future you decide to add other nodes to an Animal node, then you have avoided a potential updating bug. Then, you calculate the new position of the animal by adding the velocity multiplied by the time passed (using the new CGPoint operator extensions!). You don't have to do anything else if the animal isn't visible or if its velocity is zero. Therefore, the first instructions in the updateDelta method are

```
super.updateDelta(delta)
position += velocity * CGFloat(delta)
if hidden || velocity == CGPoint.zeroPoint {
    return
}
```

Now you have to check whether the animal collides with another game object. Because of the check you do at the start of the updateDelta method, you only do this for animals that are both visible and moving.

If the animal is moving, you need to know what tile it's currently moving into. Then you can check what kind of tile it is and whether other game objects are located at that tile. For this, you add a property called currentBlock to the Animal class. In order to calculate the tile the animal is moving into, you calculate the edge of the box surrounding the animal. If the animal is moving left, you take the left edge. If it is moving down, you take the bottom edge. The following code contains the complete header and body of the currentBlock property:

```
var currentBlock: (Int, Int) {
    get {
        var p = CGPoint()
        if let tileField = childNodeWithName("//tileField") as? TileField {
            var edgepos = position
            if velocity.x > 0 {
                edgepos.x += CGFloat(tileField.layout.cellWidth) / 2
            } else if velocity.x < 0 {
                edgepos.x -= CGFloat(tileField.layout.cellWidth) / 2
            } else if velocity.y > 0 {
                edgepos.y += CGFloat(tileField.layout.cellHeight) / 2
            } else if velocity.y < 0 {
                edgepos.y -= CGFloat(tileField.layout.cellHeight) / 2
            }
```

```
            return tileField.layout.gridLocation(edgepos)
        }
        return (-1, -1)
    }
}
```

The next step is finding out what kind of tile the animal is moving into. To do that, you use the getTileType method from the `TileField` class. This method retrieves the type of tile for a given tile position. Here is the complete method:

```
func getTileType(col: Int, row: Int) -> TileType {
    if let obj = layout.at(col, row: row) as? Tile {
        return obj.type
    }
    return .Background
}
```

Now you can go back to the updateDelta method in the `Animal` class and check whether the animal has fallen off the tile field. If so, you hide the animal and you set its velocity to zero to ensure that the animal doesn't keep moving indefinitely while it's hidden:

```
let tileField = childNodeWithName("//tileField") as! TileField
let (targetcol, targetrow) = currentBlock

if tileField.getTileType(targetcol, row: targetrow) == .Background {
    self.hidden = true
    self.velocity = CGPoint.zeroPoint
}
```

Another possibility is that the animal ran into a wall tile. If that is the case, it has to stop moving:

```
else if tileField.getTileType(targetcol, row: targetrow) == .Wall {
    self.stopMoving()
}
```

Stopping moving isn't as easy as it sounds. You could simply set the animal's velocity to zero, but then the animal would be partly in another tile. You need to place the animal at the tile *it just moved out of*. The method stopMoving accomplishes exactly that. In this method, you first have to calculate the position of the old tile. You can do that by starting from the *x* and *y* indices of the tile the animal is currently moving into. These are passed along as a parameter. For example, if the animal's velocity is the vector *(500, 0)* (moving to the right), you need to subtract 1 from the *x* index to get the *x* index of the tile the animal is moving out of. If the animal's velocity is *(0, -500)* (moving up), then you need to *add* 1 to the *y* index to get the *y* index of the tile the animal is moving out of. You can achieve this by *normalizing the velocity vector* and subtracting it from the *x* and *y* indices. This works because normalizing a vector results in a vector of length 1 (unit length). Because an animal is only allowed to move in either the *x* or *y* direction and not diagonally, you end up with a vector *(1, 0)* in the first example and *(0, -1)* in the second example. So you set the position of the animal to the position of the tile it just moved out of, as follows:

```
let tileField = childNodeWithName("//tileField") as! TileField
velocity = CGPoint.normalize(velocity)
let (currcol, currrow) = currentBlock
position = tileField.layout.toPosition(currcol  - Int(velocity.x),
    row: currrow - Int(velocity.y))
```

Finally, you set the animal's velocity to zero so it stays in its new position:

```
velocity = CGPoint.zeroPoint
```

# Meeting Other Game Objects

You still need to check whether the animal collides with another game object, such as another penguin or a shark. There are a few special types of animals:

- Multicolored penguins
- Empty boxes
- Seals
- Sharks

You can add a few methods to the `Animal` class to determine whether you're dealing with these special cases. For example, you're dealing with a seal if the type is "s":

```
var isSeal: Bool {
    get {
        return type == "s" && !boxed
    }
}
```

And you're dealing with an empty box if the type is "@" and it is boxed:

```
var isEmptyBox: Bool {
    get {
        return type == "@" && boxed
    }
}
```

The Animal class contains a few other properties that help establish the type of an animal. Have a look at the PenguinPairs5 example program.

First, you need to check whether there is another animal at the tile the animal is moving into. To do that, you retrieve the level and use the `findAnimalAtPosition` method from the LevelState class to find out whether there is another animal:

```
let lvl = GameStateManager.instance.currentGameState as? LevelState
if let a = lvl?.findAnimalAtPosition(targetcol, row: targetrow) {
    // handle the animal interaction
}
```

The findAnimalAtPosition method is straightforward; have a look at the method in the example code belonging to this chapter. First, if the other animal isn't visible, you don't have to do anything, and you can return from the method:

```
if a.hidden {
    return
}
```

The first case you solve is if the penguin is colliding with a seal. In that case, the penguin doesn't have to do anything—it simply stops moving:

```
if a.isSeal {
    stopMoving()
}
```

The next case is if the animal collides with an empty box. If that is the case, you make the moving animal invisible and you move the animal inside the box by changing the type of the empty box to the boxed version of the animal that is moving, which is represented by the uppercase version of the type character of that animal:

```
else if a.isEmptyBox {
    self.hidden = true
    a.changeTypeTo(self.type.uppercaseString)
}
```

The changeTypeTo method is a helper method that changes the type of the animal and updates the texture accordingly. Here is the complete method; it looks very similar to the code used in the initializer of the class:

```
func changeTypeTo(type: String) {
    boxed = type.uppercaseString == type
    var spriteName = "spr_animal_\(type)"
    if boxed && type != "@" {
        spriteName = "spr_animal_boxed_\(type.lowercaseString)"
    }
    texture = SKTexture(imageNamed: spriteName)
    self.type = type
}
```

If the type of the animal a is the same as the type of this animal, or either one of the animals is a multicolored penguin, you have a valid pair of penguins and make both penguins invisible:

```
else if type.lowercaseString == a.type.lowercaseString || self.isMulticolor || a.isMulticolor {
    a.hidden = true
    self.hidden = true
}
```

You also have to display an extra pair at the top left on the screen, but you deal with that in the next section.

If a penguin encounters a shark, the penguin is eaten and the shark leaves the playing field with a full belly. In the game, this means the penguin stops moving (forever) and both the shark and the penguin become invisible. The following lines of code achieve this:

```
else if a.isShark {
    a.hidden = true
    self.hidden = true
    stopMoving()
}
```

Finally, in all other cases, the penguin simply stops moving:

```
else {
    self.stopMoving()
}
```

# Maintaining the Number of Pairs

In order to maintain the number of pairs and draw it nicely on the screen, you add another class called PairList to the game. The PairList class inherits from the SKNode class. The pair list is drawn on top of a frame, which is added to the level in the LevelState constructor:

```
let goalFrame = SKSpriteNode(imageNamed: "spr_frame_goal")
goalFrame.zPosition = Layer.Overlay
goalFrame.position = GameScreen.instance.topLeft + CGPoint(x: 10 + goalFrame.center.x, y: -40)
self.addChild(goalFrame)
```

The pair list shows a row of sprites indicating the number of required and completed pairs. Because you want to indicate the color of each pair that was made, you store this information in an array as string values, each representing a pair type. This array is a property of the PairList class:

```
var colors: [String] = []
```

You pass along a parameter, nrPairs, to the initializer of the PairList class so you know how large the array should be. You then fill the array so that each element is set to the empty slot (which is represented by the sprite "spr_pairs_e"):

```
for var i = 0; i < nrPairs; i++ {
    let pairSprite = SKSpriteNode(imageNamed: "spr_pairs_e")
    pairSprite.position = CGPoint(x: CGFloat(i) * (pairSprite.size.width + 5), y: 0)
    self.addChild(pairSprite)
    colors.append("e")
}
```

You also add a method named addPair to the class, which finds the first occurrence of an empty pair (type "e") in the array and replaces it with the pair type that was passed along as a parameter:

```
func addPair(color : String) {
    for var i = 0; i < colors.count; i++ {
        if colors[i] == "e" {
            let sprite = children[i] as! SKSpriteNode
            sprite.texture = SKTexture(imageNamed: "spr_pairs_\(color)")
            colors[i] = color
            return
        }
    }
}
```

This example uses a for instruction to increment the i variable until you find an empty spot (i.e. the element in the colors array equals "e").

Now you add a useful property to check whether the player has completed the level. The level is completed if the list of pair colors no longer contains any value of "e" (meaning all empty spots have been replaced by a pair):

```
var completed: Bool {
    get {
        for color in colors {
            if color == "e" {
                return false
            }
        }
        return true
    }
}
```

Now that you have the PairList class, you can create an instance of it in the LevelState class, add it to the game world, and position it near the top left of the screen:

```
let pairList = PairList(nrPairs: nrPairs)
pairList.name = "pairList"
pairList.zPosition = Layer.Overlay1
pairList.position = GameScreen.instance.topLeft + CGPoint(x: 130, y: -40)
self.addChild(pairList)
```

And in the Animal class, you add a pair to the list if an animal encounters another penguin of the same color or one of the two animals is a multicolored penguin:

```
else if type.lowercaseString == a.type.lowercaseString || self.isMulticolor
    || a.isMulticolor {
    a.hidden = true
    self.hidden = true
    let pairList = childNodeWithName("//pairList") as! PairList
    pairList.addPair(type)
}
```

For the complete example, see the PenguinPairs5 program belonging to this chapter. Figure 20-2 shows a screenshot of a level where five pairs need to be made. In the next chapter, you will add the final touches to the Penguin Pairs game, such as showing an overlay when the level is completed and showing a hint arrow.

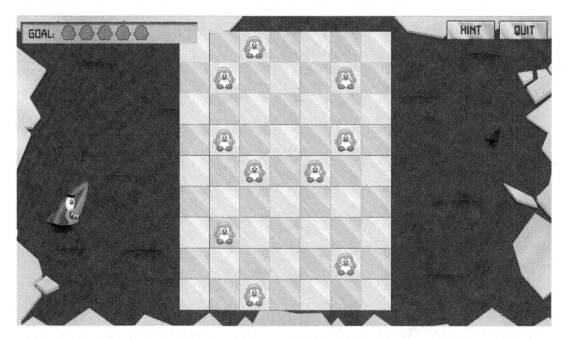

*Figure 20-2. A level of Penguin Pairs game. The goal is to make five pairs of yellow penguins*

# What You Have Learned

In this chapter, you have learned the following:

- How to define operator behavior for types such as CGPoint
- How to program a game object selector
- How to model interactions between different kinds of game objects
- How to maintain the number of pairs made by the player

# Chapter 21

# Finishing the Penguin Pairs Game

In this chapter, you will finalize the Penguin Pairs game. You will first complete the user interface by adding a hint arrow and a help overlay that is shown for a few seconds when the player starts playing each level. Then, you will learn how to reset and move on to the next level. You will complete the game by adding sound effects.

## Showing Hints

In order to finish Penguin Pairs, there are a couple more features to add to the game. As a first step, you want to be able to show a hint when the user taps a button. The hint consists of an orange arrow that is visible for a second. When you load the level in the LevelState initializer, you read the hint position and direction from the text file. Then, you create an SKSpriteNode instance, you assign the correct sprite to it, and you position it according to the information in the text file, as follows:

```
let hintx = hintArr[0].toInt()!, hinty = hintArr[1].toInt()!
hint = SKSpriteNode(imageNamed: "spr_arrow_hint_\(hintArr[2])")
hint.zPosition = Layer.Scene2
hint.position = tileField.layout.toPosition(hintx, row: hinty)
hint.hidden = true
self.addChild(hint)
```

Initially, the hint arrow is hidden. In order to temporarily display the arrow when the player taps the Hint button, you create an action stored as a property:

```
let hintVisibleAction = SKAction.sequence([SKAction.unhide(),
    SKAction.waitForDuration(1), SKAction.hide()])
```

Finally, you extend the handleInput method of LevelState to deal with the Hint button being pressed:

```
if hintButton.tapped {
    hint.runAction(hintVisibleAction)
}
```

The Hint button can only be pressed if it's visible, which in some cases it shouldn't be, such as the following:

- After the player makes the first move, the Hint button should disappear, and the Retry button should appear.
- If the player chooses to switch off hints in the Options menu, the Hint button should never be visible.

For the first case, you need to keep track of when the player makes her first move. You add an extra property firstMoveMade to the LevelState class. When you give an animal a velocity, this is done in the AnimalSelector class. Once the player has tapped an arrow and the animal is moving, you call the applyFirstMoveMade method part of LevelState:

```
let lvl = GameStateManager.instance.currentGameState as? LevelState
if animalVelocity != CGPoint.zeroPoint {
    lvl?.applyFirstMoveMade()
}
```

The applyFirstMoveMade method hides the Hint button, unhides the Retry button, and sets the firstMoveMade property to true:

```
func applyFirstMoveMade() {
    self.hintButton.hidden = true
    self.retryButton.hidden = false
    firstMoveMade = true
}
```

In the updateDelta method of LevelState, you make sure to only change the visibility of the Hint and Retry buttons if the player has not made his first move yet:

```
if !firstMoveMade {
    self.hintButton.hidden = !DefaultsManager.instance.hints
    self.retryButton.hidden = DefaultsManager.instance.hints
}
```

As you can see from the two lines of code in the if instruction, the Hint button is hidden only if DefaultsManager.instance.hints is false. The Retry button's hidden status is always the opposite of the Hint button's hidden status. So if the Hint button is visible, the Retry button isn't, and vice versa. Figure 21-1 shows a screenshot of the hint arrow in action.

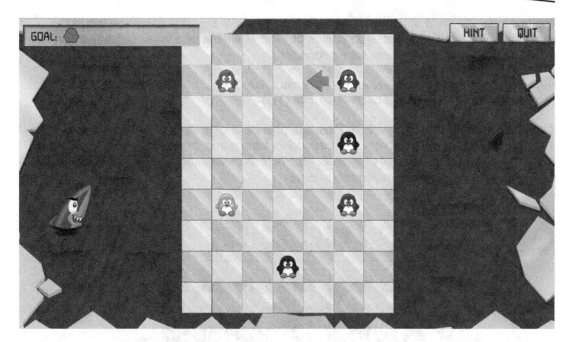

*Figure 21-1. The hint arrow shows the player the first sensible move. Hmm. . . that really helps!*

# Showing a Help Frame

It's also useful to show the player a bit of useful information when (s)he begins playing the level. Let's use a custom font to display the help text. You can load a custom font in your project using the same procedure as in the Tut's Tomb game (see Chapter 16 for more information). The first step is adding a help frame in the LevelState initializer:

```
helpFrame.position = CGPoint(x: 0, y: GameScreen.instance.bottom + helpFrame.center.y + 10)
helpFrame.zPosition = Layer.Overlay
self.addChild(helpFrame)
```

The help frame is positioned at the bottom center of the screen. On top of it, you display a text label:

```
let textLabel = SKLabelNode(fontNamed: "Autodestruct BB")
textLabel.fontColor = UIColor(red: 0, green: 0, blue: 0.4, alpha: 1)
textLabel.fontSize = 24
textLabel.text = help
textLabel.horizontalAlignmentMode = .Center
textLabel.verticalAlignmentMode = .Center
textLabel.zPosition = 1
helpFrame.addChild(textLabel)
```

The text label is a child of the help frame. In order to make sure it is shown on top of the help frame, you set it at a relative z position of 1. Now, whenever a level is reset, you add an action that shows the help frame for 5 seconds:

```
helpFrame.runAction(SKAction.sequence([SKAction.unhide(),
    SKAction.waitForDuration(5), SKAction.hide()]))
```

If you take a look at the PenguinPairsFinal example belonging to this chapter, you'll see that this same custom font is now used throughout the game, for example to show the level indices on the level buttons (see Figure 21-2). You can clearly see that using a custom font makes the game look much more professional.

*Figure 21-2.  The level menu using the custom font*

# Resetting the Level

After a player moves a couple of animals around, it can happen that the level can't be solved anymore. Instead of having to quit and restart the game, let's give the player a means to reset a level to its initial state.

Thanks to the proper implementation of the reset method everywhere throughout the game object classes, resetting a level to its initial state is really easy. You have to call the reset method on all the game objects, and then you deal with resetting things in the LevelState class itself. The only thing you need to do there is set the firstMoveMade property to false so the player can view a hint again, and run the help frame action:

```
override func reset() {
    super.reset()
    firstMoveMade = false
    helpFrame.runAction(SKAction.sequence([SKAction.unhide(),
        SKAction.waitForDuration(5), SKAction.hide()]))
}
```

> **Note**   There are many ways in which the Penguin Pairs game can be extended. For example, can you write code that determines whether a level is still solvable? You could extend the game by displaying a message to the user if that happens. You may have your own ideas about how the game could be improved. Feel free to try them by modifying and adding to the examples.

# Moving to the Next Level

When the player finishes a level (hurray!), you want to display an encouraging overlay (see Figure 21-3). When the player clicks or taps the screen, the next level is shown. The overlay is added as a property to the LevelState class, and is initially set to hidden in its initializer:

```
var levelFinishedOverlay = SKSpriteNode(imageNamed: "spr_level_finished")
```

*Figure 21-3.   The overlay shown to the player after they finish a level*

In the updateDelta method of LevelState, you check whether the pair list is completed, and if so, you show the level finished overlay, and you play a sound:

```
if levelFinishedOverlay.hidden && pairList.completed {
    levelFinishedOverlay.hidden = false
    wonSound.play()
}
```

In the handleInput method of LevelState, you check whether the player is still playing, or whether (s)he has finished the level. In the latter case, you check whether the player has tapped the screen. If so, you move to the next level. Moving to the next level is not that complicated, but it involves updating the status of each level using the DefaultManager class, finding out what the next level is, and then switching to that state. This is the complete code:

```
if !levelFinishedOverlay.hidden {
    if !inputHelper.containsTap(levelFinishedOverlay.box) {
        return
    }
    self.reset()
    DefaultsManager.instance.setLevelStatus(self.levelNr, status: "solved")
    if GameStateManager.instance.has("level\(levelNr+1)") {
        if DefaultsManager.instance.getLevelStatus(self.levelNr+1) == "locked" {
            DefaultsManager.instance.setLevelStatus(self.levelNr+1, status: "unsolved")
        }
        GameStateManager.instance.switchTo("level\(levelNr+1)")
        GameStateManager.instance.reset()
    } else {
        GameStateManager.instance.switchTo("level")
    }
}
```

Take a look at the PenguinPairsFinal example to see the complete LevelState class.

## TUTORIALS

As you've probably noticed, the first few levels of the Penguin Pairs game also serve as a tutorial that explains how the game should be played. When you create a game, players have to learn how to play it. If you don't tell the players about the challenges and goals, and how to control the game, they might get frustrated and stop playing.

Some games provide extensive help files with long text explaining the story and the controls. Players no longer want to read such documents or screens. They want to jump right into the game. You have to educate players while they're playing.

You can create a few specific tutorial levels where the player can practice the controls without drastically affecting the progress of the game itself. This approach is popular with casual gamers as an introduction to your game. Seasoned gamers prefer to immediately dive into the action. Be careful not to explain everything in the tutorial levels. Only explain the basic controls. Explain more advanced controls during the game as they're required: for example, using simple pop-up messages, or in a visible spot in a HUD.

Tutorials work best when they naturally integrate into the game story. For example, the game character might start running around in their safe home town, learning the basic movement controls. Next, the character practices fighting with a few friends. And after, that the player goes into the woods to try to shoot some birds with a bow. This will provide the practice needed for the fights later in the game.

You should make sure your tutorial levels work and that players remember the controls even if they put the game away for a couple of days. Otherwise, they may never come back to the game.

# Adding Sound Effects

To finish the game, you should add sounds and music at the right spots. As you may remember, one of the choices in the Options menu is to change the background volume. You do that using the following line of code:

```
backgroundMusic.volume = Float(musicSlider.value)
```

In the OptionMenuState class, you can find the backgroundMusic property, as well as the code to start playing the music:

```
backgroundMusic.looping = true
backgroundMusic.play()
```

Similarly, you play sound effects at appropriate moments, just as you did in the Tut's Tomb and Painter games. For example, whenever a pair of penguins is made, you play a sound effect (see the updateDelta method in the Animal class):

```
pairSound.play()
```

If you look at the PenguinPairsFinal example belonging to this chapter, you can see how the complete game works and where sound effects are played, and of course you can play the game yourself.

---

## WORKING IN TEAMS

The first generation of games was created by programmers. They did all the work. They designed the game mechanics, they created the art (which consisted of just a few pixels), and they programmed the game in an Assembler language. All the work focused on the programming. The game mechanics were often adapted to what could be programmed efficiently.

But when more memory became available, this slowly changed. Creating fancy-looking objects with a limited number of pixels and colors became an art form, and pixel artists started to play an important role in developing games. In the early days there were no drawing programs (no computer was powerful enough for that). Pixelated characters were designed on graph paper and then turned into hexadecimal numbers to be put into the game code.

With the increase of computer power and storage media like the CD-ROM, art became increasingly important, and the artists developed with it. 3D graphics and animations became common, leading to new specialists who could use the new tools and technologies developed to support such work. Nowadays artists make up the majority of game production teams.

At some point, designing the game became a separate job. Game mechanics were tuned to the interests of user groups, and were based more and more on principles from psychology and educational sciences. This required separate expertise. Stories assumed a crucial role, leading to the inclusion of writers. And the teams were extended to include producers, sound engineers, composers, and many other types of people. Today, teams for top games can consist of hundreds of people. But without the programmers, nothing would work.

# A Few Final Notes

In this part of the book, you've created a game that is quite a bit more complicated than the previous example game, Tut's Tomb. You've probably noticed that the number of classes has become quite large, and you're relying more and more on a certain design for the game software. For example, you're positioning game objects in a grid layout and using a class to handle game states. On a more basic level, you assume that game objects are responsible for handling their input and updating themselves. You may not agree with some (or all) of these design choices. Perhaps, after reading the book to this point, you've formed your own ideas about how game software should be designed. This is a good thing. The design I propose in this book isn't the only way to do things. Designs can always be evaluated and improved, or even thrown away and replaced by something entirely different. So, don't hesitate to look critically at the design I propose and try other designs. By trying different approaches to solve a problem, you can better understand the problem and become a better software developer as a result.

# What You Have Learned

In this chapter, you have learned the following:

- How to show a hint arrow and a help frame on the screen
- How to reset a level to its initial state and handle going to the next level

# Part V

# Tick Tick

The previous chapters have shown you how to build several different types of games. In this part, you will build a platform game with animated characters, physics, and different levels. The game is called *Tick Tick* (see Figure V-1), and the story revolves around a slightly stressed-out bomb that will explode within a number of seconds. Each level in the game should be finished before the bomb explodes. A level is finished if the player collects all the refreshing water drops and reaches the finish panel in time.

*Figure V-1. The Tick Tick game*

This platform game includes a number of basic elements that are found in many other games as well:

- It should be possible to play different levels.

- These levels should be loaded from a separate file so they can be changed without having to know how the game code works.

- The game should support animated characters for both the player and the enemies.

- The player should control the actions of a player character that can run or jump.

- There should be some basic physics in the game to manage falling, colliding with objects, jumping on platforms, and so on.

That is quite a list! Fortunately, you can reuse many of the classes you've already developed. The following chapters look at all the items on the list. If you want to play the complete version of the Tick Tick game, run the example program belonging to Chapter 27.

# Chapter 22

# The Main Game Structure

In this chapter, you will lay out the framework for the Tick Tick game. Because of all the work you've done for the previous games, you can rely on a lot of preexisting classes. This means you already have a basic design for handling game states and settings, a hierarchy of game objects, and more. Note that the Tick Tick game is not designed to work on very small devices such as the older iPhones, nor the iPhone 6 Plus (for which you would need 3x resolution images anyway). If you run the game on older iPhones, a big part of the game world will be clipped. On the iPhone 6 Plus, the game is playable, but some black space will appear at the borders.

## Overview of the Game Structure

This game follows a structure very similar to that of the Penguin Pairs game. There is a title screen that allows the player to go to either the level-selection menu or a help page (see Figure 22-1). To keep things simple, you won't implement an options page, although adding it would be straightforward because you could use the same approach as in Penguin Pairs. Because the menu structure is so similar, it isn't discussed here. You can see the code in the TickTick1 example that belongs to this chapter.

*Figure 22-1. The title screen of the Tick Tick game*

The LevelState class is used to represent levels and deals with maintaining the level status (locked/unsolved/solved), just as in the Penguin Pairs game. Each level is a tile-based game world, again very similar to the way Penguin Pairs is structured.

# The Structure of a Level

Let's first look at what kind of things can be in a level in Tick Tick. First, there is a background image. For now, you display a simple background sprite; there is no need to store any information about that in the level data variable. There are also different kinds of blocks the player can jump on, along with water drops, enemies, the player's starting position, and the end position the player has to reach. As in the Penguin Pairs game, you store level information in a text file, which is read when the game is started.

You define a level using tiles, where each tile has a certain type (wall, background, and so on). You then represent each tile type with a character in the text file. Just as in the Penguin Pairs game, you lay out the level as text in a two-dimensional space corresponding to the playing field. Next to the actual tiles, you also store a hint together with the level definition. Here you can see the definition of the first level in the text file:

```
Pick up all the water drops and reach the exit in time.
20 15
60
....................
..................X..
..........#########
....................
WWW....WWWW.........
---....####.........
....................
```

```
WWW.................
###........WWWWW...
...........#####...
....WWW............
....###............
..................
.1........W.W.W.W.W.
###################
```

This level definition defines a number of different tiles and objects. For example, a wall tile is defined by the # sign, a water drop by a W character, and the start position of the player by the 1 character. If there is no tile at the specific position, you use the . character. For the platform game, you need different types of tiles: a wall tile the player can stand on or collide with, and a background/transparent tile that indicates there is no block in that position. You also want to define a *platform tile*. This tile has the property that the player can stand on it like a wall tile, but if they're standing under it, they can jump through it from below. This kind of tile is used in many classic platform games, and it would be a pity not to include it here! In the text file, platform tiles are represented by a - character. Table 22-1 gives a complete list of the different tiles in the Tick Tick game.

*Table 22-1. Overview of the Different Kinds of Tiles in the Tick Tick Game*

| Character | Tile Description |
| --- | --- |
| . | Background tile |
| # | Wall tile |
| ^ | Wall tile (hot) |
| * | Wall tile (ice) |
| - | Platform tile |
| + | Platform tile (hot) |
| @ | Platform tile (ice) |
| X | End tile |
| W | Water drop |
| 1 | Start tile (initial player position) |
| R | Rocket enemy (moving to the left) |
| R | Rocket enemy (moving to the right) |
| S | Sparky enemy |
| T | Turtle enemy |
| A | Flame enemy (random speed and direction change) |
| B | Flame enemy (player following) |
| C | Flame enemy (patrolling) |

# Water Drops

The goal of each level is to collect all of the water drops. Each water drop is represented by an instance of the WaterDrop class. This class is a SKSpriteNode subclass, but you want to add a little behavior to it: the water drop should bounce up and down. You can do this in the updateDelta method. First, you compute a *bounce offset* that you can add to the current position of the water drop. This bounce offset is stored in the property bounce, which is initially set to 0. You also maintain the total game time that has passed, like so:

```
var bounce: CGFloat = 0
var totalTime: CGFloat = 0
```

To calculate the bounce offset in each game-loop iteration, you use a *sine* function. And depending on the *x*-position of the water drop, you change the phase of the sine so that not all drops move up or down at the same time:

```
totalTime += CGFloat(delta)
var t = totalTime + position.x
self.bounce = sin(t*5) * 5
```

You subtract the bounce value from the y-position of the water drop:

```
position.y -= self.bounce
```

The -= operator subtracts the bounce value from the y-position (see Chapter 5 for more about these types of operators). However, simply subtracting the bounce value from the y-position isn't correct because this is a bounce *offset*—in other words, an offset with regard to the *original* y-position. To get the original y-position, you *add* the bounce offset from the y-position in the first instruction of the updateDelta method:

```
position.y += self.bounce
```

This works because at this point, the bounce variable still contains the bounce offset from the previous game-loop iteration. So, adding it to the y-position gives you the original y-position.

In the next chapters, you add more game objects, such as the player and a variety of enemies. But let's first look at how to define the tiles in a platform game such as Tick Tick.

# The Tile Class

The Tile class is very similar to the one used in Penguin Pairs, but it has a few differences. First, you define the different kinds of tiles using an enumerated type:

```
enum TileType {
    case Wall
    case Background
    case Platform
}
```

In the Tile class, you then define a property tileType to store the type of tile that an instance represents. In addition to these basic tile types, you also have ice tiles and hot tiles, which are special versions of normal or platform tiles. In the text file, an ice tile is represented by the * character (or the @ character if it's a platform tile), and a hot tile is represented by the ^ character (or the + character for the platform version). You add two Boolean properties to the Tile class to represent these different kinds of tiles. Here are the Tile initializers:

```
convenience init() {
    self.init(imageNamed: "spr_wall", type: .Background)
}

init(imageNamed: String, type: TileType) {
    let texture = SKTexture(imageNamed: imageNamed)
    super.init(texture: texture, color: UIColor.whiteColor(), size: texture.size())
    self.type = type
}

required init?(coder aDecoder: NSCoder) {
    fatalError("init(coder:) has not been implemented")
}
```

As you can see, there is a convenience initializer that allows you to create a Tile instance of the Background type. This makes it easier to create Tile instances since you don't have to provide any parameter values. For example, the following instruction creates a simple background (transparent) tile:

```
var myTile = Tile()
```

In the Tile initializer, you use a type property that allows you to set and get the type of the tile. In the set part of the type property, you assign a new value to the tp property, and using Boolean logic, you hide the tile if it is a background tile. Here are the two lines of code that achieve this (for the full Tile class, see the TickTick1 example):

```
tileType = newValue
self.hidden = tileType == .Background
```

Now, let's look at the LevelState class and how the Tile instances are created.

# The LevelState Class

This section shows how the LevelState class is designed in Tick Tick. It's done in a way very similar to Penguin Pairs. In the initializer of the LevelState class, you do a couple of things:

- Create the background sprite game object.
- Add a Quit button.
- Create the tile-based game world from the level data.

The first two are straightforward. Have a look at the `LevelState` class in the example code to see how they work. Creating the tile-based game world is done using a separate method called `loadTile`. Depending on the tile character taken from the text file, a different `Tile` object will be created. The first step is creating a `TileField` instance with the desired height and width, taken from the text file:

```
tileField = TileField(rows: height, columns: width, cellWidth: 72, cellHeight: 55)
tileField.name = "tileField"
world.addChild(tileField)
```

As you can see, the tile field is added to a separate node called `world`, as opposed to the Quit button, which is simply added to the level node:

```
quitButton.zPosition = Layer.Overlay
quitButton.position = GameScreen.instance.topRight - quitButton.center - CGPoint(x: 10, y: 10)
self.addChild(quitButton)
```

There is a reason for this. You want to separate overlays such as the Quit button or a help frame from the actual tile-based game world because later on you are going to add *side scrolling* to this platform game. This means that the game world needs to move around on the screen, while the buttons should stay in the same place. This can only be done if the actual game world is stored in a separate node. You can then change the position of that node (and therefore also the position of the game world) without affecting any of the buttons or other overlays. Chapter 26 shows you how to add vertical and horizontal scrolling to your game.

After reading the lines defining the level from the text file, you create the `Tile` objects and add them to the `TileField` object. You use a nested for loop for this:

```
for i in 0..<height {
    var currLine = lines[height-1-i]
    var j = 0
    for c in currLine {
        tileField.layout.add(loadTile(c, x: j, y: i))
        j++
    }
}
```

The nested `for` loop examines all the characters you read from the text file. The `loadTile` method creates a `Tile` object for you, given a character and the x- and y-positions of the tile in the grid.

In the `loadTile` method, you want to load a different tile according to the character passed as a parameter. For each type of tile, you add a method to the `LevelState` class that creates that particular kind of tile. For example, `loadWaterTile` loads a background tile with a water drop on top of it:

```
func loadWaterTile(x: Int, y: Int) -> SKNode {
    var w = WaterDrop()
    w.position = tileField.layout.toPosition(x, row: y)
    w.position.y += 10
```

```
    w.zPosition = Layer.Scene1
    world.addChild(w)
    self.waterDrops.append(w)
    return Tile()
}
```

This particular example creates a `WaterDrop` instance and positions it in the center of the tile. You place each water drop 10 points higher than the tile center so it doesn't bounce over the tile below it. Look at the `Level` class to see how to create the various tiles and objects in each level. Figure 22-2 shows a screenshot of the objects in the first level (other than the player character, which you will deal with in the following chapters).

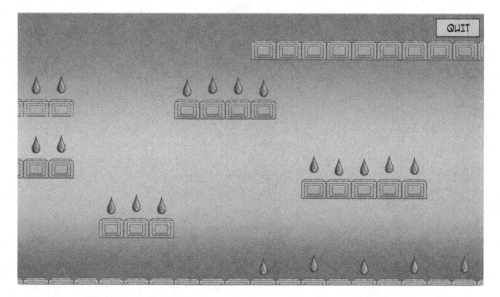

*Figure 22-2. The game world of the first level of Tick Tick*

# What You Have Learned

In this chapter, you have learned the following:

- How to set up the general structure of the Tick Tick game
- How to create a bouncing water drop

Chapter **23**

# Animation

In this chapter, you will see how to add *animations* to your game. In the games you've developed until now, game objects could move around on the screen, but adding something like a running character to a game is slightly more challenging. In this chapter, you will write a program that contains a character walking from left to right on the screen. The character is controlled by the player pressing left and right buttons on the screen.

## What Is Animation?

Before you look into how to program a character walking around on the screen, you first have to think about what animation is. To grasp this, you have to go back to the 1930s, when several animation studios (among them Walt Disney) produced the first cartoons in black and white.

A cartoon is actually a very fast sequence of still images, also called *frames*. A television draws these frames at a very high rate, about 25-30 times per second. When the image varies each time, your brain interprets this as motion. This special feature (also called the *phi phenomenon*) of the human brain is very useful, especially when you want to program games that contain moving or animated objects.

You used this feature in the previous games you developed in this book. In every iteration of the game loop, you draw a new "frame" on the screen. By drawing sprites at different positions every time, you give the impression that the sprites move. However, this isn't really what is happening: you're simply drawing the sprite at different positions many times per second, which makes the player *think* the sprite is moving.

In a similar fashion, you can draw a walking or running character. In addition to moving the sprite, you draw a slightly different sprite every time. By drawing a sequence of sprites, each of which represents part of a walking motion, you can create the illusion that a character is walking on the screen. An example of such a sequence of sprites is shown in Figure 23-1.

*Figure 23-1. A sequence of images representing a walking motion*

There are different reasons for putting animations in games. When you create 3D games, animation is normally necessary to enhance realism, but for 2D games this isn't always the case. Still, animations can considerably enrich a game.

Animation brings objects to life. But it doesn't have to be complicated. The simple animation of a character closing and opening its eyes results in a strong feeling that the character is alive. Animated characters are also easier to relate to. If you look at a game like *Cut the Rope*, the main character (named Om Nom) is simply sitting in a corner. But from time to time the character makes some funny moves to show you it's there and wants you to bring it food. This creates a very effective motivation for the player to continue playing the game.

Animations also help draw the player's attention to a certain object, task, or event. For example, having a small animation on a button makes it clearer to the player that they have to press the button. And a bouncing water drop or a rotating star indicates that this object should be collected or avoided. Animations can also be used to provide feedback. When a button moves downward when you tap on it with your finger, it's immediately obvious that the button tap was successful.

However, creating animations is a lot of work. So think carefully beforehand about where animations are needed and where they can be avoided, to save time and money.

# Texture Atlases

For animated characters, you usually design one sequence of sprites for each type of movement. Some animations consist of only a few sprites. For example, the Tick Tick game contains a rocket that flies through the screen. The rocket is animated using three frames only (see Figure 23-2).

*Figure 23-2. The frames of the rocket animation*

Other animations may have many more frames. An example is the bomb explosion animation in Tick Tick, which has 49 frames. As you add more animations to your game, the number of sprites needed (in 1x, 2x, and for some games even 3x resolutions) can dramatically increase. This puts a strain on the device in terms of memory necessary to store all the image data, but also processing power to load the images from files and display them on the screen fast enough. A very common trick to reduce image loading time is to put multiple sprites on a single image. For example, you could put all the buttons needed for the title screen in the same file, and when you need to display a button, you show that part of the image representing the button. The SpriteKit framework has a neat solution for this called a *texture atlas*. A texture atlas is basically a collection of sprites/textures that is optimally stored in as few image files as possible.

If you have a lot of images in your game, texture atlases help make the game load much faster. The nice thing is that as a developer, you don't have to worry about how the sprites are stored in the image file. You simply tell the Xcode environment that all the sprites in a folder belong to an atlas.

In order to use texture atlases in Xcode, you can simply put sprites in a folder that has a name ending with .atlas, and then drag that folder into the project. For example, in the AnimationSample project belonging to this chapter, you can see two atlases: spr_player_run.atlas and spr_player_idle.atlas (representing running and idle animations). If you look inside spr_player_run.atlas, you see that it contains quite a few different sprites. There is one important naming convention that you need to remember for texture atlases: if you use sprites at different resolutions, you should add "@1x," "@2x," or "@3x" at the end of the file name to indicate the resolution of the sprite. Other than that, you can choose any sprite name you like. In this case, name each sprite the same at its atlas name, add a number, and then indicate the resolution of the sprite.

Creating a texture atlas in your code is very simple. This is how you create a texture atlas from the spr_player_run.atlas file:

```
let atlas = SKTextureAtlas(named: "spr_player_run")
```

You can now access specific textures within the atlas as follows:

```
let texture = atlas.textureNamed("spr_player_run0")
```

The texture names in the atlas correspond to the names that you give the files, minus the resolution indication. You can then use this texture to create a node and add it to the game world:

```
let spriteNode = SKSpriteNode(texture: texture)
addChild(spriteNode)
```

# The Animation Class

For animated characters, you usually design one sequence of sprites for each type of movement. The example in Figure 23-1 is the sequence for animating a running character. This is where texture atlases are a very useful tool. You can define each frame as a separate sprite in a texture atlas. In the AnimationSample project, I did exactly this. As a next step, let's design a few useful classes and methods for loading and playing animations. The basic class for representing animations is called Animation, and it is a part of the AnimationSample project. In addition to sprites stored in a texture atlas, an animation requires extra information. For example, you want to indicate how long each frame should be shown on the screen. You also want to be able to *loop* your animation, meaning that once you reach the last frame, you immediately move back to the first frame again, leading to a continuous, infinite animation. Looping an animation is very useful: in the case of a walking character, for instance, you only have to draw one walk cycle and then loop the animation to get a continuous walking motion. Not all animations should be looped, though. For example, a dying animation shouldn't be looped (that would be very cruel to the character). To deal with all these situations, the Animation class has a number of properties. Here is a part of the class:

```
class Animation: SKSpriteNode {
    var action = SKAction()

    init(atlasNamed: String, looping: Bool, frameTime: NSTimeInterval) {
        // to do
    }

    required init?(coder aDecoder: NSCoder) {
        fatalError("init(coder:) has not been implemented")
    }

    ...
}
```

As you can see, the Animation class is a subclass of SKSpriteNode. So, if you create an instance of Animation, you can directly add it to the game world. The Animation class has one single property, action. It refers to the action that plays the actual animation. The action is created in the initializer. As you can see, the initializer expects a few parameters: the name of the atlas that contains the animation frames, a Boolean indicating whether the animation should be looping or not, and the time between consecutive frames. Depending on the values of these parameters, you will create a different animation action.

The first step is loading the texture atlas. For convenience, let's also store the number of textures that the atlas contains in a variable:

```
let atlas = SKTextureAtlas(named: atlasNamed)
let numImages = atlas.textureNames.count
```

Now, let's extract all the textures from this atlas and store them in an array. Later on, you can define an action that uses this array of texture to produce the animation. First, declare and initialize an array of SKTexture objects:

```
var frames: [SKTexture] = []
```

The next step is to retrieve all the textures from the atlas. This is where the naming of the animation frames is useful. Let's use a for loop to retrieve all the frames and add them to the array of textures:

```
for i in 0..<numImages/2 {
    let textureName = "\(atlasNamed)_\(i)"
    frames.append(atlas.textureNamed(textureName))
}
```

A few things happen in this bit of code. First, there is a variable i in the range between 0 and numImages/2. The reason you need to divide the number of images in the atlas by two is because the atlas contains images for both the 1x and 2x resolution. Inside the for loop, you first construct the texture name by adding a number behind the name of the atlas. Then, you use the textureNamed method to retrieve the actual texture and append it to the array of textures.

Now you can call the initializer of the superclass. The node is initialized with the first texture in the array:

```
super.init(texture: frames[0], color: UIColor.whiteColor(),
    size: frames[0].size())
```

Then, you need to create the actual action that animates the node, as follows:

```
let animateAction = SKAction.animateWithTextures(frames,
    timePerFrame: frameTime)
```

Depending on whether the animation should loop, you need to repeat the action indefinitely. This is handled in the following if instruction:

```
if looping {
    action = SKAction.repeatActionForever(animateAction)
} else {
    action = animateAction
}
```

# Supporting Multiple Animations

The Animation class provides the groundwork for representing an animation. An animated game object may contain a number of different animations, so you can have a character that can perform different (animated) actions such as walking, running, jumping, and more. Each action is represented by an animation. Depending on the player input, you change the animation that is currently active. Let's define a class that makes it easy to deal with multiple animations. In the AnimationSample project, this class is called AnimatedNode.

To store the different animations, you use an array. For each animation you need, you add an instance of the Animation class to the array. So, AnimatedNode has the following property:

```
var animations : [Animation] = []
```

To make loading and playing animations more convenient, you add two methods to the class, loadAnimation and playAnimation. The first method creates an Animation object and adds it to the animations property:

```
func loadAnimation(atlasNamed: String, looping: Bool = false,
    frameTime: NSTimeInterval = 0.05, name: String,
    anchorPoint: CGPoint = CGPoint(x: 0.5, y: 0)) {

    let anim = Animation(atlasNamed: atlasNamed, looping: looping, frameTime: frameTime)
    anim.name = name
    anim.anchorPoint = anchorPoint
    animations.append(anim)
}
```

The `loadAnimation` method expects a few parameters, some of which have default values for convenience. First, you need to provide the name of the atlas that is used for the animation. Then, you can indicate whether the animation should be looping, and the time between frames. Also, each animation needs to have a unique name, so that you can retrieve and activate it later on. Finally, you can optionally provide an anchor point for the node that is created. Here, the anchor point is set to the bottom middle of the sprite by default. In the case of Tick Tick, this is a useful default value, since animated characters such as the player will walk over tiles. Having the sprite origin at the bottom center makes calculations a bit easier, as you'll see later.

In the method body, you create the `Animation` instance, assign it a name and set its anchor point, and finally, you add it to the array of animations.

In the `playAnimation` method, you have to select the animation that needs to be played, add it to the node, and start the animation action. First, you check whether the animation you want to play is already a child of the node. In that case, the animation is already playing and you don't have to do anything else, so you can return from the method:

```
func playAnimation(name: String) {
    if childNodeWithName(name) != nil {
        return
    }
    ...
}
```

Next, you use a `for` loop to find the animation with the chosen name. Once you have found it, you remove any children that this node has, add the animation to the node, and start the action.

```
for anim in animations {
    if anim.name == name {
        self.removeAllChildren()
        self.addChild(anim)
        anim.runAction(anim.action)
        return
    }
}
```

# The Player Class

To use the `AnimatedNode` class introduced in the previous section, you inherit from it. Because the player will control the animated character, let's define a `Player` class that is a subclass of `AnimatedNode`. In this class, you load the animations belonging to the player and handle the input from the player. In the `Player` initializer, you load the animations that are needed for this character. In this example, you want the character to walk or stand still.

So, you load two animations by calling the loadAnimation method twice. You make both of these animations loop by setting the looping parameter to true:

```
class Player: AnimatedNode {

    var velocity = CGPoint.zeroPoint

    override init() {
        super.init()
        loadAnimation("spr_player_idle", looping: true, name: "idle")
        loadAnimation("spr_player_run", looping: true, name: "run")
    }

    required init?(coder aDecoder: NSCoder) {
        fatalError("init(coder:) has not been implemented")
    }
    ...
}
```

Note that the actual idle animation of the player has only a single frame, so it doesn't make a difference in this case whether the idle animation loops or not. The AnimationSample application has one single game state, which is an instance of MainState. In this game state, you add a few buttons to the screen to control the player character, as well as the player character itself. For the complete code, see the MainState.swift file.

You need to handle the player's input in this class. When the player presses the left or right button on the screen, the velocity of the character should change. You do this in the handleInput method, using an if instruction:

```
let walkLeftButton = childNodeWithName("//button_walkleft") as! Button
let walkRightButton = childNodeWithName("//button_walkright") as! Button

var walkingSpeed = CGFloat(300)
if walkLeftButton.down {
    self.velocity.x = -walkingSpeed
} else if walkRightButton.down {
    self.velocity.x = walkingSpeed
} else {
    self.velocity.x = 0
}
```

---

**Note**  I chose a value of 300 for the walkingSpeed parameter. Play around with this value and see how it changes the character's behavior. Choosing the right value for parameters such as this one has a big influence on gameplay. It's important to choose values that are "just right." Testing gameplay with a variety of players can help you determine what these values should be so that the gameplay feels natural.

Using the sprites shown in Figure 23-1 allows you to animate a character walking to the right. To animate a character walking to the left, you could use another set of sprites. However, there is an easier way to accomplish this: by *mirroring* the sprite in the code. Mirroring is quite easy in SpriteKit. You can use scaling to accomplish this. If you want to mirror the node so that the character is walking to the left, you assign it a negative *x* scale, as follows:

```
self.xScale = -1
```

You only want to set a negative *x* scale if the player velocity is negative. So, you add the following if instruction to the handleInput method of the Player class:

```
if self.velocity.x < 0 {
    self.xScale = -1
} else if self.velocity.x > 0 {
    self.xScale = 1
}
```

I applied a little trick here. I only change the *x* scale if the velocity is either greater than or less than 0. If the velocity is exactly 0, nothing happens. The effect of this is that when the character stops moving, it keeps looking in the direction it was moving in, which is the behavior I desire.

In the updateDelta method, you select which animation to play based on the velocity. If the velocity is zero, you play the idle animation; otherwise you play the run animation:

```
override func updateDelta(delta: NSTimeInterval) {
    super.updateDelta(delta)
    position += velocity * CGFloat(delta)

    if self.velocity.x == 0 {
        self.playAnimation("idle")
    } else {
        self.playAnimation("run")
    }
}
```

As you can see, you also call the updateDelta method of the superclass, and you add the velocity multiplied by the passed time to the player's current position, so that the player can move around.

If you run the program, you will see an animated character that you can control by touching the left and right buttons (see Figure 23-3). Note that if the character walks off the visible screen, it doesn't just "stop" off-screen—it keeps going. So, if you touch the right button for 5 seconds, you need to touch the left button for 5 seconds as well to get the character back.

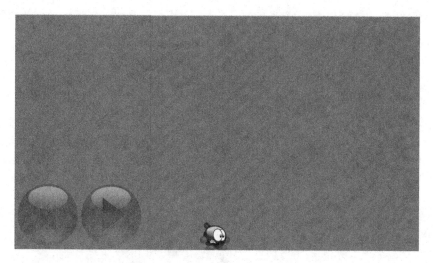

*Figure 23-3. An animated character moving from left to right on the bottom of the screen*

One way around this behavior of being able to walk off the edge of the screen is to implement wrapping: if the character walks off the right side of the screen, it reappears on the left, and vice versa. You can implement wrapping quite easily by adding an `if` instruction to the code that checks the current position of the character and, depending on that position, chooses to move the character to the other end of the screen. Can you change the example yourself to add wrapping?

# What You Have Learned

In this chapter, you have learned the following:

- How to use texture atlases to more efficiently deal with large numbers of images

- How to create and control an animation

- How to build an animated game object consisting of multiple animations

# Chapter 24

# Platform Game Physics

In the previous chapter, you learned how to create an animated character. You also learned how to build a tile-based game world by reading level data from a text file. One of the most important aspects is still missing: defining *how the character interacts with the game world*. You can make a character move from left to right, but if you simply place the character in the level, it can only walk on the bottom of the screen. This isn't enough. You want the character to be able to jump on top of tiles and fall down if it moves off a tile, and you don't want the character to fall off the edge of the screen. For these things, you need a physics system.

You could use the existing physics engine provided with the SpriteKit framework, but there are a few reasons why it makes sense to roll your own engine specifically for platform games. Since the physics engine largely determines how the game plays, you need to be able to tweak the parameters of the engine to suit the game. If you write your own physics engine, you have a lot more control over how it behaves. Also, your own engine might use fewer resources than the SpriteKit physics engine; platform games generally don't need hyperrealistic physics, so you can make do with simpler rules and algorithms. Another important reason to write your own physics engine is that some parts of platform game behavior are difficult to integrate with an existing physics engine. For example, the Tick Tick game has special tiles that you can jump through when you stand below them. This kind of behavior is hard to encode using a traditional physics engine. And finally, although writing your own physics engine can be quite a challenge, it's a great exercise in understanding physics and translating it into code that actually works!

In the Tick Tick game, the main physics behavior will be implemented in the Player class, since the player is the main character interacting with the game world. There are two main aspects to dealing with physics: giving the character the ability to jump or fall, and handling collisions between the character and other game objects, and responding to these collisions.

# Locking the Character in the Game World

The first thing you do is lock the character in the game world. In the example in the previous chapter, the character could walk out of the screen without any problem. You can solve this by placing a virtual pile of wall-type tiles to the left and right of the screen. You then assume that your collision-handling mechanism (which you haven't written yet) will ensure that the character can't walk through these walls. You only want to prevent the character from walking out of the left or right side of the screen. The character should be able to jump out of sight at the top of the screen. The character should also be able to fall off the game world through a hole in the ground (and die, obviously).

In order to build this virtual pile of wall tiles on the left and right sides of the screen, you have to add some behavior to the grid of tiles. You can do this in the `TileField` class, which represents the tile-based game world. This class has a method named `getTileType`, which returns the type of the tile given its column and row index on the grid. The nice thing about this method is that you allow these indices to fall *outside* of the valid indices in the grid. For example, it would be fine to ask for the tile type of the tile at position (-2,500). First, you check if there is a tile at the provided location in the grid, and if so, you return its tile type:

```
if let obj = layout.at(col, row: row) as? Tile {
    return obj.type
}
```

Then, you check whether the column index is out of range. If so, you return a wall tile type:

```
if col < 0 || col >= layout.columns {
    return .Wall
}
```

In all other cases, you return a background tile type:

```
return .Background
```

The complete `TileField` class can be found in the example program TickTick2 belonging to this chapter.

# Setting the Character at the Right Position

When you load the level tiles from the text file, you use the character 1 to indicate the tile on which the player's character is starting. Based on the location of that tile, you have to create the `Player` object and set it at the right position. For this, you add a method named `loadStartTile` to the `LevelState` class. In this method, you calculate the character's starting position based on its location in the grid. Because the character's origin is the *bottom-center* point of the sprite, you calculate this position as follows:

```
var startPosition = tileField.layout.toPosition(x, row: y)
startPosition.y -= CGFloat(tileField.layout.cellHeight / 2)
```

Note that you first calculate the position using the `toPosition` method of the grid layout. Since this gives you the center of the tile, you subtract half of the cell height from the y-position to end up at the bottom of the tile. You then create the `Player` object and add it to the game world:

```
var player = Player(startPos: startPosition)
player.name = "player"
player.zPosition = Layer.Scene1
world.addChild(player)
```

Finally, you still need to make an actual tile here that can be stored in the grid because each character should represent a tile. In this case, you can create a background tile that is placed where the character is standing:

```
return Tile()
```

# Jumping …

You've seen how a character can walk to the left or right. How can you deal with jumping and falling? In the TickTick2 example, you add a jump button on the bottom right of the screen. When the player presses that button, the character jumps. This basically means the character gets a *positive* y velocity. This can be done easily in the `handleInput` method of the `Player` class:

```
if jumpButton.tapped {
    self.jump()
}
```

The `jump` method is as follows:

```
func jump(speed: CGFloat = 680) {
    self.velocity.y = speed
}
```

So, the effect of calling the `jump` method without providing any parameter value is that the y velocity is set to a value of 680. I chose this number somewhat randomly. Using a bigger number means the character can jump higher. I chose this value so the character can jump high enough to reach the tiles but not high enough that the game becomes too easy (then the character could just jump to the end of the level).

There is a minor problem with this approach: you always allow the player's character to jump, no matter what the character's current situation is. So, if the character is currently jumping or falling down a cliff, you allow the player to make the character jump back to safety. This isn't really what you want. You want the character to jump only when standing on the ground. This is something that you can detect by looking at collisions between the character and wall or platform tiles (which are the only tiles that the character can stand on). Let's assume for now that your yet-to-be-written collision-detection algorithm will take care of this and keep track of whether the character is on the ground by using a property:

```
var onTheGround = false
```

Sometimes it's necessary to sketch out a class in English (as opposed to Swift) beforehand to allow you to write other parts of a game. This is also true in the case of collision detection. You can't test a collision-detection algorithm until you build it in, but you don't want to build it in until you've created the algorithm and tested it. One has to happen first, so you must mentally know what's going on with the other and plan it or keep notes.

If the onTheGround property is true, you know the character is standing on the ground. You can now change the initial if instruction so it only allows a character to jump from the ground and not from the air:

```
if jumpButton.tapped && self.onTheGround {
    self.jump()
}
```

# ... And Falling

The only place where you're currently changing the y velocity is in the handleInput method, when the player wants to jump. If the y velocity indefinitely keeps the value of 680, the character moves up in the air, outside of the screen, out of the planet's atmosphere, and into outer space. Because you're not making a game about bombs in space, you have to do something about this. What you forgot to add to the game world is *gravity*.

You can follow a simple approach to simulate the effect of gravity on the character's velocity. You subtract a small value from the velocity in the y-direction in each update step, similar to what you did in the Painter game for the ball:

```
self.velocity.y -= CGFloat(1300 * delta)
```

If the character has a positive velocity, this velocity slowly becomes smaller until it reaches zero and then starts to increase again in the negative direction. The effect is that the character jumps to a certain height and then starts falling down again, just like in the real world. However, the collision-detection mechanism now becomes even more important. If there is no collision detection, the character will start falling down at the start of the game!

# Collision Detection

Detecting collisions between game objects is a very important part of simulating interacting game worlds. Collision detection is used for many different things in games: detecting whether the character walks over a power-up, detecting whether the character collides with a projectile, detecting collisions between the character and walls or floors, and so on. You used collision detection in the previous games discussed in this book. In Tut's Tomb, the physics engine dealt with detection collisions between objects. In the Painter game, you performed a simple collision detection yourself using bounding boxes. Here is a snippet of code from the PaintCan class:

```
var ball = GameScene.world.ball
if self.box.intersects(ball.box) {
    color = ball.color
    ball.reset()
}
```

What you're doing here is detecting a collision between the ball and the paint can by checking if their bounding boxes intersect. This isn't a very precise way of checking collisions. Neither the ball nor the paint can resemble a box. As a result, in some cases a collision is detected when there is none, and sometimes a collision isn't detected when the sprites are actually colliding. Still, many games use *simplified shapes* such as circles and rectangles to represent objects when they do collision detection. Because these shapes bind the object within, they're also called *bounding circles* and *bounding boxes*. The Tick Tick game uses *axis-aligned* bounding boxes, meaning you don't consider boxes whose sides aren't parallel to the *x*- and *y*-axes.

Doing collision detection using bounding boxes isn't always precise enough. When game objects are close to each other, their bounding shapes may intersect (and thus trigger a collision), but the actual objects don't. And when a game object is animated, its shape may change over time. You could make the bounding shape bigger so the object fits in it under all circumstances, but that would lead to even more false collision triggers. There are some solutions for this. For example, instead of using boxes and circles, you could also create an outline of the sprite by drawing lines around it. If you create a *convex* outline (meaning the outline doesn't contain any holes or inward pointing sections), you can use the separating axes theorem to determine if there is a collision between two such outlines. Dealing with this is outside of the scope of this book, but suffice to say that it will be slightly more resource intensive than dealing with boxes and circles.

Yet another solution, which is even more resource-hungry, is to check for collisions on a per-pixel basis. Basically, you can write an algorithm that walks over the non-transparent pixels in the sprite (using a nested for instruction) and checks whether one or more of these pixels collides with one of the pixels in another sprite (again, by walking through them using a nested for instruction). Because such highly detailed collision detection is costly, especially if you want your game to run smoothly on older iDevices, you'll use simple collision detection using bounding boxes in the Tick Tick game, even though you'll learn a few tricks to make the collision handling more natural.

## Retrieving Bounding Boxes

To handle collisions efficiently in your game, you use the box property from the SKNode class that returns the bounding box of the sprite:

```
var box: CGRect {
    get {
        var boundingBox = self.calculateAccumulatedFrame()
        if parent != nil {
            boundingBox.origin = scene!.convertPoint(boundingBox.origin,
                fromNode: parent!)
        }
        return boundingBox
    }
}
```

Note that you convert the bounding box origin to the scene coordinate frame. This ensures that the bounding box position is expressed in *world coordinates*. When doing collision detection, you want to know where the objects are in the world—you don't care about their local positions in a hierarchy of game objects.

# Handling Character-Tile Collisions

In the Tick Tick game, you mainly need to detect collisions between the character and the tiles. You do this in a method called `handleCollisions`, which you call from the `updateDelta` method in the `Player` class. The idea is that you do all the calculations for jumping, falling, and running first (you did this at the beginning of this chapter). If there is a collision between the character and a tile, you correct the position of the character so that it no longer collides. In the `handleCollisions` method, you walk through the grid of tiles and check whether there is a collision between the character and the tile you're currently examining.

You don't need to check all the tiles in the grid, only those close to the character's current location. You can calculate the closest tile to the character's position as follows:

```
let tiles = childNodeWithName("//tileField") as! TileField
let (x_floor, y_floor) = tiles.layout.gridLocation(self.position)
```

Now you can use a nested `for` instruction to look at the tiles surrounding the character. In order to account for fast jumping and falling, you take more tiles into account in the y-direction. In the nested `for` instruction, you then check whether the character is colliding with the tile. However, you only need to do that if the tile is *not* a background tile. The code to do all that is as follows:

```
for (var y = y_floor - 1; y <= y_floor + 2; ++y) {
    for (var x = x_floor - 1; x <= x_floor + 1; ++x) {
        let tileType = tiles.getTileType(x, row: y)
        if tileType == .Background {
            continue
        }
        let tileBounds = tiles.getTileBox(x, row: y)
        if !tileBounds.intersects(box) {
            continue
        }
        ...
    }
}
```

As you can see, you don't directly access the `Tile` objects. The reason is that sometimes the x or y index can be negative because the character is near the edge of the screen. Here you see the advantage of using the `getTileType` method you added to the `TileField` class. You don't care if you're really dealing with a tile: as long as you know its type and bounding box, you can do your job.

In the nested `for` instruction, you also see a new keyword: `continue`. This keyword can be used in `for` or `while` instructions to stop executing the current iteration of the loop and continue to the next one. In this case, if the tile is of type `Background`, the rest of the instructions are no longer executed, and you continue to increment x and start a new iteration to check the next tile. The result is that only tiles that aren't of type `Background` are considered. The `continue` keyword is related to `break`, which stops the loop entirely. Unlike `break`, `continue` only stops the current iteration.

This code doesn't always work correctly, though. Particularly when the character is standing on a tile, rounding errors when calculating the bounding box can lead to the algorithm thinking the character isn't standing on the ground. The character's velocity is then increased, and the character may fall through the tile as a result. To compensate for any rounding errors, you decrease the y origin of the bounding box by 1:

```
let tileBounds = tiles.getTileBox(x, row: y)
var bbox = box
bbox.origin.y -= 1
if !tileBounds.intersects(bbox) {
    continue
}
// handle the collision
```

# Dealing with the Collision

Now that you can detect collisions between the character and the tiles in the game world, you have to determine what to do when a collision happens. There are a couple of possibilities. You could let the game crash (not good if you want to sell your game to many people), you could warn users that they shouldn't collide with objects in the game (resulting in a lot of pop-up messages), or you could automatically correct the position of the character if it collides with an object.

In order to correct the character's position, you need to know how bad the collision was. For example, if the character walked into a wall on the right, you have to know how far to move the character to the left to undo the collision. This is also called the *intersection depth*. Let's extend the CGRect type with a method called calculateIntersectionDepth that calculates the intersection depth in both x- and y-directions for two CGRect objects. In this example, these rectangles are the bounding box of the character and the bounding box of the tile it's colliding with.

The intersection depth can be calculated by first determining the minimum allowed distance between the centers of the rectangles such that there is no collision between the two rectangles:

```
let minDistance = CGPoint(x: (self.size.width + rect.size.width)/2,
    y: (self.size.height + rect.size.height)/2)
```

Then you calculate the *real* distance between the two rectangle centers:

```
let distance = CGPoint(x: self.midX - rect.midX, y: self.midY - rect.midY)
```

Now you can calculate the difference between the minimum allowed distance and the actual distance to get the intersection depth. If you look at the actual distance between the two centers, there are two possibilities for both dimensions (x and y): the distance is either negative or positive. For example, if the x distance is negative, this means rectangle rect is placed to the right of rectangle this (because rect.midX > self.midX). If rectangle self represents the character, this means you have to move the character to the *left* to correct this intersection. Therefore, you return the x intersection depth as a *negative* value, which can be calculated as -minDistance.x - distance.x. Why? Because there is a collision, the distance between the two rectangles is smaller than minDistance. And because distance is negative, the expression -minDistance.x - distance.x gives the difference between the two as a *negative* value. If distance is positive, the expression minDistance.x - distance.x gives the *positive* difference between the two. The same reasoning holds for the y distance. You can then calculate the depth as follows:

```
if distance.x > 0 {
    depth.x = minDistance.x - distance.x
} else {
    depth.x = -minDistance.x - distance.x
}
if distance.y > 0 {
    depth.y = minDistance.y - distance.y
} else {
    depth.y = -minDistance.y - distance.y
}
```

Finally, you return the depth vector as the result of this method:

```
return depth
```

For the complete method, see the Math.swift file in the TickTick2 example belonging to this chapter. When you know that the character collides with the tile, you calculate the intersection depth using the method you just added to the CGRect type:

```
let depth = box.calculateIntersectionDepth(tileBounds)
```

Now that you've calculated the intersection depth, there are two ways to solve this collision: move the character in the x direction, or move the character in the y direction. Generally, you want to move the character the least possible distance to avoid unnatural motions or displacements. So, if the x depth is smaller than the y depth, you move the character in the x direction; otherwise you move it in the y direction. You can check this with an if instruction. When comparing the two depth dimensions, you have to take into account that they may be negative. You solve this by comparing the absolute values, using the fabs function:

```
if fabs(depth.x) < fabs(depth.y) {
    // move character in the x direction
}
```

Do you always want to move the character if there is a collision with a tile? Well, that depends on the tile type. Remember that TileType is used to represent three possible tile types: TileType.Background, TileType.Wall, and TileType.Platform. If the tile the character is colliding with is a background tile, you definitely don't want to move the character. Also, in the case of moving in the x direction, you want the character to be able to *pass through* platform tiles. Therefore, the only case where you want to move the character to correct a collision is when it's colliding with a *wall* tile (TileType.Wall). In that case, you move the character by adding the x depth value to the character position:

```
if tileType == .Wall {
    self.position.x += depth.x
}
```

If you want to correct the character position in the y direction, things become slightly more complicated. Because you're dealing with movement in the y direction, this is also a good place to determine whether the character is on the ground. In the beginning of the handleCollisions method, you set the isOnTheGround property to false. So, the starting point is to assume that the character is *not* on the ground. In *some* cases, it's on the ground, and you have to set the property to true. How can you check if the character is on the ground? If it isn't on the ground, it must be falling. If it's falling, then the *previous* y-position is smaller than the current position. In order to have access to the previous y-position, you store it in a property at the end of each call to the handleCollisions method:

```
self.previousYPosition = self.position.y
```

Now you can use the previous y-position to determine if the character is on the ground. First, you calculate the difference between the previous and the current y-positions:

```
let ydifference = self.position.y - self.previousYPosition
```

If the current global y-position minus this difference is equal to or larger than the top of the tile the character is colliding with and the tile is *not* a background tile, then the character was falling and has reached a tile. If so, you set the isOnTheGround property to true and the y velocity to 0 so the character stops falling. You also correct the current y-position so the character no longer intersects the tile:

```
if box.minY - ydifference >= tileBounds.maxY && tileType != .Background {
    self.onTheGround = true
    self.velocity.y = 0
    self.position.y += depth.y
}
```

The only other case you still have to deal with is if the character is not falling down, but jumping and has reached a wall tile. In this case, you simply want to correct the character position so it no longer intersects with the wall tile, which is covered in the following if instruction:

```
else if tileType == .Wall {
    self.position.y += depth.y
}
```

Figure 24-1 shows a screenshot of the TickTick2 example. I created a simple level here that you can use to test the physics engine. The level is smaller than the screen of most iDevices, so there is some black space surrounding the level. In Chapter 26, I'll show you how to add sidescrolling to the game so that you can create larger levels and still be able to play them on devices with varying screen sizes.

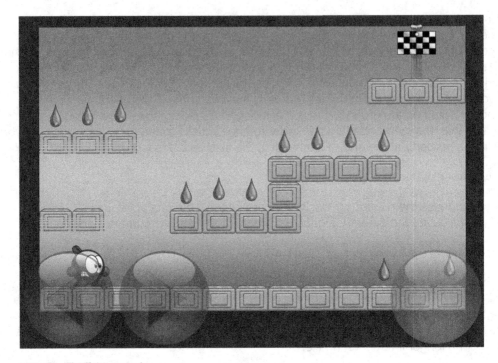

*Figure 24-1. The TickTick2 example*

# What You Have Learned

In this chapter, you have learned the following:

- How to constrain a character within the environment
- How to simulate jumping and falling
- How to deal with collisions in games

# Chapter 25

# Intelligent Enemies

As the next step in developing the Tick Tick game, let's introduce some peril to the player by adding dangerous enemies. If the player touches an enemy, the player dies. The enemies generally aren't controlled by the player (that would make it too easy). Therefore, you need to define some kind of smart (or stupid) behavior. You don't want these enemies to be too smart: the player should be able to complete the level. After all, that is the goal of playing a game: winning it. What is nice is that you can build different types of enemies that exhibit different types of behavior. As a result, the player has different gameplay options and must develop different strategies to complete the level.

Defining the behavior of an enemy can lead to some very complex code, with many different states, reasoning, path planning, and much more. You will see a few different types of enemies in this chapter: a rocket, a sneezing turtle (seriously), Sparky, and a couple of different patrolling enemies. This chapter doesn't deal with how the player should *interact* with enemies—you'll only define their basic behavior.

## The Rocket

One of the most basic enemies is a rocket. A rocket flies from one side of the screen to the other and then reappears after some time has passed. If the player comes in contact with the rocket, the player dies. In the level description, you indicate with the *r* and *R* characters that a rocket enemy should be placed in a level. For example, consider this level description:

```
Many, many, many, many, many rockets...
20 15
30
....................
r..W...........X....
...--..W.......--...
....W.--........W..R
...-............--...
r..W......W....W....
...--....--....--...
```

```
....W...........W...
...--........W.--...
r..W.........--.W....
...--...........-...
....W...........W..R
...--...........--...
.1................
#####..####..#####
```

A lowercase *r* means the rocket should fly from left to right, and an uppercase *R* means it should fly from right to left (see Table 22-1 in Chapter 22).

# Creating and Resetting the Rocket

Let's create a Rocket class that represents this particular kind of enemy. You inherit from the AnimatedNode class because the rocket is animated. The Rocket class has a few properties: a velocity, its starting position in the level, and a property called spawnTime, which is needed to keep track of when the rocket should appear. In the initializer, you need to load the rocket animation and play it, and then you need to check whether the animation should be mirrored. Because the animation has the rocket moving to the right, you need to mirror it if the rocket moves to the left. You also store the starting position of the rocket so you can place it back at that position when it moves out of the screen. Here is part of the Rocket class definition:

```
class Rocket: AnimatedNode {

    var startPosition: CGPoint = CGPoint.zeroPoint
    var spawnTime: CGFloat = 0
    var velocity = CGPoint.zeroPoint

    init(moveToLeft: Bool, startPos: CGPoint) {
        startPosition = startPos
        super.init()
        loadAnimation("spr_rocket", looping: true, frameTime: 0.5, name: "default")
        playAnimation("default")
        if moveToLeft {
            self.xScale = -1
        }
        reset()
    }
    ...
}
```

The last instruction in the initializer is a call to the reset method. In this method, you set the current position of the rocket to the starting position, hide the rocket (it should initially be invisible), and set its velocity to zero. You also use the random number generator to calculate a random time (in seconds) after which the rocket should appear and start moving. You store this time in the property spawnTime. You put these instructions in a separate reset method because you call this method later as well, after the rocket has flown out of the screen.

# Programming the Rocket Behavior

The behavior of the rocket is (as usual) encoded in the updateDelta method. Basically, a rocket exhibits two main types of behavior: either it's visible and moving from one end of the screen to the other, or it's invisible and waiting to appear. You can determine which of the two states the rocket is in by looking at the value of the spawnTime property. If this property contains a value larger than zero, the rocket is waiting to be spawned. If the value is less than or equal to zero, the rocket is visible and moving from one end of the screen to the other.

Let's look at the first case. If the rocket is waiting to be spawned, you simply subtract the time that has elapsed since the last updateDelta call from the spawn time:

```
if spawnTime > 0 {
    spawnTime -= CGFloat(delta)
    return
}
```

The second case is slightly more complicated. The rocket is moving from one end of the screen to the other. So, you set the hidden status to false and you calculate the rocket velocity depending on the direction it's moving:

```
hidden = false
self.velocity.x = 600
if self.xScale < 0 {
    self.velocity.x *= -1
}
```

Finally, you have to check whether the rocket has flown outside of the level. If that is the case, the rocket should be reset. You check whether the rocket is outside of the level using the bounding box of the tile field. If this bounding box doesn't intersect the rocket's bounding box, you know the rocket is outside of the level, and you reset it:

```
let tileField = childNodeWithName("//tileField") as! TileField
if !tileField.box.intersects(self.box) {
    self.reset()
}
```

This completes the Rocket class, except for interaction with the player, which is something you will look at in more detail in Chapter 26. For the complete class, see the TickTick3 example code belonging to this chapter. Figure 25-1 shows a screenshot of the level defined in the first section of this chapter. Note that the level is only partly visible since it is bigger than the screen of the device.

*Figure 25-1. A level with many rockets flying around*

# A Patrolling Enemy

The rocket is a type of enemy that basically has no intelligent behavior. It flies from left to right or vice versa until it flies out of the level, and then it resets itself. You can also add enemies that are slightly smarter, such as a *patrolling* enemy. Let's set up a few different types of patrolling enemies that you can add to the game.

## The Basic PatrollingEnemy Class

The PatrollingEnemy class is similar to the Rocket class. You want the patrolling enemy to be animated, so it inherits from the AnimatedNode class. You also need to define the *behavior* of the enemy in the overridden updateDelta method. The basic behavior of the patrolling enemy is that it walks from left to right and back again. If the enemy character reaches a gap or a wall tile, the enemy stops walking, waits for some time, and turns around. You can place enemies at arbitrary positions in the level. For the player, you define some rudimentary physics like falling and jumping. You don't do that for the PatrollingEnemy class because the enemies you define for this game only walk from left to right and back.

In the initializer of the PatrollingEnemy class, you load the main animation for the patrolling enemy character (an angry-looking flame, as shown in Figure 25-2). Initially, you set a positive velocity so the enemy starts walking to the right. You also initialize another property called waitTime that keeps track of how long the enemy has been waiting on one of the edges of the platform it's walking on:

```
class PatrollingEnemy: AnimatedNode {

    var waitTime: CGFloat = 0
    var velocity = CGPoint(x: 120, y: 0)
```

```
override init() {
    super.init()
    loadAnimation("spr_flame", looping: true, frameTime: 0.1, name: "default")
    playAnimation("default")
}
...
}
```

*Figure 25-2.  A few patrolling enemies*

In the updateDelta method, you have to distinguish between two cases: the enemy is walking or waiting. You can distinguish between these states by looking at the waitTime property. If it contains a positive value, the enemy is waiting. If the property contains a value of zero or less, the enemy is walking. When the enemy is waiting, you don't have to do much. Just as you did in the Rocket class, you subtract the elapsed game time from the waitTime property. If the wait time has reached zero, you need to turn the character around. Here is the code to do that:

```
if waitTime > 0 {
    waitTime -= CGFloat(delta)
    if waitTime <= 0 {
        self.turnAround()
    }
}
```

The turnAround method simply mirrors the animation and inverts the velocity:

```
func turnAround() {
    xScale = -xScale
    velocity.x = 120 * xScale
}
```

If the enemy currently is walking, not waiting, you need to find out whether it has reached the edge of the platform it's walking on. It has reached an edge in two cases: either there is a gap, so the enemy can't move any further, or a wall tile is blocking the way. You use the enemy's bounding box to find this information. If the enemy is walking to the left, you check the tile to the left of the enemy. If the enemy is walking to the right, you check the tile to its right. You can calculate the column index of the target tile as follows:

```
let tileField = childNodeWithName("//tileField") as! TileField
var (col, row) = tileField.layout.gridLocation(self.position)
if xScale < 0 {
    col -= 1
} else {
    col += 1
}
```

Next, you have to check whether the enemy has reached a wall tile or the border of the platform. If the tile *below* the tile at the calculated indices is a background tile, the enemy has reached the border of the platform and must stop walking. If the tile at indices (col, row) (in other words, the tile right next to the enemy) is a wall tile, the enemy also has to stop walking. In order to stop walking, you assign a positive value to the wait time and set the x velocity to zero:

```
if tileField.getTileType(col, row: row - 1) == .Background ||
    tileField.getTileType(col, row: row) == .Wall {

    waitTime = 0.5
    velocity = CGPoint.zeroPoint
}
```

# Different Types of Enemies

You can make the patrolling enemy slightly more interesting by introducing a few varieties. Here you can use the power of inheritance to write a few subclasses of the PatrollingEnemy class to define different enemy behaviors.

For example, you can create an enemy that is a bit more unpredictable by letting it change direction once in a while. At that point, you can also change the enemy's walking speed to a random value. You do this by defining a class called UnpredictableEnemy that inherits from the PatrollingEnemy class. So, by default, it exhibits the same behavior as a regular enemy. You override the updateDelta method and add a few lines of code that randomly change the direction in which the enemy is walking as well as its velocity. Because you reuse most of the `PatrollingEnemy` class code, the `UnpredictableEnemy` class is rather short. Here is the complete class definition:

```
class UnpredictableEnemy: PatrollingEnemy {

    override func updateDelta(delta: NSTimeInterval) {
        super.updateDelta(delta)
        if waitTime <= 0 && randomCGFloat() < 0.01 {
            self.turnAround()
            self.velocity.x = randomCGFloat() * 300 * xScale
        }
    }
}
```

As you can see, you use an `if` instruction to check whether a randomly generated number falls below a certain value. As a result, in a few cases the condition will yield `true`. In the body of the `if` instruction, you first turn the enemy around, and then you calculate a new x velocity. Note that you multiply the randomly generated velocity by the x scale. This is to ensure that the new velocity is set in the right direction. You also first call the `updateDelta` method of the base class so the right animation is selected, collisions with the player are dealt with, and so on.

Another variety I can think of is an enemy that follows the player instead of simply walking from left to the right and back again. Again, it inherits from the `PatrollingEnemy` class. Here is a class called `PlayerFollowingEnemy`:

```
class PlayerFollowingEnemy: PatrollingEnemy {

    override func updateDelta(delta: NSTimeInterval) {
        super.updateDelta(delta)

        let player = childNodeWithName("//player") as! Player
        let direction = player.position.x - self.position.x
        if direction * velocity.x < 0 && player.velocity != CGPoint.zeroPoint {
            self.turnAround()
        }
    }
}
```

This class defines an enemy that follows the player if the player is moving. This is done by checking whether the enemy is currently walking in the direction where the player is standing (only taking the x direction into account). If not, the enemy turns around. You place a limitation on the enemy's intelligence by doing that only if the player isn't moving in the x direction (in other words, the player's x velocity is zero).

You should never make enemies too smart. In addition, don't make them too fast—it would be a short game if enemies walked appreciably faster than the player while following them. Enemies are there to be beaten by the player so the player can win the game. Playing a game where the enemies are too smart or unbeatable isn't a lot of fun, unless you like dying over and over again!

# Other Types of Enemies

Yet another enemy you can add to the game is a sneezing turtle (see Figure 25-3). Why a turtle, you ask? And why a sneezing one? Well, I don't really have an answer to that question. But the idea behind this enemy is that it has both a negative and a positive side. On the negative side, the turtle grows spikes when it sneezes, so you shouldn't touch it. But if the turtle isn't sneezing, you can use it to jump higher. Because you aren't dealing with interaction just yet, you only add the animated turtle for now. The turtle can be used to jump for 5 seconds, then it sneezes and grows spikes for 5 seconds, after which it returns to the previous state for 5 seconds, and so on.

*Figure 25-3. Don't jump on the spiky turtle!*

The enemy is represented by the Turtle class, which is set up in a fashion similar to the previous enemies. A turtle has two states: it's idle, or it has sneezed and therefore has dangerous spikes. In this case, you maintain two member variables to keep track of which state the turtle is in and how much time has passed in that state: the waitTime property tracks how much time is left in the current state, and the sneezing property tracks whether the turtle is sneezing. Again, in the updateDelta method, you handle the transition between the two phases, much as you did for the rocket and the patrolling enemies. I don't go into further detail here because the code is very similar to the other enemy classes. You can see the complete code in the TickTick3 program belonging to this chapter.

Sparky is the final enemy type that you add to the game. Just like the other enemies, Sparky has two states (see Figure 25-4). Sparky is a very dangerous, electricity-loving enemy. He hangs quietly in the air until he receives a bolt of energy, which makes him fall down. While Sparky is hanging in the air, he isn't dangerous; but as soon as he falls, don't touch him! See the Sparky class to see the code.

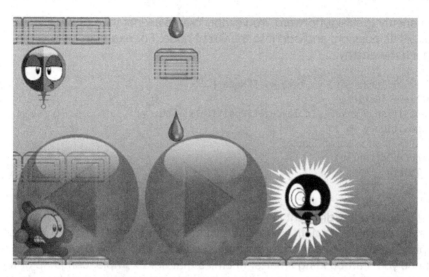

*Figure 25-4. Sparky is dangerous when he is electrified*

---

**ENEMY SOFTWARE ARCHITECTURE**

All these different types of enemies look different and behave differently, but they generally have a common class design. You could probably design a better way to define these enemies by using a couple of generic classes that let you define states and transitions between them. There could be conditions attached to each transition, such as that a certain amount of time must have passed or that an animation should be finished playing. Such a structure is called a *finite state machine*. It's a very common technique used in artificial intelligence systems. If you're up to the challenge, try to write a finite state machine library and redefine the existing enemies to use it!

---

# Loading the Different Types of Enemies

Now that you've defined different varieties of enemies, the only thing left to do is load them when you read the level data from the text file. The sprites for the different enemies are identified using characters.

Depending on the character you read when loading the level, you call a different method to load the enemy by adding a few cases to the switch instruction in the LevelState class:

```
case "R":
    return loadRocketTile(x, y: y, moveToLeft: true)
case "r":
    return loadRocketTile(x, y: y, moveToLeft: false)
case "A", "B", "C":
    return loadFlameTile(c, x: x, y: y)
case "S":
    return loadSparkyTile(x, y: y)
case "T":
    return loadTurtleTile(x, y: y)
```

Loading an enemy is straightforward. You simply create an instance of the enemy you would like to add, set its position, and add it to the `world` node. For example, here is the method for loading a turtle enemy:

```
func loadTurtleTile(x: Int, y: Int) -> SKNode {
    var turtle = Turtle()
    turtle.position = tileField.layout.toPosition(x, row: y)
    turtle.position.y += 20
    turtle.zPosition = Layer.Scene1
    world.addChild(turtle)
    return Tile()
}
```

You've now defined a few different kinds of enemies with varying intelligence and capabilities. It's up to you to define enemies that are smarter, more devious, or even more stupid, depending on the needs of your game. You didn't apply any physics to the enemies; however, once you start building smarter enemies that, for example, can jump or fall, you'll need to implement physics just as you did for the player. As an exercise, try to think how you can make these enemies more capable without having to rely on physics. Can you let them move faster when the player is nearby? Can you create an enemy that launches particles toward the player? The possibilities are endless, so try these things for yourself!

# What You Have Learned

In this chapter, you have learned the following:

- How to define different kinds of enemies
- How to use inheritance to create variety in enemy behavior

Chapter **26**

# Adding Player Interaction

In this chapter, you will add more interaction between the player and the objects in the level. Currently, the player can walk around, and a basic physics system allows the player to jump, collide with wall tiles, or fall out of the screen. First, you will look at a very simple kind of interaction: collecting water drops. Then you will see how to create the behavior that allows the player to slide over ice. You will also focus on the part of the program that deals with the various player-enemy interactions in the game. Finally, you will add vertical and horizontal scrolling to the game.

## Collecting Water Drops

The first thing to add is the possibility for the player to collect water drops. A player collects a water drop if the bomb character collides with that drop. In that case, you make the drop invisible.

Making a drop invisible once a player collects it isn't the only way to approach the problem of drawing only the uncollected drops, but it's one of the easiest solutions. Another approach is to maintain a list of water drops that have been collected and then add only those drops that the player still has to find to the game scene, but this technique requires a lot more code.

The place where you check whether the player collides with a water drop is in the WaterDrop class. The reason is clear: as before, each game object is responsible for its own behavior. If you handle these collisions in the WaterDrop class, each water drop checks whether it collides with the player. You write this code in the updateDelta method. The first step is to retrieve the player:

```
let player = childNodeWithName("//player") as! Player
```

If the water drop is currently visible, you check whether it collides with the player using the `intersects` method from `CGRect`. If so, you set the hidden status of the drop to `true`. You also play a sound to let the player know the water drop has been collected:

```
if player.box.intersects(self.box) && !self.hidden {
    self.hidden = true
    waterCollectedSound.play()
}
```

Later, you can determine whether the level is completed by checking the visibility of each water drop. If all of the water drops are invisible, you know the player has collected all of them.

# Ice Blocks

Another type of interaction you can add to the game is special behavior when the player is walking over ice. When the player moves over ice, you want the character to continue sliding at a constant rate and not stop moving when the player releases the button. Even though continuing to slide isn't completely realistic (in real life you would slide and slow down), it does lead to predictable behavior that the player can easily understand, which in many cases is more important than achieving realism. To implement this, you have to do two things:

- Extend the `handleInput` method to deal with moving over ice.
- Calculate whether the player is standing on ice.

You keep track of whether the player is standing on ice in a property called `walkingOnIce` in the `Player` class. Let's assume for now that this property is updated somewhere else, and let's look at extending the `handleInput` method. The first thing you want to do is increase the player's walking speed when the character is walking on ice. You can do that as follows:

```
var walkingSpeed = CGFloat(300)
if self.walkingOnIce {
    walkingSpeed *= 1.5
}
```

The value by which the speed is multiplied is a variable that influences the gameplay. Choosing the right value is important—too fast, and the level becomes unplayable; too slow, and the ice isn't different from a regular walking surface in any meaningful way.

If the player isn't walking on ice but is instead standing on the ground, you need to set the x velocity to zero so the character stops moving when the player is no longer pressing one of the touch buttons. To achieve this, you add the following `if` instruction at the beginning of the `handleInput` method in the `Player` class:

```
if self.onTheGround && !self.walkingOnIce {
    self.velocity.x = 0
}
```

Then you handle the player input. If the player is pressing the left or right touch button, you set the appropriate x velocity:

```
if walkLeftButton.down {
    self.velocity.x = -walkingSpeed
} else if walkRightButton.down {
    self.velocity.x = walkingSpeed
}
```

The only thing you still need to do is find out whether the player is walking on ice and update the walkingOnIce property accordingly. You already use the handleCollisions method to look at the tiles surrounding the player, so to extend that method to also check whether the player is walking on ice, you only need to add a few lines of code. In the beginning of this method, you assume the player isn't walking on ice, just like you assume that the player isn't on the ground:

```
self.walkingOnIce = false
```

The player can only walk on ice if they're on the ground. You check whether they're on the ground in the following if instruction:

```
if box.minY - ydifference >= tileBounds.maxY && tileType != .Background {
    self.onTheGround = true
    self.velocity.y = 0
    self.position.y += depth.y
}
```

To check whether the tile the player is standing on is an ice tile, you have to retrieve the tile from the tile field and check its ice property. You can do this in an if instruction combined with the let keyword, as follows:

```
if let currentTile = tiles.layout.at(x, row: y) as? Tile {
    // do something with the tile
}
```

Inside the if instruction, you update the walkingOnIce property. You use a logical *or* operator so that if the player is only partly on an ice tile, the property is also set to true:

```
self.walkingOnIce = self.walkingOnIce || currentTile.ice
```

Because you use the logical *or* to calculate whether the player is walking on ice, you take all surrounding tiles into account. The effect is that the character keeps moving until it isn't standing on an ice tile anymore (not even partly). Run the TickTick4 example to see how the player character now interacts with ice.

# Enemies Colliding With the Player

The final kind of interaction to add is collisions with enemies. In many cases, when the player collides with an enemy, it causes the player's death. In some cases, you have to do something special (such as jumping extra high when jumping on the turtle). On the player side, you have to load an extra animation that shows the player dying. Because you don't want to handle player input after the player has died, you need to update the player's current alive status. You do this using a property called alive that is set to true when the Player instance is created. In the handleInput method, you check whether the player is still alive. If not, you return from the method so you don't handle any input:

```
if !self.alive {
    return
}
```

You also add a method called die to let the player die. There are two ways the player can die: by falling in a hole out of the game screen and by colliding with an enemy. Therefore, you pass a Boolean parameter to the die method to indicate whether the player died by falling or by colliding with an enemy.

In the die method, you do a couple of things. First, you check whether the player was already dead. If so, you return from the method without doing anything (after all, a player can only die once). You set the alive variable to false. Then, you set the velocity in the x direction to zero, to stop the player from moving to the left or right. You don't reset the y velocity, so the player keeps on falling: gravity doesn't cease to exist when you die. Next, you determine which sound to play when the player dies. If the player falls to their death, the sound produced is quite different from dying by an enemy's hand (don't try this for real; just take my word for it). If the player dies because of a collision with an enemy, you give the player an upward velocity as well. This upward velocity isn't very realistic, but it does provide for a nice visual effect (see Figure 26-1). Finally, you play the die animation. The complete method is as follows:

```
func die(falling: Bool = false) {
    if !alive {
        return
    }
    alive = false
    velocity.x = 0
    if falling {
        playerFallSound.play()
    } else {
        velocity.y = 600
        playerDieSound.play()
    }
    self.playAnimation("die")
}
```

*Figure 26-1. The player dies after colliding with an enemy*

You can check in the updateDelta method whether the player is falling to death by calculating if the player's y-position falls outside of the level. If this is the case, you call the die method:

```
let tiles = childNodeWithName("//tileField") as! TileField
if self.box.maxY < tiles.box.minY {
    self.die(falling: true)
}
```

At the start of the updateDelta method, you call the update method of the superclass to ensure that the animation is updated:

```
super.updateDelta(delta)
```

Next, you do the physics and collisions (which still need to be done, even if the player is dead). Then you check whether the player is alive. If not, you're finished, and you return from the method.

Now that the player can die in various gruesome ways, you have to extend the enemy classes to deal with collisions. In the Rocket class, you add a method called checkPlayerCollision that you call in the rocket's updateDelta method. In the checkPlayerCollision method, you simply check whether the player collides with the rocket. If that is the case, you call the die method on the Player object. The complete method is as follows:

```
func checkPlayerCollision() {
    let player = childNodeWithName("//player") as! Player
    if player.box.intersects(self.box) {
        player.die()
    }
}
```

In the case of the patrolling enemy, you do exactly the same thing. You add the same method to that class and call it from the updateDelta method. The version in the Sparky class is slightly different: the player should die only if Sparky is currently being electrified. Therefore, you change the method as follows:

```
func checkPlayerCollision() {
    let player = childNodeWithName("//player") as! Player
    if player.box.intersects(self.box) && self.waitTime <= 0 {
        player.die()
    }
}
```

Finally, the Turtle enemy adds even more behavior. You begin by checking whether the turtle collides with the player. If that's not the case, you simply return from the checkPlayerCollision method because you're done:

```
let player = childNodeWithName("//player") as! Player
if !player.box.intersects(self.box) {
    return
}
```

If a collision occurs, there are two possibilities. The first is that the turtle is currently sneezing. In that case, the player dies:

```
if sneezing {
    player.die()
}
```

The second case is that the turtle is in waiting mode, and the player is jumping on the turtle. In that case, the player should make an extra-high jump. An easy way to check whether the player is jumping on the turtle is to look at the y velocity. Assume that if that velocity is negative, the player is jumping on the turtle. So, you call the jump method to make the player jump extra high:

```
else if player.velocity.y < 0 && player.alive {
    player.jump(900)
}
```

And of course, you only want to do this if the player is still alive.

You now have finished programming the main interactions between the characters and objects in the game. There is one more kind of "interaction" to add to the game: the interaction between the player character and the device screen.

# Adding Horizontal and Vertical Scrolling

You've probably noticed that the levels were generally larger than the screen of any of the Apple devices. Especially on the iPad, a big part of the left and right side of each level isn't visible on the screen. In order to make sure that the game works as it should on all devices, you should add a mechanism that shows the relevant part of the level to the player while playing. The most common way to achieve this in platform games is by adding scrolling behavior. This means that as the player is moving through the game world, the world scrolls along with the player on the screen. In a sense, the device screen becomes a moving virtual camera that sees a part of the game world. Some games only allow horizontal (side) scrolling, other games also allow vertical scrolling. In Tick Tick, you will add both horizontal and vertical scrolling.

Fortunately, it is really easy to add scrolling to the Tick Tick game because you already made most of the preparations. Inside the LevelState class, the world node currently contains all of the items belonging to the level. The overlays (such as the Quit button or the walk and jump buttons) are not a part of the node. That's a good thing because you don't want the buttons to move out of the screen as the level starts scrolling!

To keep things simple, let's make a very basic scrolling mechanism that tries to follow the player. You will do this in the updateDelta method of LevelState. The first step is to call the super class method (so that all the objects in the level are updated), and retrieve the player:

```
super.updateDelta(delta)
let player = childNodeWithName("//player") as! Player
```

Now you need to make the virtual camera follow the player. A very naïve way to do this would be to simply set the world position to be the same as the player position:

```
world.position = -player.position
```

Notice the minus sign here. If the player moves to the *right*, the world needs to move to the *left* so that you can still see the player. The result of this particular instruction is that the player will always be shown exactly in the middle of the device screen, since the world position is now compensating for the player position, and the anchor point of the game scene is set at the center of the screen. Although this approach works well, you need to solve a problem. Now that the camera is following the player, it is possible that when the player approaches the edge of the level, you will see empty space. This is not desirable. You want to *clamp* the world position between its allowed maximum and minimum values so that the camera will never be partly outside of the world.

How do you calculate these values? Let's first look at one example. Suppose that the player is moving to the right and that the camera is following the player. This means that the world node will be displaced to the *left*. How much can you move the world node to the left until you start seeing empty space? If you move the world half of the width of the level to the left, then half of the screen of your device will show empty space. In order to fix this, you need to add back half of the width of the device screen so that the left edge of the world matches up exactly with the left edge of the device. This gives you the leftmost allowed position of the screen:

```
let minx = CGFloat(-tileField.layout.width/2) + GameScreen.instance.size.width/2
```

See Figure 26-2 for an illustration. In it, the player has moved so far to the right that the world position has to be clamped to avoid showing empty space. Similarly, you can also find the rightmost value that is allowed for the world position:

```
let maxx = CGFloat(tileField.layout.width/2) - GameScreen.instance.size.width/2
```

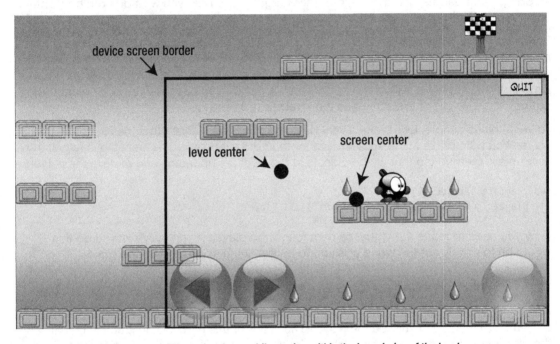

*Figure 26-2. The screen camera follows the player while staying within the boundaries of the level*

And you can do the same thing for the y axis:

```
let miny = CGFloat(-tileField.layout.height/2) + GameScreen.instance.size.height/2
let maxy = CGFloat(tileField.layout.height/2) - GameScreen.instance.size.height/2
```

The only thing left to do is to clamp the world position between these minimum and maximum values:

```
world.position.x = clamp(-player.position.x, minx, maxx)
world.position.y = clamp(-player.position.y, miny, maxy)
```

Now scrolling works in both horizontal and vertical directions, and you make sure that there is never any empty space shown on the device screen (unless your level size is smaller than the device size). Check out the TickTick4 example to see the scrolling in action. In Chapter 27, you will finish this game by adding mountains and moving clouds in the background. You will also add the code that manages transitions between the levels.

---

```
TO DIE, OR NOT TO DIE?
```

I made a choice in this section that the player dies immediately when they touch an enemy. Other options are to give the player several lives or to add a health indicator for the player that decreases every time the player touches an enemy.

Adding multiple lives or a health indicator to a game can make the game more fun, but you also have to be sure the levels are still difficult enough. As a challenge, try to extend the Tick Tick game with a health bar for the player.

---

# What You Have Learned

In this chapter, you have learned the following:

- How to program various kinds of player interactions with water drops and enemies
- How to program ice tile behavior
- How to cause the player to die in certain situations
- How to add horizontal and vertical scrolling to a game

# Chapter 27

# Finishing the Tick Tick Game

In this chapter, you will finish the Tick Tick game. First, you will add a timer so that the player has a limited amount of time to complete each level. Then, you will add a few mountains and clouds to the background to make the game visually more interesting. Finally, you will write the code that allows the player to progress through the level.

## Adding a Timer

Let's first look at adding a *timer* to the game. You don't want the timer to take up too much screen space, so you use a text version of it. The Timer class inherits from the SKNode class, and it contains a background frame as well as a label node showing the remaining time. You want to be able to pause the timer (for example, when the level is finished), so you add a Boolean property called running that indicates whether the timer is running. You store the time remaining in a property called timeLeft. The number of seconds that the player has for each level is read from the text file and is stored in a property called totalTime. When the reset method is called, the timer is set to the total time, and it will start counting down. Here is the complete reset method:

```
override func reset() {
    super.reset()
    self.timeLeft = totalTime
    self.running = true
}
```

Now the only thing you still need to do is implement the updateDelta method to program the timer behavior. As a first step, you only update the timer if it's running and if there is still time left. If that's not the case, you return from the method:

```
if self.timeLeft < 0 || !self.running {
    return
}
```

Then, you subtract the elapsed game time from the current remaining time:

```
self.timeLeft -= delta
```

Next, you create the text that you want to print on the screen. You could simply print the number of seconds on the screen, but let's make the timer a bit more generic so it's also possible to define a timer that can handle minutes as well as seconds. For example, if you want to define a timer that counts down from two minutes, you initialize it as follows:

```
self.timeLeft = 120
```

You want to display "2:00" instead of "120" on the screen. To do this, you need to calculate in the updateDelta method how many minutes are left. First, you round up the current number of seconds. This is necessary because you want to show "2:00" on the screen between the 119th and 120th second. You use the ceil method for this:

```
let roundedTimeLeft = Int(ceil(timeLeft))
```

In addition to the ceil method, you have also seen the floor method, which rounds down. So ceil(0.1) yields 1, floor(0.1) yields 0. The number of minutes and seconds is then calculated as follows:

```
let minutes = roundedTimeLeft / 60
let seconds = roundedTimeLeft % 60
```

Now that you've calculated the number of minutes and seconds remaining, you can create a string that you draw on the screen:

```
textLabel.text = "\(minutes):\(seconds)"
if seconds < 10 {
    textLabel.text = "\(minutes):0\(seconds)"
}
```

You set the color of the text to yellow so it better fits the design of the game:

```
textLabel.fontColor = UIColor.yellowColor()
```

Finally, you want to warn the player if they don't have a lot of time left to finish the level. You do this by alternating between red and yellow when printing the text on the screen. You can do this with an if instruction and a clever use of the remainder operator:

```
if timeLeft <= 10 && seconds % 2 == 0 {
    textLabel.fontColor = UIColor.redColor()
}
```

Although calculating things with time in this manner is sufficient for the Tick Tick game, you might find yourself wanting to do more complex time or date representations. Swift has the NSDate class, which represents time, and you can use it in combination with the NSDateFormatter class, which allows you to specify exactly how you want to represent a date and/or time as a string.

# Making the Timer Go Faster or Slower

Depending on the kind of tile the player is walking on, time should go faster or slower. Walking on a hot tile increases the speed at which time passes, whereas walking on an ice tile decreases it. To allow for a timer that runs at different speeds, you introduce a *multiplier* value in the Timer class. This value is stored as a property, which is initially set to 1:

```
var multiplier = 1.0
```

Taking this multiplier into account while the timer is running is fairly easy. You simply multiply the passed time by the multiplier in the updateDelta method, and you're done:

```
self.timeLeft -= delta * multiplier
```

Now that you can change the speed at which time passes, you can do this depending on the kind of tile the player is walking on. In the Player class, you already maintain the walkingOnIce property, which indicates whether the player is walking on an ice tile. In order to handle hot tiles as well, you define another property called walkingOnHot, in which you keep track of whether the player is walking on a hot tile. To determine the value of this property, you follow the same approach you did for the walkingOnIce property. In the handleCollisions method, you initially set this property to false:

```
self.walkingOnHot = false
```

Then you add one line of code to update the value of the property depending on the current tile the player is standing on:

```
self.walkingOnHot = self.walkingOnHot || currentTile.hot
```

For the complete code, see the Player class belonging to the TickTickFinal example.

Using the walkingOnIce and walkingOnHot properties, you can now update the timer multiplier. You do this in the player's updateDelta method:

```
let timer = childNodeWithName("//timer") as! Timer
if self.walkingOnHot {
    timer.multiplier = 2.0
} else if self.walkingOnIce {
    timer.multiplier = 0.5
} else {
    timer.multiplier = 1
}
```

From a game design perspective, it's probably a good idea to explicitly let the player know that walking on a hot tile shortens the time left for finishing the level. You can do this by briefly showing a warning overlay, showing a smoke animation around the player character, or changing the timer's display color. You can also play back a warning sound. Another possibility is to change the background music to something more frantic, to make the player realize something has changed.

---

## ADAPTING TO THE SKILLS OF THE PLAYER

Changing the speed of the timer can make a level much easier or harder. You could extend the game so that in some cases the timer stops or moves back a few seconds if the player picked up a special item. You could even make the level progression adaptive so that if the player dies too often, the maximum number of seconds per level is increased. However, be careful about doing this. If you help the player in a too-obvious way, the player will realize it and adapt their strategy to it (in other words, the player will play worse in order to make the levels easier). Also, the player may feel they aren't being treated seriously. A better way to deal with adapting the maximum time per level is to allow the player to (partly) transfer time left over from previous levels to the current level. That way, difficult levels can be made easier, but the player has to do something to make that happen. You could also consider adding difficulty levels, where a more difficult level has a faster timer but also better benefits such as more points, extra items to pick up, or extra abilities for the player. Casual game players can then select the "Can I play, Daddy?" difficulty level, whereas skilled players can opt for the extremely challenging "I am Death incarnate" level.

---

# When the Timer Reaches Zero

When the player doesn't finish the level on time, the bomb explodes, and the game is over. A Boolean property in the `Player` class indicates whether the player has exploded. You then add a method called `explode` to the class that sets the explosion in motion. This is the complete method:

```
func explode() {
    if !alive || finished {
        return
    }
    alive = false
    exploded = true
    velocity = CGPoint.zeroPoint
    position.y -= 100
    playAnimation("explode")
    playerExplodeSound.play()
}
```

First, the player character can't explode if the character wasn't alive in the first place, or if the player finished the level. In either of those cases, you simply return from the method. Then, you set the alive status to `false` and the exploded status to `true`. You set the velocity to zero (explosions don't move). Then, you play the "explode" animation. This animation is stored in a texture atlas and consists of 49 frames of an explosion. Finally, you play an appropriate sound.

Because gravity also no longer affects an exploded character, you only do the gravity physics if the player isn't exploded:

```
if !self.exploded {
    self.velocity.y -= CGFloat(1300 * delta)
}
```

In the updateDelta method of the LevelState class, you check whether the timer has reached zero, and if so, you call the explode method:

```
let timer = childNodeWithName("//timer") as! Timer
if timer.timeLeft < 0 {
    player.explode()
}
```

## PRODUCING GAME ASSETS

If you want your game to look good, you need nice game assets. Good game assets that show coherency will make your game more attractive to customers. This includes not only the visuals but also the sound effects and background music. Generally, sound and music are underestimated, but they're important factors in establishing ambience. Watching a film without sound is a lot less fun than watching it with music that emotionally supports what is happening and sound effects that give body to what the characters are doing. Games also need music and sound effects, just like films.

To get started, you can buy premade packs of sprites. Here are a few web sites where you can get sprites for free, buy sprites, or hire artists who can create sprites for you:

- www.supergameasset.com
- www.graphic-buffet.com
- www.hireanillustrator.com
- opengameart.org
- www.3dfoin.com
- www.content-pack.com

Just like sprites, you can also buy music and sound effects for your games. Take a look at these web sites:

- www.soundrangers.com
- www.indiegamemusic.com
- www.stereobot.com
- audiojungle.net
- www.arteriamusic.com
- soundcloud.com

If you've already created a few games using these stock assets, it will be much easier for you to set up connections with other indie developers. The games you develop will form a portfolio that shows your capabilities as a game developer.

# Adding Mountains and Clouds

To make the level background a bit more interesting, let's add mountains and moving clouds to it. The LevelState class of the TickTickFinal example has a separate method called addBackgrounds in which you add the sky background, mountains, and moving clouds. First, let's have a look at how to add a few mountains. Depending on the width of the level, you calculate how many mountains and clouds you will add to the background:

```
let nrItems: Int = Int(tileField.layout.width) / 150
```

To add the mountains to the background, you use a for instruction. In the body of that instruction, you create a sprite node, give it a position, and add it to the backgrounds node that contains all the background objects.

This is the complete for instruction:

```
for _ in 1...nrItems {
    let mountainSpriteName = "spr_mountain_\(arc4random_uniform(2))"
    let mountain = SKSpriteNode(imageNamed: mountainSpriteName)
    mountain.zPosition = Layer.Background1
    mountain.position = CGPoint(x: randomCGFloat() * (tileField.layout.width +
        mountain.size.width) - tileField.layout.width / 2,
        y: -CGFloat(tileField.layout.height)/2 + mountain.size.height/2)
    backgrounds.addChild(mountain)
}
```

The first step is to create the sprite node. You want to choose randomly between the different mountain sprites that you have. Because there are two mountain sprites, you create a random number (either 0 or 1) to select between them. You use the number to create the file name that corresponds to that sprite. You position the sprite at the Background1 layer, which is on top of the sky node, but behind the actual scene.

Then you calculate the position of the mountain. The x-position is chosen randomly, and you use a fixed y-position so the mountain is at the appropriate height (you don't want mountains hanging in the sky). Finally, the mountain object is added to the backgrounds node.

For clouds, you do something slightly more complicated. You want the clouds to move from left to right or vice versa, and if a cloud disappears from the screen, you want a new one to appear. To do this, you add a Cloud class to the game, which is a subclass of SKSpriteNode. For each cloud you want to add to the background, you create an instance of this class. You assign it a higher layer value than the background itself and the mountains. This ensures that the clouds are drawn in front of the mountains. Again, you use a for loop to create a number of cloud instances:

```
for _ in 1...nrItems {
    var cloud = Cloud()
    cloud.zPosition = Layer.Background2
    backgrounds.addChild(cloud)
}
```

The Cloud class has a property velocity, since it has to move on the screen. In the initializer, you load a random cloud sprite (there are five different ones provided with the example). Here is the complete initializer:

```
init() {
    let cloudSpriteName = "spr_cloud_\(arc4random_uniform(5))"
    let texture = SKTexture(imageNamed: cloudSpriteName)
    super.init(texture: texture, color: UIColor.whiteColor(), size: texture.size())
}
```

When the level is reset, each Cloud instance gets a random position and velocity. The method responsible for that is the setRandomPositionAndVelocity method in the Cloud class. This method first sets a random y-position and a random x velocity (either positive or negative):

```
self.position.y = randomCGFloat() * tileField.layout.height -
    tileField.layout.height / 2
self.velocity.x = (randomCGFloat() * 2 - 1) * 20
```

Note in the second instruction, you calculate a random number between -1 and 1 and then multiply that number by 20. This allows you to randomly create clouds with either a positive or a negative x velocity.

The setRandomPositionAndVelocity method either places the cloud somewhere in the level (which is what you want when the player first starts the level) or it places the cloud just outside the screen so it can start moving in the screen (which is what you want if the cloud has moved outside of the level). A Boolean parameter called placeAtEdgeOfSceen allows you to choose where the cloud should be placed. For the complete method, see the Cloud class of the TickTickFinal example belonging to this chapter.

The Cloud class also has an updateDelta method, in which you check whether the cloud has exited the screen. If the cloud has exited the screen, you reset it by calling the setRandomPositionAndVelocity with the placeAtEdgeOfScreen parameter set to true. A cloud can exit the screen either on the left side or on the right side. You can calculate the minimum and maximum x values for which the cloud has completely exited the screen:

```
let minx = -tileField.layout.width / 2 - self.size.width / 2
let maxx = tileField.layout.width / 2 + self.size.width / 2
```

Now you can use an if instruction to determine if the cloud has exited the screen, and if so, call the setRandomPositionAndVelocity:

```
if position.x < minx || position.x > maxx {
    setRandomPositionAndVelocity(true)
}
```

Figure 27-1 shows a screenshot of a level that has mountains and moving clouds in its background.

*Figure 27-1. A Tick Tick level with mountains and moving clouds in the background*

# Showing the Help Frame

To complete each level, you also briefly show a frame with a hint, using a nice custom font to make the text look attractive. In the LevelState initializer, you add the frame as well as the hint text:

```
helpFrame.position = CGPoint(x: 0, y: GameScreen.instance.top - helpFrame.center.y - 10)
helpFrame.zPosition = Layer.Overlay
self.addChild(helpFrame)

let textLabel = SKLabelNode(fontNamed: "SmackAttackBB")
textLabel.fontColor = UIColor(red: 0, green: 0, blue: 0.4, alpha: 1)
textLabel.fontSize = 16
textLabel.text = help
textLabel.horizontalAlignmentMode = .Center
textLabel.verticalAlignmentMode = .Center
textLabel.zPosition = 1
textLabel.position = CGPoint(x: 45, y: -5)
helpFrame.addChild(textLabel)
```

To temporarily show the help frame, you define an action and run it when the `reset` method of `LevelState` is called. Here is the complete `reset` method:

```
override func reset() {
    super.reset()
    levelFinishedOverlay.hidden = true
    helpFrame.runAction(SKAction.sequence([SKAction.unhide(),
        SKAction.waitForDuration(5), SKAction.hide()]))
}
```

# Finalizing the Level Progression

To complete the game, you still need to deal with the event that the player has lost or won a level. You approach this in a fashion similar to how you handled it in the Penguin Pairs game, by adding the overlays for winning and losing the game, and showing them only if the player has either lost or won the game. To determine whether the player has finished a level, you add a `completed` property to the `LevelState` class that checks for two things:

- Has the player collected all of the water drops?
- Has the player reached the exit sign?

Both of these things are fairly easy to check. To check whether the player has reached the end sign, you can see whether their bounding boxes are intersecting. Checking whether the player has collected all the water drops can be done by verifying that all water drops are invisible. This is the complete property:

```
var completed: Bool {
    get {
        for w in waterDrops {
            if !w.hidden {
                return false
            }
        }
        let player = childNodeWithName("//player")!
        let exit = childNodeWithName("//exit")!
        return exit.box.intersects(player.box)
    }
}
```

In the `updateDelta` method of the `LevelState` class, you check whether the level was completed. If so, you call the `levelFinished` method in the `Player` class, which plays the "celebration" animation:

```
if self.completed && levelFinishedOverlay.hidden {
    levelFinishedOverlay.hidden = false
    player.levelFinished()
    timer.running = false
}
```

You also stop the timer because the player is done. Similarly, you also have a gameOver property that determines whether the player has lost the game:

```
var gameOver: Bool {
    get {
        let player = childNodeWithName("//player") as! Player
        let timer = childNodeWithName("//timer") as! Timer
        return !player.alive || timer.timeLeft < 0
    }
}
```

In the updateDelta method, you then set the visibility of the Game Over overlay according to this property:

```
gameoverOverlay.hidden = !self.gameOver
```

The code to deal with transitions between levels is fairly straightforward and is almost a copy of the code used in the Penguin Pairs game. Have a look at the code in the TickTickFinal example to see how this is done.

You've now seen how to build a platform game with commonly occurring elements such as collecting items, avoiding enemies, game physics, going from one level to another, and so on. Perhaps you also noticed that the Tick Tick game doesn't run very fast in the iOS simulator (although on recent iDevices it should run fine). Here you see that the cost of using high-quality artwork, many animations, (physical) interactions between objects, and so on, does add up in terms of computation. On the other hand, to make Tick Tick a game that is commercially viable, a lot of work still needs to be done. You probably want to define more of everything: more levels, more enemies, more different items to pick up, more challenges, more sounds. You may also want to introduce a few things that I didn't address: playing with other players over a network, maintaining a high-score list, playing in-game movies between levels, and other things you can think of that would be interesting to add. Use the Tick Tick game as a starting point for your own game, but always keep in mind that ideally your game should be playable on as many devices as possible, which places limits on the complexity of the games you create.

## SELLING YOUR GAME

Now that you're programming your own games, you may have started to think about how to get them out in the real world. Maybe you don't want to create a game just for the achievement, but to make some money with it. Fortunately, with the App Store, getting your game published is easy. In order to be able to publish apps, you need to become an Apple developer, for which you'll have to pay a yearly fee. After that, the challenge lies in making your game visible. On iOS, more than 300 new games appear every day. Most of them are played by just a few people. So how do you make your game stand out?

First of all, you need to produce a quality game. If the game isn't good, people won't play it. Find other people with other skill sets to help you. Don't be overambitious: you aren't going to create the next *Halo*! Set reasonable goals. Start with small but excellent games. Don't trust your own judgment: talk to others about your game, and let them play prototypes to make sure players actually like it. When your game is nearing completion, make a marketing plan. Post about the game wherever you can, make a press kit, create a video, send information to blogs and other web sites, and so on. People will only play your game when they hear about it. Don't expect that this will happen automatically after you've published your game on the App Store; you need to make a plan. Before your game is out, build a network of potential players—people who are interested in what you do. Create a Facebook group for your company and/or the game you're creating. Be sure to communicate with followers on social networks such as Twitter. Encourage others to play your game and write about it.

# What You Have Learned

In this chapter, you have learned the following:

- How to add a timer to a level
- How to create animated backgrounds consisting of mountains and clouds

# Index

# Get the eBook for only $5!

Why limit yourself?

Now you can take the weightless companion with you wherever you go and access your content on your PC, phone, tablet, or reader.

Since you've purchased this print book, we're happy to offer you the eBook in all 3 formats for just $5.

Convenient and fully searchable, the PDF version enables you to easily find and copy code—or perform examples by quickly toggling between instructions and applications. The MOBI format is ideal for your Kindle, while the ePUB can be utilized on a variety of mobile devices.

To learn more, go to www.apress.com/companion or contact support@apress.com.

Printed in the United States
By Bookmasters